What others have said a

This book is a MUST read!!
So many different topics in one that I've often wanted to address but not really known where to start!! Working through this book its really helped me to dig deep into the heart of my soul and awaken parts I didn't even think existed! Beautiful pieces of work which includes poems that draw you into exactly what the author was feeling as well as shinning a reflective light on yourself too
5 Stars - Naomi - Amazon Purchase
****

Beautiful and necessary book. Speaking straight to the Soul...grounding and touching for ones who are already in tune with their Spirit, accounts of the Author shows that we are actually experiencing collective awakening. This title is necessary for ones who are just stepping out on this most beautiful journey called " know thyself" - u need to read this book, it will shift your perception and help you to manifest the reality u wish to live in.
5 Star Eve - Amazon Purchase
****

Amenti is truly connected and an inspiration.
I highly recommend this book for those seeking deeper insight
5 Star A.Dwek- Amazon Purchase
****

We are all here to serve a purpose but not all of us know how to go about it... This book will definitely help you along your journey to discover your true path and help you understand yourself inside and out .I personally recommend you give this book a read and start your journey of true understanding. Love. Blessings. Peace
5 Stars C.Neckles
****

Beautifully Written and Amazingly structured. If ever wrote a Starseed book, it would be just like this one! Great Read and very insightful
Rainbow.Rahmie - Artist and Healer

12 Seeds To Awaken Your Spirit

From Star to Seed and Back Again

By Amenti the Awakener

(Makeda-Amenti)

Published by

Halls of Amenti
Publishing

© 2017 Amenti the Awakener. All rights reserved.

ISBN: 9781976756924

No part of this publication may be reproduced, stored in, or introduced into a retrieval system, or transmitted in any form or by any means (electronic, mechanical, photocopying, recording, or otherwise) without prior consent of the copyright owner.

Table of Contents

What others have said about this book 1

Dedication (Livi-cation- Celebration of Life) 21

Acknowledgements 22

The Message 23

Preface 25

HOW THIS BOOK WAS CREATED 32

One Night in 2012 33

How to use this book? 39

The Importance of the Number 12 39

SACRED GEOMTERY - THE KEY TO LIFE 40

From the Star to the Seed – The Beginning of All Life 41

The Seed of Life 44

Growing Through the Tree of Life 46

The Divine Lights 47

The 5 Platonic Solids 48

Other Important Sacred Geometry Symbols 50

From Star to Seed….and Back Again 52

Journey to the Stars 54

Seed 1 56

Understand the 56

Laws of the Universe 56
    SEED 1 – UNDERSTAND THE LAWS OF THE UNIVERSE 57

The Universal Laws 59

Nurturing The Seeds	63
Journal Page	65
Seed 2	66
Know Thyself	66
SEED 2 – KNOW THYSELF	67
Know Thyself- How far back can you go?	69
Out of the Mouths of Babes and Suckling's	71
My Beginning	76
I Remember – Part I I Let Go	77
I Remember – Part II My Descent – 'Down the rabbit hole'	78
I Am the Way Shower	85
My Sacred Cup	87
Nurturing the Seeds	100
Seed Two- KNOW Thyself	100
Time to Do the Work	100
Air – Know Your Mind	100
Earth – Know your Body	101
Water – Know your Emotions	101
Fire - Know your Passion	102
Spirit – Know Your Spirit	103
Love – The Spirit of Love	104
Golden Seeds of Wisdom	105
Star Seed Journey	106
Soul journey – Journey to connect your higher self	106
Guided Journey to Meet your Higher Self	106
Journal Page	109

Seed 3 110
SEED 3 – UNDERSTAND THAT YOU ARE ENERGY 111
   Your Body's Natural Energy System 111

Understanding Energy 111

Hand Energy Sensing 112

Exercise 112

Exercise for Developing Hand Sensitivity 113
   Your Body's Natural Energy System 114

The Human Aura 114
     The Etheric Layer 115
     Emotional Layer 115
     Mental Layer 115
     Astral Layer 116
     Etheric Template Layer 116
     Celestial Layer 116
     Ketheric Template Layer 117
   The Chakras – Your Personal Energy and Information System 117
     The Chakra System 117

Understanding your 7 Chakras- What are they? 120

Spotlight on the 7 Chakras 121
     1. First - Base Chakra – (colour: Red) 121
     2. Second - Sacral Chakra– (colour: Orange) 121
     3. Third - Solar Plexus Chakra– (colour: Yellow) 122
     4. Fourth - Heart Chakra– (colour: Green) 122
     5. Fifth - Throat Chakra– (colour: Blue) 123
     6. Sixth - Brow Chakra– (colour: Indigo) 123
     7. Seventh - Crown Chakra – (colour: Violet) 124
     My Journey 124
   The Journey of Ascensions through the chakras 127
     Ascension through the Lower Chakras 127
     Passing through the gateways of the heart 127

Galactic or Collective Consciousness Chakras 130

Higher Level Chakras 130
8. Earth Star (seed) Chakra – Ancestral Gateway 130
9. Universal Heart or Higher Charka – Unity Consciousness 131

10. Cosmic or Causal Charka (Divine Masculine) 131
11. The Soul Star (Divine Feminine Centre)..................................... 131
12. Stellar Gateway/the Womb (Enlightenment – I Am Consciousness) 132
The Importance of Grounding and Protecting Your Energy Field 133
Grounding Exercises 134
Energy Protection 136

You are what you Eat 139

Food and The Elements 139
Rainbow Food Colour Chart 142

Chakra Cleanse – Power Up 144

Nurturing the Seeds 145
Seed 3 - Understanding yourself as Energy 145
Time to Do the Work 145

Earth –Root Chakra.. 145
Root Chakra Affirmations 146

Water - The Energy of Movement and Flow............................. 147
Sacral Chakra Affirmations 148
Fire – Solar Plexus - Your Inner Sun 148
Solar Plexus Affirmation 150
Love - The Heart Chakra - The Gateway to understating our connection to all that is 150
Heart Chakra Affirmations 151

Air –The Throat Chakra - The Space of Sacred Expression......... 152
Throat Chakra Affirmations 153

9

Spirit – Third Eye and Crown Chakra- Your inner eyes and connection to all things 154
Third Eye Affirmations 155
Crown Chakra 155
Crown Chakra Affirmations 155

Journal Page 156

Star Seed Journey- Soul Journey 157

12 Chakra Activation and Cleansing Meditation 157
Guided Meditation 157

Journal Page 160

SEED 4 – UNDERSTAND POWER OF YOUR THOUGHTS AND EMOTIONS 162

The Power of the Mind 162

The Power of Your Thought 165
- 1. Beta (14-40Hz) — The waking consciousness 165
- 2. Alpha (7.5-14Hz) — The deep relaxation wave 165
- 3. Theta (4-7.5Hz) — Vibrational Field of Change 166

The Power of Emotions 168

The Power of Your Words 171

Everything is Vibration and Frequency 173
Confusion Illusion 178

Freedom is a Frequency 181
Joy 185

Journal Page 186
Star Seed Journey 187
Soul Journey 187

Getting the Measure of your Fears 187

Guided Meditation 187

Journal Page	189
Seed 5	190
Make Peace	190
With Your	190
Past	190
SEED 5 – MAKE PEACE WITH YOUR PAST, TO UNLOCK YOUR POWER'	**191**
Childhood- The Foundation in Your Book of Life	191
The Healing Power of Forgiveness	193
Key to our Legacy	202
Nurturing the Seeds	211
Seed 5- Make Peace with Your Past	211
Time to Do the Work	211
Air – Clear Your Mind	211
Earth – Know your Body	211
Water – Know your Emotions	212
Fire – Know your Passion	212
Spirit – Know Your Spirit	213
Love – The Spirit of Love	213
Golden Seeds of Wisdom	214
Journal Page	215
Seed 6	216
Embrace Your Shadow	216
SEED 6 – EMBRACE YOUR SHADOW	**217**
Embracing Your Shadow	217
Balancing the Ego	218

Projection- our external mirrors	219
Tempering the Ego	219
Shadow healing work	221
Embracing My shadow	225
Be True to You	229
Duality Reality	230
Sides of the Same Coin (Love and Hate)	232
Don't Pretend	234
The Biggest Enemy	239
#ReleaseTheFear	242
Rebirth	245
Nurturing the Seeds	247
Seed 6 – Healing the Shadow	247
Time to Do the Work	247
Air – Know Your Mind	247
Earth – Know your Body	248
Water – Know your Emotions	248
Fire - Know your Power	249
Spirit – Know Your Past	249
Love – The Spirit of Love	250
Golden Seeds of Wisdom	251
Star Seed Journey	252
Soul Journey	252
Journey to Meet with Your Ego	252

Journal Page	254
SEED 7 – BE OPEN TO CHANGE	256
Alchemy – The Key to Understanding the Journey of Life	256
The Healing Power of Transformation	260
The Alchemy of Me	263
Nurturing the Seeds	264
Seed 7- Be open to change	264
Time to Do the Work	264
Air – Change Your Mind	264
Earth – Know your Body	265
Water – Change your Emotions	265
Fire – Know your Passion	266
Spirit – Change Your Spirit	266
Love – The Spirit of Love	266
Golden Seeds of Wisdom	266
Journal Page	267
SEED 8 – UNDERSTAND AND LEARN FROM YOUR RELATIONSHIPS	269
Relationships	269
Home and family Relationships	270
Friendships	271
Authority / Duality Reality	272
Work relationships	274
Romantic Relationships	275
Soul mate Relationships	278

Twin Flame Relationship	279
Letter to My Sister	285
Letter to My Mother	288
Letter to My Dad	292
Nurturing the Seeds	296
Seed- 8 Understand Your Relationships	296
Time to Do the Work	296
Air – Know Your Mind	296
Earth – Know your Body	296
Water – Know your Emotions	297
Fire - Know your Passion	297
Spirit – Know Your Spirit	297
Love – The Spirit of Love	298
Star Seed Journey	299
Guided Meditation Journey	299
Journal Page	301
Golden Seeds of Wisdom	302
Seed 9	303
Connect	303
to	303
Source	303
SEED 9 – CONNECT WITH SOURCE AND SPIRIT	304
Spirituality and Religion	305
What is Religion?	305
What is Spirituality?	310

Why is it important to develop Spiritual Practice? 313

My Journey with Spirit 314

Understanding Spiritual Power and Spiritual Practice 319

Understanding your Spiritual Power 324

Spiritual Power is an invisible force, abundant in nature, allowing for the betterment of all. 325

The importance of Spiritual Development 326

Connection with Your Ancestral and Spiritual Guides 327

Connecting with Your Higher Self 329

Understanding your Spiritual Power 330

> Spiritual power is very much connected to our emotions, faith and our experience of having our prayers answered or feeling the tangibility of the protection, guidance and present of Source, the Most High. 330
>
> Spiritual Power is an invisible force, abundant in nature, allowing for the betterment of all. 331

How to cultivate Spiritual Power 332

Meditation 333

Prayer 335

Affirmations 336

Developing your intuition 338

The Importance of Daily Spiritual Practice 340

Listening to Uplifting Music 341

Sekhmet Invocation 343

The Soul-U-tion 344

Nurturing the Seeds 346

Seed 9 - Connecting with Source 346

Time to Do the Work 346

....Air - The Mind/ Intellect/ Etheric 347
- Earth 347
- Water 347
- Fire 347
- Spirit 348
- Love 348
- Golden Seeds of Wisdom 349

Journal Page 350

Star Seed Journey 351

Soul Journey - Journey to Meet Your Spirit/ Ancestral Guardian 351

Guided Meditation Journey 351

Journal Page 353

Seed 10 354

The Alchemy of Ecstasy 354

SEED 10 – THE ALCHEMY OF ECSTASY 355

The Power of Intimacy, The Power of Alchemy 355

Let's Talk About Sex 355

The Dark Side of Sex 357

Understand the Healing Nature of Sexual Energy 358

The Sacred Art of Tantra 359

The Power of the Orgasm 360

Kundalini 361

Sacred Sex 361

The Art of Making Love	362
Sacred Sexuality	363
The Alchemy of Ecstasy – The Healing Nature of Sex	364
My Sacred Intention :-) My Divine Mate	366
In to me see (Intimacy)	370
Sacred Sexual Power	371
The Sacred Alchemy of You and Me	378
BLESSED risings :-)	381
Nurturing the Seeds	384
Seed 10 – Sacred Sexual Power	384
Time to Do the Work	384
Air – Know Your Mind	384
Earth – Know your Body	384
Water – Know your Emotions	385
Fire - Know your Passion	385
Spirit – Know Your Spirit	385
Love – The Spirit of Love	385
Golden Seeds of Wisdom	386
Journal Page	387
SEED 11 – UNDERSTAND THE POWER OF LOVE	389
Love	389
Love Connects Us All	389
Understanding The Various types of Love	392
1. Eros - Erotic Love	392
2. Philla - Affectionate Love	392
3. Storge - Familiar Love	393
4. Ludus - Playful Love	393
5. Mania - Obsessive Love	394

    6. Pragma - Enduring Love 395
        7. Phiautia - Self Love 395
        8. Agape - Selfless Love 396

The Purpose of Relationships 397

The Five Love Languages 398

    1. Words of Affirmation -Statement: *"Actions speak Louder than words"*... 398
    2. Quality Time - Statement: "Spending time with me, shows your love and affection" 399
    3. Receiving Gifts - Statement: "Showering me with gifts shows me your love me".. 399
    4. Acts of Service - Statement: "The things you do; shows me your Love"... 400
    5. Physical Touch - Statement: "The way you touch me and make me feel" 400
    Take a Moment to Reflect 401

Love languages quiz... 401

Love is the Elixir 402

Nurturing the Seeds 406

Seed - 11 Love is Your Super Power 406

Time to Do the Work 406

    Air – What Do you think about Love 406
    Earth – Know your Body 406

Water – What does Love Feel Like 407

    Fire - Know your Passion... 407
    Spirit – The Spirit of Love 407

Love – The Love That Is 408

    Golden Seeds of Wisdom 408

Journal Page 409

SEED 12 – BE THE MASTER OF YOUR REALITY	411
How to Create You Own Reality	412
Step Up, Step Out	414
It's time to Step up and Step Out!	414
Keep your Head	416
Nurturing the Seeds	417
Seed 12 – Step Up, Step Out	417
Time to Do the Work	417
Air – Master Your Mind	417
Earth – Master your Body	418
Water – Know your Emotions	418
Fire – Know your Passion	418
Spirit – Know Your Spirit	418
Love – The Spirit of Love	418
A Brand New Day	419
Step up, Step out	422
Journal Page	427
From Star to Seed….and Back Again	429
Other Books by Amenti the Awakener	432
Current	432
Forthcoming	432
About the Author	433
Holistic Health Expert, Light Worker and Spiritual Teacher	433
Your Review	435

Dedication (Livi-cation- Celebration of Life)

This book is dedicated to anyone who has ever known deep down in their heart, that there is more to this life than they have been told.

This book is for anyone who knows that they are more than they have been told they are.

This book is for all the Knowledge Seekers, and Wisdom Keepers, Wounded Healers and Free Speakers.

This book is for the Kings and the Queens
and for those who dare to dream.

This book is for the Mothers, the Fathers, the Sisters, the Brothers

This book is for the Rainbow, Crystal, and Indigo Children and the Young at Heart

This book is for Me and this book is for You

This book is for all who know Love to be true

and all those who are searching for their way back home

This book is for everyone, for everyone should know

the secrets within it, revealed in plain sight

For all to enjoy and find delight

To be part of a journey of remembering…

This Book is for You!

Now Turn the Page......And Let's Begin

Acknowledgements

I would like to take this moment in time, to Give thanks to the Most High One, Source Divine. For inspiring me within the guidance to speak, and giving me experience and knowledge to teach. I give thanks for all that I AM, all that I Was and All That I AM...to become.

I GIVE THANKS to DJEHUTI/THOTH and all of my guides and My GREAT GRANDMOTHER for guiding me and supporting me along the way. I Give Thanks to all of the people that supported me on my journey and have helped to bring this book together.

I GIVE THANKS to My Mother and Father, first and foremost, for giving birth to me, for without them, there would be no story. I GIVE THANKS to my Sisters, Brother, Aunties, Uncles and Nan for all your love and support.

A Special THANK YOU to my partner in Co-Creation and My children for supporting me and empowering me to succeed.

I GIVE THANKS to my Co- Pees (My closest friends) also for your love, lessons and encouragement.

I GIVE THANKS to my many mentors along the way especially RAS Campbell and Caroline Shola Arewa (My Spiritual Mama) for all the guidance.

To All the Clients and students that I have worked with through the Years, Organisations like NATURAL NOVEMBER and THE CALABASH HUB and DAY OF THE GODDESS for the continuous love and support.

To Tony at Overcome Foundation - Thank you so much for the support.

And to Me... Well Done!

The Message

We are Healing

Shedding

Connecting

Releasing

Loving

Creating

Affirming and Being

These are magical times

With more magical times ahead

Feel the fear and move through it

For it has so much to share

Clarity awaits you

For those who chose to hear

The whispers from the Heavens

Pouring down Divine Love and Care

To support you on your journey

Your strength will take you there

Open your heart to the truth in you

Bask in your love and share

This is a time of choosing

A dream that's coming true

Be loving, open and willing

That's all you have to do

The transformation is upon us

As we herald the grand cross

There is wisdom in each moment

How we receive it, is down to us

Be gentle to yourself, dear ones

And in the Creator, place your trust

And feel your spirit call you home, to shake off all the rust

Release from the cocoon you've created

To shield you from all your pain

Prepare the rebirth

And you'll be whole again

Make ready your intentions

Make them strong and true

Take a breath

Take a step

And the journey begins

Trust and you'll know what to do

Djehuti - TEHUTI

Seeds are magic, potent vessels of nature.

They hold entire intelligent blueprints for life.

They can lie dormant for ages before the conditions are ripe for them to burst into life. As a beautiful metaphor for consciousness, a seed represents the Divine Design within all things.

KRYSTAL EYZE

Preface

We are currently living in magical and transforming times. The earth is shifting, the weather is changing, people are evolving and doing amazing things and we are asking more questions about the world we live in.

Whether you're conscious of it or not we are in the midst of change.

There are many prophecies, scriptures and ancients' texts which have spoken of this time, the catastrophes that would take place and also the potential for great change in humanity; to evolve further than our wildest dreams or expectations.

Many texts such as the Bible and Emerald Tablets also speak of a time, when the world would see a birth of new beings, who would come to earth to help to raise the vibration of the people and the planet herself, and be a part of a sacred mission to usher in great change and the return of our sacred gifts.

Edgar Cayce (the sleeping prophet 1877-1945), one of the most documented psychics of all time said the following: "Great numbers of Children will be born who understand the electronics and atomic power as well as other forms of energy. They will grow into scientist and engineers of a new age which has the power to destroy civilization unless we learn to live by spiritual laws."

He predicted that theses 'special' children would be born with special gifts and characteristics that were once prevalent on the Earth but has since been phased out of our genetic pool. He goes on to say that their healing abilities, insight, energy, love and gifts will reveal itself to humanity to help to raise our collective consciousness.

In West Indian and African cultures, it has been said that our Ancestors reincarnate and return and many of the wise ones return as old souls at specific times in history, to bring back healing, ancient knowledge and insight to uplift and inspire the people through great shifts of consciousness and change.

The Indigos are another form of this energy, as we move into more evolved times, all the souls who were present at the beginning of the cycle. Are now reincarnated back on earth at the end of the old and to bring in the new.

These beings in human form, would come to the planet and have human experiences and look just like me and you, but they would be endowed with special qualities and gifts; heightened states of awareness and perception and empower us in new ideals of love, action, strength, fairness and enlightenment that will seem ahead of its time and a potent and welcoming force to bring in the winds of change.

These beings bring knowledge, wisdom and information from the higher realms and in their own experience through life; gain a passion for humanity and purpose; which inspires others to see the greatness in themselves, fight against illusion, unfairness and suppression and pave the way for the rebirth of this whole dimension into a higher state of being.

These beings have an innate knowing of other dimensions, and the understanding of life and death and the experiences beyond this realm...

They come with knowledge that expands the consciousness of those they are around and they lead by example and empowerment of others in to the next experience of man: Unity Consciousness and the Golden age; where we humans can live at our highest potential purpose and power.

They have come to break down old social ideals that no longer serve the greatest good of all and liberate and inspire others to free themselves from the illusion of separation and come together in true Oneness, Harmony and Unity.

There are many names for these beings, the Shining ones, the Indigo Children, Crystal children, 144000, Star children, Children of the Light amongst others.

Throughout the history of man, there have always been ones, who have manifested on this realm to be a guidance to others through the experience of their lives.

Hailie Selassie, Solomon, Yeshua or Jesus, Mohammed and all the prophets of the worlds history came to this Earth as human beings and through their life experience, their challenges, their struggle, and then their own self-awareness, reflection and then righteous action, became leaders and examples for us to follow.

Through their deep connection with their highest and lowest self, their Creator and their will, the inner voice, their conviction, self-reflection and purpose, they became a guiding force for others and brought in new ideals and change for the people of Earth.

The role of an indigos, old souls and others is to bring forth great change through experience, gnosis and divine wisdom and a purpose to help us see outside of the current limitations of our society and how we see ourselves.

We each have special gifts, and have chosen to be born at this time, on this Earth to help humanity to awaken to its true identity and to re-embody its sacred gifts and divinity.

Christ 'himself' said that we would go on to do greater miracles than he and this is the time of awakening that consciousness with ourselves. And in order to do that, we must seek to 'lighten' ourselves, to know ourselves fully in both darkness and light and to gain mastery of self and share the knowledge of that journey with others.

> ***To know thyself…. This is the true enlightenment!***

As we are collectively coming to the understanding that there is more to this life that we currently know of, it offers us opportunity to tap into some of the hidden and deeper aspects of our purpose on this Earth and opening up to the expansive potential of the human experience.

Have you ever wondered why the Ancients Egyptians, Sumerians, Atlanteans and other civilizations were able to create and do things that we can only dream about?

Have you ever wondered about the source of your origin or why you're no longer able to fly?

We as a civilization, in this realm of duality, have had to experience both the best and highest of our self (Atlantis/Kemet) and the lowest of our selves (Roman empire, slavery past 2000 years).

The age of Pieces, which was the age of separation and duality, gifted us with the experience of learning from our consequences and the illusion of separation from Source, when out of balances with divine order and harmony.

The coming age of the Aquarius, the age of information and the pouring out of knowledge offers us the opportunity to consolidate our learning, and return back to the Divinity of our grace and in line with our original purpose and intention.

The Ancients knew that this time would come, and many scriptures speak of the end, and yes it is the end, the end of the old, the end of separation and the birth of unity consciousness and oneness, the next stage of evolution in our human story.

From homo sapient to homo luminous.

I remember, from a very young age, I had a level of awareness that even at first I didn't understand, but my connection to the creator and my level of soul consciousness from beyond enabled/empowered me to navigate my way through life with a heightened level of awareness, past life memories, the ability to ask Spirit and know all things, read people, see energy and many other gifts and hidden abilities which allowed me to be what I AM....a Spirit having an earthly experience!

My life was full of ups and down just like most other people, but with many twists and turn and sprinkles of magic, to make it all the more multi-dimensional.

One of my gifts being my gift of communication and the ability to understand and feel the pain of others, articulate it and heal it through sound and expression. I also had a special gift which allowed me to connect with the heart and spirit of others, regardless of colour, creed or race. I could speak in the language of their soul, in the language of love, truth and Divine Wisdom.

I went through sexual abuse, childhood trauma, spiritual abuse, you name it, but all with a level of consciousness that allowed me to understand the higher soul learning of each experience and an overwhelming knowing within that all was for a purpose. I chose these experiences so I could feel, embody, cry, release, heal, forgive, shed, love and expand and know my greatness so that I could support others in doing the same thing and turn their lead into gold!

Throughout all of my endeavours, the voice of my higher self and The Most-High 'God" never left me, or allowed me to feel alone, even though at times I felt alone in this world. I used the power of words and song to express what I was feeling and to heal the trauma I had experienced. My love of writing allowed me to put pen to paper and document all of my experiences from my soul's highest perspective, whilst offering understanding which allowed the healing in me to unfold.

I knew one day that the words I wrote and the expressions and understanding of the experiences I had, would soon be called upon to help others to see the light in their own darkness and turn their base metals and experiences into the Gold that would bring them their power and their purpose.

The transformative experience of life on this realm is a journey that many embark on without navigation. We are thrust into life and can aimlessly walk through it totally affected by everything and a slave to the experience rather than in your true guise as the Master and Creator of your reality.

It is a divine truth that nothing happens to us without reason because we have intended and created every single part of this journey and this life.

Our true power in this realm comes in the form of Spiritual Alchemy, the process of turning your lead into gold, your pain into your power, your passion into your purpose.

Within these pages you will find my sacred expression, my highs and my lows, my spirit messages and my insights and nuggets of wisdom that allowed me to grow from a seed to a star and remember my true divinity.

I, along with my guides, bring forth this workbook in the hope that it will assist someone in their own healing and help them to remember the greatness in them and who they truly are. To know that they are so strong and perfect that they chose to come here and carry the burden of not only themselves but their family and their ancestors.

To remind them of the special gift that it is to be here at this time and the power of turning your lead into your gold, your story into your power, and your pain into your purpose.

I hope it awakens and inspires you and if nothing else just allows you a little snippet of me with love.

So I give this gift to you 12 Seeds to Awaken the Spirit, the life of a spirit having a human experience :-) Enjoy

HOW THIS BOOK WAS CREATED

"Stars cannot Shine without Darkness, and Seeds can not Grow without Light. Such is the true balance in the nature of Life"

As I reflect on how this book came to be and introduce to you my latest creation, I am filled with a profound sense of gratitude and excitement for the journey I have taken, but most importantly for the gift I am about to share with you and how it may (I hope) empower, influence or inspire you as much as it did me to experience it.

This book was birthed through my inner guidance, healing and transformation. It's been a long time in the making only because, this book is a testament to my own personal journey, and I had to grow into what I know so to speak.

I long resisted the guidance to write and create my own book and gift to humanity. An avid lover of books and all thing literature I knew one day that my own purpose was to write books that would be read and enjoyed by many for years to come.

But little did I know that as much as I knew it to be my purpose, I was also scared of my own truth and success.

12 seeds to Awaken your Spirit is unlike any other book I've read because I had to become the book, as I grew, the information grew and has become an example of my journey and experience thus far.

The journey began a while ago, and to be honest, I know it started way before that, in the Heavens, but the journey that marks the start of this particular healing creation started in 2012, which was an auspicious time and beginning of a change in reality and consciousness for many.

One Night in 2012

One night in 2012, in Dublin, whilst visiting a dear healer and sister friends of mine, Ruth, I was guided to channel and connect with the spirit of Djehuti, (Tehuti/Thoth to the Greeks) the Ancient Egyptian/Kemetic deity, who had long been a guide and mentor in spirit for me.

Ruth and I, both being trained in Channelling and Sacred Arts, set up a sacred and safe space for communication. As he spoke through me, he stated that he wanted to work more closely with me as part of my purpose to bring forth Divine knowledge and guidance to empower the people in my community in this time. He said that I should start by holding an open channelling event that evening with a few close others, so I could practice channelling his energy and so he could connect with those present and bring forth spiritual insight.

I had to admit that I was quite nervous by this as I had only channelled a few times before and it was not something I thought I would do again, however from just the small channelling that had just taken place in Ruth's therapy room, I could already feel some energy shifting within my body, my heart and throat chakra pulsated and my mind felt open.

Djehuti had instructed us that I would find a blue stone on my travels that would help to open the connection with him and prepare me for the channelling event.

So said, so done. As we were on our travels, we stopped by a shop that had this amazing blue Larimar stone that just spoke to me. It was the shape of a tear drop and sat just on my throat chakra when I tried it on.

Larimar is an Ancient Atlanteans stone found off the coast of the Dominican Republic where it is said that Atlantis sank. Djehuti or Thoth as he is also known, is also an Ancient High priest from the civilization of Atlantis and it is said that when Atlantis was about to be destroyed by its people, Thoth/Djehuti and other Atla Priests set a plan to flee Atlantis and set up a new foundation on Earth.

The reason why this stone was of so much significance for me at this time was because Larimar was once a stone that was popular in the times of Atlantis. Its properties include, enhancing connection with higher energies, opening the way for communications and channelling, it empowers your heart chakra and your universal heart chakra which is your energy centre of unconditional love.

But most importantly when I placed it on my throat, I felt my throat chakra open up and I knew that I could now speak with a knowing and trust that all would be well for the channelling

Larimar is a stone deeply connected to the energy of Atlantis and I had wanted a piece for so long. It was quite a big piece and as I hadn't planned to be making a purchase, I was unsure about whether I could buy it at the time. However, when I asked the man behind the counter, he said that the original piece was £77 but it had gone down today to £44. I smiled to myself and that was exactly what I had and I knew it was confirmation that was on the right path.

That evening, although I was filled with a little fear and doubt, having never channelled publicly before, I carried out the channelling and it was an amazing experience for all involved. The magic that was channelled and felt had me buzzing and everyone congratulated and thanked me for being of service. I was honoured to have been involved in the connection and happy for the wisdom shared.

But that night, as everyone left, I felt this buzzing energy inside of me. It was a nervous and anxious energy but also felt like something was building inside, coming up to be cleared.

Before I had come to Dublin I was at a crossroads in my life. I was faced with dealing with some challenges that had affected me since childhood, and although I had thought that I had dealt with them, the fact they were resurfacing, left me feeling tired and confused, so I went to Dublin to relax, review and gain some clarity.

Up until now, I hadn't focused on anything from back home but now all of a sudden it all came flooding back to my mind.

Like an avalanche of memories and emotion, thoughts and feelings came crashing through my mind. As each image came, I felt a stab or jab in my body. My heart, my back, my throat! All the memories of my reacting to the trauma trapped in my body, my whole head and the room around me started to spin.

The room going round, faster and faster. Insides feeling more and more twisted.

Nausea building and building…. I scramble around for somewhere to sit or to lie down to ground and find my balance.

And I fall back onto the chair behind me an allow the chaos to enfold me, consume me….no longer fighting, no longer resisting

Just releasing, just release….and let go

Release….and let go

I let go…

And as I do, as I surrender fully and completely to the process, to the chaos, to my pain and confusion…. I realised that everything had stopped!

Everything has stopped.

The room has stopped spinning.

The Nausea had stopped

And silence on the backdrop of my heartbeat, filled the air.

In this moment, I felt like nothing and everything, all at the same time.

I felt safe and vulnerable, real and unreal, loved and love, connected to all and connected to nothing at all!

So, I stayed in this space for a while and just allowed myself to Just Be!

Something that felt so hard to do at home!

I basked in the energy of feeling close to source, feeling close to home.

Home...

And that was all I could remember before this surge of energy came rushing up from my root chakra, bursting through my sacral, igniting my solar plexus, coursing through my heart and exploding from throat to my crown on a sea of tear and emotions and I opened up, released and I let go!

I cried, I cried, I cried, I cried.

I whaled, I whaled, I whaled.

I moaned, I moaned, I moaned

And I held myself so deeply and tightly and I Love, Loved, Loved ME!!!

I had so much energy flowing through my body.

It was as though the past had flashed before my eyes, but I was re connecting with my original intention for creating the obstacles I did in my life, and remembering the qualities and life experience.

I knew it would gift me with the tools and true knowing of self, locked and hidden within the pain and trauma, that would help me to understand and achieve my purpose on this realm.

By living a life of conscious reflection. To go through a multitude of human burdens and experiences, in a short space of time.

With a level of consciousness and awareness that world allow me to experience, embody, understand, learn, resolve, heal and transmute, that would allow others to know that they too can get through everything they have chosen and help them to remember who they are.

But now it was time to unpack my own pain and transform it into my purpose.

And it was at that point that I heard the spirit of Djehuti say, "it's time to write" …. And was the beginning of 12 Seeds to Awaken Your Spirit – From Star to Seed and Back Again.

In that night I wrote 44 poems or healing expressions, which honoured my story and allowed me to transform my understanding of my experience into the healing that I required to be conscious of my choices and experience. As I wrote, tears flowed, joy was evoked, I laughed, I reminisced and I found my power! I turned my pain into my power and reignited my purpose whilst healing myself.

Any time, I have read these poems or heling verses to others, they have been deeply touched and have commented on how the way that the words are expressed, connect them with the story and their own personal experience. But also, they feel that they are 'healed' or inspired by the journey within the message, which empowers them with a new understanding of the experiences of themselves or others.

The poems and prose facilitate a process of alchemical healing within, inspiring and empowering us all to transform our lead into gold and our purpose in to our power

From that night my whole life changed and I stepped even further into my purpose to learn, to serve and be a Divine Oracle for the people in my community and who seek healing and understanding and a sometimes 'alternative' perspective on life as a human having a spiritual experience.

When I looked back on the video recording of the channelling event a few weeks later, I was shocked and surprised to see how the whole thing manifested itself and how spirit and reality became one. And I would one day share the result of my own healing, with others so they too can get whatever they need from it and from my journey.

Since that time in Dublin, I have wanted to write the book that was gifted to me by my own healing, but little did I realise that I would still have some growing and experiencing to do before I could really embody and share the truth that is my purpose.

In life we go through a continuous flow of death and rebirth, change and transformation, release and growth, which are sometimes layered like the skin of an onion – just as you feel you have removed one layer, or healed, then something else pops up challenging you to push yourself even more.

'12 seed was a call to me to be something more than the limitation that I had set myself and to Step Up and Step Out into my purpose. The Golden seeds of wisdom are the keys that helped me to unlock the door to my true potential and assist me in navigating my way back to the star- in me! And it is my wish, that it will do the same for you! Enjoy!

How to use this book?

The format of this book was created in a way that would allow me to share a little of my journey and experience, include some of the Healing Prose that Spirit channelled through my healing, and also share some practical tools and wisdom that can assist others on their journey to seed to star and back again.

It is a practical workbook that will allow you to take the first steps towards getting to know yourself and awakening your spirit. Life is a constant unfolding and the more that we seek to learn about ourselves the more there is to learn and the more that we learn the more we become.

You are here to be your most powerful and loving self and it will take many experiences to help you to become just that.

You can use this book to support you on that journey and also as a reflective tool, once complete, to show you just how far you have come.

The Importance of the Number 12

This is a magical or a divine number that affects us humans in many more ways than one for it is the perfect numeral to represent how vibrations affect our DNA and souls. It is also said to signify the "end or a whole. The number twelve has a special meaning in nature which is representative in math and math can help you decipher the secret mysteries of nature.

You will see the fact that there is only one true square number, (144) 12 x 12 = 144, which we know as Pure Math Harmony Vertically and Horizontally. This can be easily seen in music, but this also affects our DNA and how we react to these "vibrations.

The number 12 is an important one when it comes to numerology since it signifies completion. It also belongs to the star sign Pisces who is known to be a spiritual sign that is in constant touch with the energies of the universe

The number 12 is made up of two numbers, 1 and 2. 1 is a prime number and signifies the beginning and the singular nature of the universe. It is also related to completion, perfection, harmony, motivation, achievement and independence. 2, on the other hand, is all about seeing two sides of any situation, diplomacy, partnership and the mutable nature of life.

The number 12 is the result of 4×3, 4 elements – 4 corners of the earth – 4 cardinal points. When these are multiplied 4 x 3, three being the sacred number of God, the result is 12 – the perfect number.

Some other awesome 12 facts:

1. *Represent the manifestation of the Trinity to the four corners of the horizon - 3 X 4.*
2. *Symbolize the command and the good, and governs the space and the time, that is to say the operation of the Cosmos, from where its designation of cosmic number.*
3. *Number attributed to the government of the world or the cosmos.*
4. *It is the creative capacity, and in some religions, it expresses also the Divine Mother.*
5. *Twelve is the number of what is completed, which forms a whole, a perfect and harmonious unit.*

Some other important number 12 principles

1. *12 strands of DNA*
2. *12 signs of Zodiac*
3. *12 chakras*
4. *12 original tribes of humanity*
5. *12 Solar and Lunar months and more*

SACRED GEOMTERY - THE KEY TO LIFE

"All Consciousness, including human, is solely based on Sacred Geometry"

The Flow of Life Vol 2 – Drunvalo Melchizedek

From the Star to the Seed – The Beginning of All Life

Sacred geometry is a universal language that describes the inner workings of nature and the intrinsic order of the universe. It is the natural sanction that unites all forms of life… from microbes, plants, animals and humans to the motions of the planets and stars. It shows the connection and interrelated

Everything is creation has a significant purpose and intention and therefore everything also has an underlying geometric template which links it to the Cosmos, To the Creator.

We as Human beings are a manifestation of that expressed consciousness and the same energy and make up is the substance of the stars is the same substance that created us. And even more so everything that is in the Cosmos is within us. We are the stars, that were birthed in the heavens and have descended into consciousness and life on another dimension playground.

Our purpose is to come and experience more of ourselves is this limited form and to bring more of our soul consciousness, the true essence of who we are into this physical body and reality.

We as collective co-creators, create a reality of experience through our collective thought, emotions and actions. However, we are all connected to the One Universal Mind, the Creative Source of all that is and therefore here to experience ourselves as a differentiated aspect of the One. To be Creator of our own reality and experience and to attain the experience of Decadence into the Material and Ascension, a remembering of one's original source and intention.

Once the experience the illusion of separation has been experienced and understood, then we integrate that knowledge and awareness and bring down more of our source light, our God essence into our being and raise the vibration of the physical human experience and that of the planet as well.

We are at a crucial time in our human story where we are transitioning into another, higher dimensional experience, where we get to experience more of our self at a higher vibration. We are remembering the lost aspects of our soul's consciousness and what it truly means to be and Child of the Creator.

We are being called to heal and awaken to who we truly are. To raise our awareness of self and everything around us, and understanding our true nature and connection to all things

By consciously examining our life experiences, we are learning to see and experience reality beyond the limitation of the 5 senses, and awaken to the latent power that is within you.

Know thyself is one of the first steps towards becoming a master of your reality and making that vibrational shift and allowing more of you to manifest within you. To know yourself is to know God, to know the Universe and to know all, as all is within you! And to return to a place of oneness and harmony with all things, all creation and work in alignment with the all that is to manifest all that you need and require, for this experience of life.

You see, in this time we are being encouraged to remember that we are the stars who have made their descent from the cosmos, to the Earth. We have been planted deep into her centre, as golden seeds of light consciousness. During this descent, we become lower in our vibrational rate in order to match the frequency matter and the material. During this process we lose a lot of the remembrance of who we are and what we came here for, only vague memories will be left in our consciousness to help us to remember.

And as we embed within her, in the depths of her fertile womb, a new life is created and a new Star-seed, which is you, is about to begin a journey of awakening and unfolding. Learning and embodying and experiencing so that it can learn to understand it self and in doing so, understand the very nature of God and the Universe.

Whilst here you have a personal mission, which is the sum total of your experience and the lessons that your soul consciousness has chosen to learn and also one for humanity. Each one has a purpose that is of benefit to the whole and many of us are here to raise the vibration of the planet to support her rebirth in her next stage.

As we learn from our life experiences, understand our true nature and how we connect to all things and then intentionally embody the light and raise our own vibration, we empower the creation of a new reality and remember that we are the stars!

Each one of us has everything that we need hidden inside of us and it our job in this time to uncover and explore more of who we are and how we came to be here. You were created with a unique divine geometric blue print that is You and everything about you is Perfect, Whole and Complete.

But to experience yourself you must separate from the whole, or even experience the illusion of separation in order to then see yourself within the whole.

You are here to experience you I relation to you, working in harmony or against You, as everything is You!

The journey from Star to Seed and Back again is the story of You and how you came to be here, what you are here to do, and how to be a master of reality here on earth, before you make your Ascension back to the stars.

The Seed of Life

Sacred geometry holds the divine blueprint to all things and in order to understand yourself fully you must understand the nature of creation and reality.

The Universe is the Great Cosmic Womb of creation and as with all life, everything begins with a seed. Whether a seed sound or a literal seed, the whole of creation is birthed from the seed. And so are. Sacred geometry helps us to understand our nature and connection to all things.

The Seed of Life is a Sacred Geometric symbol, which is the source of all creation. It is universal symbol of creation and contains the blueprint for all life.

It demonstrates that all of creation is formed from the same divine blueprint and all have the same potential to experience Source at its varying levels

The Seed of Life

In sacred geometry, it is formed from a relationship of 6 circles around one. In fact, 6 circles will ALWAYS fit exactly around a 7th circle of the same size. Some also say that there is an 8th circle in the middle of the flower as well.

Each circle fits into this pattern like a lock and key, forming a dynamic field of possible geometric relationships which reveal the most fundamental shapes of Creation.

These 7/8 circles mirror our chakras, the colours of the rainbow & even musical scales! It forms a foundation upon which the infinite, fractal nature of life can be understood. They are also said to represent the number of cells in the nucleus of a human embryo at its first stage of embryo development

The creator's consciousness exists within the Sphere, and the only thing that really exists is the membrane of the sphere itself.

The **Seed of Life** is a stage before the shape known as the **Flower of Life** which produces the "Fruit of Life". The Fruit of life is the **blueprint of the universe**; it contains every atom, molecular structure, life form and eventually everything in existence. Therefore, all things existing can be built from the shape of the **seed of life**. The 7 circles within the seed of life represent the 7 days of creation and the soul sounds of creation.

Seed or 'Bija' is also the name given to the 7 tones of creation and mantras and chants. This is related to the seed of sound that is the basis of all creation.

The seed of life is the consciousness of Source Creator in all things and is the blueprint for all life in the Universe.

All life begins from as a seed. Whether It be a seed of intention, a seed within the womb, or a seed within the ground, all of us come from the same source.

That's seed, that golden seed of consciousness, that descended from the cosmos and is now You, is full of source potential and with the right soil and nutrients, will become a full and vibrant tree, ready to make its ways back to the stars. The process of transformation taken by the seed is a great example of the alchemical process that we embark on during our time her on the earth plane. We start out as a seed in the womb of our mother and sperm of our father, but as that seed is being planted a star is also being born in the heavens. Think back to the story of Jesus and the 3 wise men who looked to the stars to predict the time and place of his birth.

This is the same for each and every one of us.

Growing Through the Tree of Life

The Tree of life is also another significant sacred geometry symbol that is symbolic of our growth and development here on this planet in our journey from star to see and back again.

It fits within the sacred geometry of the seed of life which blooms in the Flower of Life, originally called the Flower of Amenti (include quote from tablet 13), 13 being the goddess number of creation, the holder of the divine egg and seed of life.

And this tree is symbolic of Mother Earth and the nourishment that she gives to sustain all life with all the nutrients and elements its need to grow.

The Tree of life is also integral element of philosophy and study originating from Ancient Judaism and the beginning of Christianity and the Orthodox religions. It can be seen as a complex and multi-faceted philosophy but as its most basic level it represents the wisdom to see the Divine within.

The Kabbalah teaches that in order to move inward closer towards to Most High and Source within, it is necessary to understand the stages and the creation of Universal reality. It is formed from 10 'Sefirot' which are considered to be 'Divine Lights' acting as channels for consciousness.

Growing Through the Tree of Life

The Tree of life is also another significant sacred geometry symbol that is symbolic of our growth and development here on this planet in our journey from star to see and back again.

It fits within the sacred geometry of the seed of life which blooms in the Flower of Life, originally called the Flower of Amenti (include quote from tablet 13), 13 being the goddess number of creation, the holder of the divine egg and seed of life.

And this tree is symbolic of Mother Earth and the nourishment that she gives to sustain all life with all the nutrients and elements its need to grow.

The Tree of life is also integral element of philosophy and study originating from Ancient Judaism and the beginning of Christianity and the Orthodox religions. It can be seen as a complex and multi-faceted philosophy but as its most basic level it represents the wisdom to see the Divine within.

The Kabbalah teaches that in order to move inward closer towards to Most High and Source within, it is necessary to understand the stages and the creation of Universal reality. It is formed from 10 'Sefirot' which are considered to be 'Divine Lights' acting as channels for consciousness.

The Divine Lights

Keter/Da'at The two opposing forces of God	*Crown and highest of the 10* *Corresponds with the super-conscious realm of experience. Representing the aura and consciousness of Man*
Chochmah - Wisdom	*The first power of conscious intellect within creation*
Binah – Understanding	*The second power of conscious intellect within Creation*
Da'at - Knowledge	*The third and final power of conscious intellect*
Chesed – Loving kindness	*The first emotive attributes of Creation*
Gevurah - Might	*The second emotive attributes of Creation*
Tipharet – Beauty	*The third emotive attributes of Creation*
Netzach – Victory	*The forth emotive attribute within Creation*
Hod – Splendour	*The fifth emotive attribute of Creation*

| Yesod – Foundation | *The sixth emotive attribute of Creation* |
| Malkut –Kingdom /Earth | *The seventh emotive attribute of Creation* |

Sacred Geometry is the blueprint of Divine Consciousness and every one of us and everything we need can be experienced through the study of sacred geometry as a study of self and the universe.

Each one of us were birthed from the stars; we all have a purpose; and it was written that we would come at this time and do great things and bring great change and healing to this planet.

Every one of us has a divine reason for being here and the quicker that we embrace the unfolding and take the steps towards choosing to live from our highest self, then humanity will experience a higher consciousness of Love and Self Mastery and truly restore balance and harmony amongst each other and on our planet again.

But before all of that, we have some work to do.

The 5 Platonic Solids

The 5 platonic solids are also sacred geometrical shapes that are connected to the Seed of life and all of creating. They form the building blocks of manifesting source into form. There are 5 all together and they connect with different aspects of reality and dimensions and are also found within all thing. The 5 platonic solids are the Cube, Icosahedron, Tetrahedron, Octahedron and the Dodecahedron.

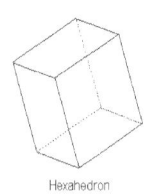

The **Cube** is also known as the hexahedron and is a six sided figure with square faces. The cube is associated with the element of earth and the base Chakra. The cube represents the connections with the foundations of the earth to the foundations of the heavens.

The **Icosahedron** structure represents movement, flow and change. It has 20 sides all of which are equilateral triangles. This shape can be found all throughout nature in various forms. It is said to be connected with the element of water and sacral charka and offers help in balancing the emotions. Working with the Icosahedron can also help facilitate regenerating and healing energy into physical reality.

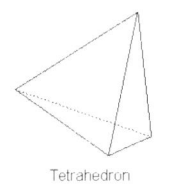

Tetrahedron is a four-sided pyramid, each of its sides being an equilateral triangle. This platonic solid is connected to the element of fire, the solar plexus chakra and is associated with creativity, motivation, inspiration, will power and self-respect.

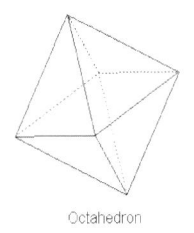

Octahedron is composed of eight equilateral triangles, four of which meet at each vertex. This shape is associated with the element of air and the throat chakra which is our centre of expression through vibration and sound. Our hearts truth is found in the Octahedron as it aids communication of self-love and compassion. The Octahedron reminds us that we all have the wisdom to know when to express our truth or when to be silent.

The **Dodecahedron** has 12 faces and 20 vertices, each face being a pentagon. The Dodecahedron is associated with spirit and consciousness and is attributed to the third eye chakra which shows the truth beyond illusion by helping us see the divine connection with all things. Some have believed that the Dodecahedron represents an idealized form of Divine thought, will or ideas. To contemplate this symbol was to engage in meditation upon the Divine.

Other Important Sacred Geometry Symbols

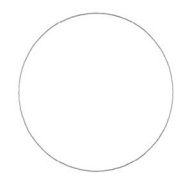

A **sphere** is a perfectly round geometrical object in three-dimensional space that is the surface of a completely round ball. This shape is associated with the crown chakra which is elementally linked to cosmic energy and opens the connection to the infinite source of creation. By understanding the sphere we are able to release limitations and through conscious focus we create union with a higher power. Through understanding the mysteries surrounding these ancient and universal shapes we can gain cosmic knowledge of our infinite connectedness to the universe and beyond.

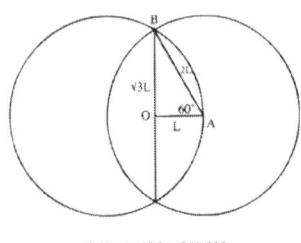

THE VESICA PISCIS

The **Vesica piscis** is a type of lens, a mathematical shape formed by the intersection of two disks with the same radius, intersecting in such a way that the center of each disk lies on the perimeter of the other. In Latin, "vesica piscis" literally means "bladder of a fish", reflecting the shape's resemblance to the conjoined dual air bladders ("swim bladder") found in most fish. In Italian, the shape's name is mandorla ("almond"). The Vesica Piscis, is a very special symbol, in that it represents the Divine Feminine and the Sacred entry into the womb, and also the connection between Male and Female and the Union between the two. In Magic and Ritual practice, it is also used a symbol for manifestation and creation. The first circle symbolizes the past, the second represents the Future and the space in between, equals the Present.

You can write down and create anything that you want to bring into your life now, by writing it into the middle space. I have completed this ritual many times and have been very successful. Why don't you try it out yourself?

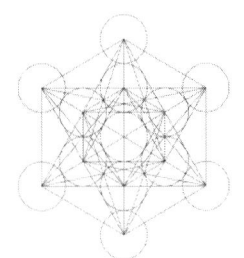

The **Merkaba or Star Tetrahedron** is comprised of two interlocking tetrahedron shapes – one pointing up to the heavens, channelling energy down from the Universe to the earth plain, and one pointing downwards, drawing energy up from the earth beneath. The Merkaba is powered by love and corresponds to the heart chakra which is the centre of our being. The Star Tetrahedron contains all manner of possibilities as well as for healing and even to transcend into other dimensions of existence. It also contains all the other platonic solids within.

The **Flower of Life** (also known as the Flower of Amenti) The "Flower of Life" can be found in all major religions of the world. In Egypt, the source of all the monotheistic religions, the "Flower of Life" can be found in the ancient Temple of Abydos. The flower of life contains all sacred symbols and also, a secret symbol created by drawing 13 circles out of the Flower of Life.

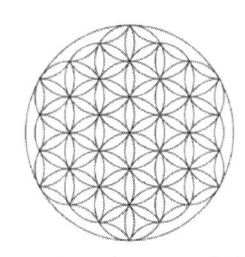

By drawing this symbol, one can discover the most important and sacred pattern in the universe. This is the source of all that exists; it's called the Fruit of Life. It contains 13 informational systems. Each one explains another aspect of reality. Thus these systems are able to give us access to everything ranging from the human body to the galaxies. The Flower of Life is also the Womb of Creation, as everything in creation can be created from this shape.

These sacred geometry symbols hold the codes for creation and they are powerful to connect with and use. When you start to draw them, you awaken the consciousness within them and start to understand its connection to all things. Working with them individually is said to help with our connection to nature and the higher realms of the cosmos; to find the common pattern which links us all at a molecular as well as at a spiritual level.

From Star to Seed....and Back Again

We are the star-seeds, that have travelled from the Universe to be planted in the fertile soil of Mother Earth. On the journey from star to seed, our purpose is to acknowledge ourselves a part of everything and connected to everything. To know that we are much more than our physical bodies, that we are, in fact a powerful divine spark of consciousness, a manifestation of Source creator energy and that we have all chosen to come experience ourselves externally and i relation to all. As a sacred golden seed, planted into the fertile soil of Mother Earth, we are empowered to learn, experience, grow and to essentially make your way back to source, as light, as a Star.

Mother Earth in a multi-dimensional entity, she is living and breathing and houses and sustains all life on this planet, including us.

She nurtures us all with her natural elements and minerals that keep us balanced, healthy and nourished and maintains a homeostasis for all on the planet, so that all can be nourished and grow.

She used Fire, as active principal, that brings the warmth of the sun and which can either cause a dessert or nourish fertile lands.

The Water, which forms the main substance on the planet and provide sustenance for all life, is cleansing and purifying.

Air is uplifting and liberating, subtle yet powerful, transforming and calming; and allows us to transcend above the heights and experience her beauty from a different perspective

And Earth is the lush rich and fertile womb of the planet that nourishes and provided the foundation for all to grow and the abundance to sustain all life.

All is kept in a harmonious balance in order to provide the right environment to nurture golden seeds. When this balance is out of alignment, we see the things that we currently see manifesting in our world.

Hurricanes, tsunamis and chaotic weather are effects of the imbalance and purging that is taking place within us also, as we and the earth are one.

The concept and practice of using the elements to nurture our golden seed, allows us a frame work of understating and practical application that can support us in our learning, development and experience of the game of life and ultimately assist us in gaining self-mastery and resolving our life lessons while completing our collective goals during our time here. It has been a useful practice for me and forms the framework for the healing work I carry out with my clients

Included in this book is a section to make notes, however it is highly recommended that you get yourself a journal specifically for doing the soul or seed nurturing work within the book.

Journaling will allow you to truly get the best out of the experience and gain a deeper understanding of self and take the steps to make changes.

Some exercises may be physical and some will encourage you to take challenging steps and challenge your fears. View this process with an open heart and be willing to try. Nourish your seeds with love, compassion and change; and you will be gifted with a transforming experience.

Within our own lives, we can use the archetypes of the elements to nurture us as the seeds and so therefore, within this are the tools that facilitate the self-development work and the active nourishing of our own seeds. The 'nourishing the seeds' section provides practical tools, exercises and guidance which can assist you with digging deeper with the topics discussed and providing the first steps towards your own self-healing and awareness.

These are tools that I have learned along the way that have helped me to nurture the seed in myself and I trust that you will find them just as useful.

Journey to the Stars

Following the nurturing the seeds section at the end of each chapter, you will also find a section called 'Star Seed Journey'. The purpose of the star seed journey aspect of the book is to help you to connect further to your higher consciousness and to offer you opportunities to experience yourself from different angles and perspective.

These will be offered in the form of guided meditation and visualisations; some will take place in the Halls of Amenti.

Our purpose now, in this time, is to remember who we truly are. To awaken from our sleep and remember the reason why we came here and what it is we are truly here to do.

So many of us, have been here before and are here again, at the turn of the age to restore balance and harmony, with in ourselves and the planet, to fulfil our life purpose and mission and to once again bring heaven to earth through our divine beings.

When we make the choice to truly ascend, to truly live our highest truths and release from the lessons of the past, of duality and separation and illusion, we transcend and transmute all the experiences of the lower aspects of our being. When we turn our shadow into light and balance our heart against the feather, then we become the living 'Gods'- experiencing long life, holistic health and longevity.

This is my understanding of the true return of the Christ Consciousness and the restoration of the Divine spirit within us, within the flesh.

Tewahedo to the Ethiopians and Smai Tawi to the Ancient Egyptians. The ultimate purpose of life to bring heaven onto Earth, in balance harmony and oneness.

And this is the vibration and experience of the fifth dimension, which is the 5th element, the vibration of Love and oneness and the experience of Unity Consciousness.

So, as we get ready to embark on a conscious journey from star to seed, I share with you my experience and wisdom with the intention that you will find practical tools and guidance of benefit and get to know my journey and your journey, a little better.

I do this in the hope that it may inspire and empower or at the very least bring a smile to your face or offer some food for thought.

The first step of any journey is usually the hardest, but together we can take step in the right direction and awaken you to the true power of your spirit and who you truly are so you can be a master of your reality, find your life purpose and turn your lead into gold.

Now Let's begin!

Seed 1

Understand the

Laws of the Universe

"He who knows theses understandingly, possess the Magic Key, before whose touch, all the doors to the temple fly open

The Kybalion

SEED 1 – UNDERSTAND THE LAWS OF THE UNIVERSE

> *"The Principals of Truth are Seven; he who knows this, understandingly, possess the Magic Key before whose touch all doors of the Temple fly open"*
>
> *Kybalion*

The Universal Laws are the laws that were passed down through the wisdom of Thoth/Tehuti who was later know as Hermes, through a book called The Kybalion.

This sacred wisdom passed on the knowledge of the understanding of how everything in the Universe works and therefore how we can understand ourselves and master our reality.

Many know about the Law of Attraction which was made popular by the book called 'The Secret,' but the Law of Attraction is only one part of the puzzle and in order to truly master your reality and understand yourself, you need at least a basic understanding of the Universals Laws.

1. There 7 original Sacred Laws that govern the Universe and everything in Creation.

2. In the Hermetic and Ancient Kemetic Cultures, there were 7 universal laws (sometimes called the Hermetic Laws) that formed the foundation of a training or initiates in the highest spiritual and political orders. This was considered vital knowledge and wisdom that enable you to be master of many.

3. The knowledge of these keys is crucial in helping us understand the true nature of reality and in order to effectively create balance in our lives, it is said that we need to learn to master and navigate our experience through understanding our relation and connection to everything that is.

4. These laws, formed the foundation for understanding one's 'Self' as part of the universe, and to all there is, and offers us the tools that help us to maximize our potential and opportunity and become masters of our own reality.

5. Everything in the Universe and in creation has a purpose, nothing is without consciousness and the Ancients before us understood this as the foundation of all learning and living.

6. Later, throughout history, more universal laws were understood and presented and in this current time there are said to be 12 universal laws, with 12 representing the whole and vibration of creation.

"Everything happens according to Law; that nothing ever "merely happens"; that there is no such thing as Chance; that while there are various planes of Cause and Effect, the higher dominating the lower planes, still nothing ever entirely escapes the Law."
The Kybalion

The Universal Laws

1. **The Law of Mentalism** – "The All is Mind; The Universe is Mental"

   The Law of Mentalism demonstrates that everything is connected to the One Source of Divine Mind. The All. Everything we see and experience in our physical world originates from the invisible mental realm. And that there is one single Universal Consciousness. All is everything and everything is in the All.

2. **The Law of Correspondence** – "As above, So Below, As within, So without"

   The of correspondence demonstrates that everything that manifests in the material world, has its counterpart in the immaterial world. All is connected. As Above so below. Your outer life is a direct reflection of your inner life. And everything the exists in the Universe exists within you also. There is no separation. Everything in the Universe, including You and I is connected to the One Sustaining Source of All Creation. All is One

3. **The Law of Vibration** - "Nothing Rests, Everything moves and Everything vibrates"

   Everything in the Universe moves or travels and vibrates with the infinite energy of source. The same principles that apply to our thoughts, feeling, desires and wills, even in the etheric world. Each sound, thing and though has its own unique vibrational frequency unique to itself. We match the frequency of a vibration and align with it. i.e. we can thing a happy thought and match with the vibrations of joy

4. **The Law of Cause and Effect** – "Every cause has its effect; every effect has its cause; everything happens according to law, chance is but a name for Law not recognized, there are many plans of causation, but nothing escapes the law"

This Law demonstrates that everything happens in accordance with Divine law and also that every action has a reaction. Chance and luck do not exist and that we humans choose to see things as chance and luck out of ignorance of the understating of the universal laws. The Law of Cause and Effect applies to all planes of existence. On the Spiritual plan cause and effect are instantaneous, as you think it or say it, it is. But our concept of time creates a delay between the cause and the eventual effect. But when you focus on your intention with desire and visualization, then what you want will instantly manifest in the spiritual world. You just have to maintain that vibration and have patience and trust to allow it to manifest. It also connects to the Law of Compensation in that what we reap, we sow.

5. **The Law of Gender** – "Gender is everything; everything has its Masculine and Feminine Principals, Gender /manifests on all planes"

This law embodies the truth that everything has both male and female principals of aspect within them as the Creator/Source does. Men have feminine energy running through them as well as Masculine and the same for women. The gender principals are always at work and represent oneness. On the physical plane. Gender manifests itself as 'sex' Male or Female. However, in the higher realms of experience, it manifests itself in other ways for example through androgynous beings and also in nature via asexual plants or animals. One of the biggest tipping points and healing intentions now for us collectively, is for the Masculine Male energy to reconnect with its Divine Feminine energy and principals within. In the patriarchal systems that we have created, there has been a suppression of this understanding which has caused a crisis in healing for men on the planet. We are now currently seeing more of this energy being rebalanced as the Men get deeper connected with their emotions and nurturing their awareness and experience of, creative feminine principals

6. **The Law of Polarity-** "Everything is Dual; everything has poles; everything has its pair of opposites; like and unlike are the same;

opposites are identical in nature, but different in degree; extremes meet; all truths are but half-truths, all paradoxes may be reconciled."

This law outlines that everything has its polar opposite. Where there is love, there is hate. There are two sides to everything and every truth has its false. This is the lesson of duality that we have to experience on this realm but that we are also moving out of the experience of. As we use our free will combined with experience, we will choose to align with either polarity or experience. We will either choose love and be love, or choose hate and be hate in the form of polarization, finding the balance or oneness between the two extremes. Ultimately all is one, but just at differing extremes.

7. **The Law of Rhythm** – "Everything flows out and in; everything has its tides; all things rise and fall; the pendulum swing manifests in everything; the measure of the swing to the right and the measure of the swing IS the measure of the swing to the right; rhythm compensates". Similar to the waves of the oceans and the coming in and out of the tide, so is the nature of the Universe and all life. This law is perfectly expressed by the infinity symbol, as it too demonstrates the coming together and separating nature of everything within the Universe. Everything has its time and everything has its season. All things have the opportunity to experience and grow from different and varying perspectives. I like to also think of this law when I feel like I am going through a rough path and I tell myself "this too shall pass." This law helps us all to weather any storm and also tune into the opportunities available to us.

8. **The Law of Action** – Action must be employed in order for us to manifest our desires or intentions on earth or on this plane. If we do not act, we cannot materialize our intentions. We must engage in actions that support our desired wishes and intentions.

9. **The Law of Divine Oneness** – This is based on the understanding that everything is connected to everything else, seemingly outside of itself. And that everything that we do; every thought, every action, every deed, has an effect on the whole.

10. **The Law of Perpetual Transformation of Energy** – All persons have within them everything that they need to change and transform their own life. We have the power to change any condition or situation that we have manifested for ourselves. Higher energies transform and consume lower ones, so if we change our perspective on a situation, through understanding of the law, we can change the effect it has on us.

11. **The Law of Relativity**- Each person will experience or receive a certain amount of tests in their lives to help them strengthen their light and to help them to learn to stay connected to the heart when trying to solve problems. This law encourages us to compare our situations with that of others so that we can also know that there is always someone going through something worst and empowers us in the ability to master your own reality. There will be tests on this journey, but ultimately they are there to strengthen you and empower you to stay in the vibration of love. For this is all there really is. All is else is experience.

12. **The Law of Compensation** – When we put out good in the world, it is returned to us in the way of blessings and gifts. But equally, when we do negative or bad things, they also bear fruit and will come back on us. So we are guided to be mindful with your intentions and actions.

The Laws of the Universe govern all of Creation, including us as well. So our understanding and knowledge of them, will empower us greatly towards knowing ourselves.

These Laws help us to understand the nature of the Universe and our connection to all things. Don't forget, we are but a small speck of

Divine consciousness, but all part of the same great big ball of consciousness and light. The very same stuff in the heavens in within you, as above so below.

When you understand and apply these spiritual laws to your life, you become a navigator and creator of your own reality and a true alchemist and child of the Source. Things no longer happen to you, but happen because of you and you start to understand the infinite and magnificent power within you as a true Divine Sovereign being.

"We do not live in a world of dreams, but in a Universe which while relative, is real so far as our lives and actions are concerned. Our business in the Universe is not to deny its existence, but to LIVE, using the Laws to rise from lower to higher--living on, doing the best that we can under the circumstances arising each day, and living, so far as is possible, to our biggest ideas and ideals. The true Meaning of Life is not known to men on this plane. If, indeed, to any--but the highest authorities, and our own intuitions, teach us that we will make no mistake in living up to the best that is in us, so far as is possible, and realising the Universal tendency in the same direction in spite of apparent evidence to the contrary. We are all on The Path--and the road leads upward ever, with frequent resting places."

Nurturing The Seeds

In this Chapter, we discussed the Universal and Spiritual Laws of the Universe. Although these concepts may seem 'new' to some of you, you may have already experienced them at work in your life.

The following exercise will help you to ascertain your understanding of the laws and also identify where you may have experienced this already at play in your life.

Below, is a list of Spiritual or Universal Laws. In your journal write down, in your own words, the description of the Law.

Also include a description or experience of this law in your daily life. This will help to further consolidate the learning from the chapter, so that you ensure you have an understanding of it, before you move on.

****

1. 1. **The Law of Mentalism**
2. 2. **The Law of Correspondence**
3. 3. **The Law of Vibration**
4. 4. **The Law of Cause and Effect**
5. 5. **The Law of Gender**
6. 6. **The Law of Polarity**
7. 7. **The Law of Rhythm**
8. 8. **The Law of Action**
9. 9. **The Law of Divine Oneness**
10. 10. **The Law of Perpetual Transformation of Energy**
11. 11. **The Law of Relativity**
12. 12. **The Law of Compensation**

Journal Page

Use this page to make any notes of your experience.

Seed 2

Know Thyself

"Knowing others is intelligence; knowing yourself is true wisdom.

Mastering others is strength; Mastering yourself is true power."

-Lao Tzu, Chinese Taoist Philosopher

SEED 2 – KNOW THYSELF

> *"The more you know yourself, the more clarity there is. Self-knowledge has no end- you don't come to an achievement; you don't come to a conclusion. It is an endless river*
>
> *Jiddu Krishnamurti*

The fundamental requirement for achieving permanent, genuine and valuable progress in life, is to Know Thyself. This concept has been taught by sages throughout the history of time. Many people do not know themselves, even though they believe that they do, they are merely existing through life without a sense of purpose, reacting to circumstances in an often incoherent and un structured way. Some people do not even take the time to question anything or ponder on life. They have a life full of work and schedules and never seek to look beyond the veils of their imposed and limited experience.

But what does it mean to truly Know thyself.

To know thyself is one of the first rules or steps, towards starting any journey of personal spiritual development of any kind. And it can be quite a difficult task to undertake, which will require self-discipline, honesty and self-examination.

It can sometimes be a challenging and upsetting process where you may have to face up to challenges that you don't want to face. But it is the truth that those same challenging problems are the very things preventing you for experiencing true happiness.

To know thyself is to become a master of your reality. It means that you know who and what you are and you know your ability to create and attract all that you need. And the journey towards becoming the master of your own reality, starts with the small yet complicated task of taking a moment with yourself and doing a review on You!

To know where you are going and how to get there, you must where you have been and who you truly are deep inside.

You must get to know all aspects of yourself. What you like, what you don't like, where you come from etc.

But you must also seek to know who you are from a higher perspective and level.

Are you one that has always felt like you were not from here? Have you felt different and a desire to know more about your true identity.

1. What's your Ancestry?

2. What constellation did you descend from?

3. Who are you really? What is your purpose?

These questions and more, set us on a journey of discovery towards unfolding the elaborate tapestry that is Us, Me, You.

This is the first step on the journey, because once you begin to ask the question or make the intention to know yourself truly know yourself on all levels, you open the way for you to journey through many aspects that make up your understanding of who you are and some of your discoveries may even challenge all that you knew before.

But know that this is just the first step. To truly see transformation and healing in oneself, it is important to recognize and identify all the aspects of self that are holding you back and to release and transform those 'negative' aspects of yourself.

It means you must go into your past, deep into your past and look at how it has crafted and moulded you into who you are now, and then you still have to ask yourself if who you are now, is really who your Truly are at all.

You must carry out a conscious assessment of your life experience and seek to learn and heal and resolve. And you may find that you also need to experience some areas a little more. All is a part of getting to Know Thyself.

Until your higher self has received a full spectrum of necessary and valuable experience, the cycle of reincarnation into the physical body continues, until the lessons have finally been learned and all of the has been learned it integrated and applied to one's life, to a point where your higher self is free from all restrictions and illusions of the physical plane. With knowing ourselves, we also must take on the responsibility of non-judgment of self or others, as in doing so we create a projection of our own self-judgments and ideals and standards.

We are all one within the universal Mind but we also must take responsibility for our own growth and development and our journey.

With so many different angles and routes to self-discovery, it can be difficult to know where to start but I suppose the best place to start is right at the beginning.

Know Thyself- How far back can you go?

How far back into your memory can you go?

How much do you remember of you journey here?

Can you remember your birth? Being in your mother's womb?

Can you remember when you were 3? Is that your first memory or can you go back even further to before you were born.

Some people are born with a distinct knowing of how they came here and even when they were born. Through healing therapies like past life, future life and life between life regression, we are also able to access these latent and distant memories and experience them in our minds and bodies.

Birth, and being born, can be both a joyful and/or traumatic time for both mother and most importantly for the new soul that is coming into form. It is proven that the mental and emotional states of the mother and father, can influence the energy and mood of the child when born and some people find that traumas and fears that they have in their adult lives are directly contributed to when they were born and trauma of that experience.

Through the practice of connecting with and exploring your birth story, you can find out insightful tips about yourself that can help you to make powerful changes in your life.

My first memory, is very poignant in my mind and I remember it like yesterday.

The first image that I see, when I go into my memory bank, is of me as light, a swirling ball of multi-coloured energy, hovering above my mother's belly.

Around me I see, tall angelic-like beings, mainly of light, and I remember this feeling of warmth and love and motherly nurturing that cascaded from their hearts to mine. They were preparing my energy to fit into my new body and this was quite late on in the third trimester of the pregnancy.

It is said that the soul can enter the physical body at different stages in the pregnancy, mainly dependant of the age of the soul. Old souls, and those who bring in higher levels of consciousness and soul awareness, usually enter the body at the later stages of pregnancy, when the body and organs are more developed.

The next thing I knew, I was in this small body and out of my mother's womb, and into the bright new world. I didn't cry at first, as I struggled to fit my soul energy into this tiny little body.

But with a wriggle and a squeeze, I was out and let out a whelp of proclamation…I had arrived.

In later years, I asked my mother if the story of my birth was true and importantly whether I cried or not at first. She confirmed that this was true. This was further confirmation of the memory that I had of my birth.

The planting of the Golden seed that is me, into the fertile womb of Mother Earth.

Out of the Mouths of Babes and Suckling's

As I have mentioned before, it has always been foretold that the children that will be born in these times will have access to Divine Gnosis, Awakened or heightened physical or spiritual gifts, and also access to past life memories spanning millions of years.

A few years back, I experienced an interaction with a young boy, the youngest I had worked with, and I received first hand insight into how far back into his soul memory he was able to access or remember. Both his mother and I were enthralled by his account and lived and breathed every moment of his soul memory with him. We both felt honoured and blessed to be in the presence of such a beautiful, intelligent and loving spirit. Below is the account of what he shared with us

My client, whom I'd been seeing for a while, had a young son, around 6 years old and she had been sharing with him her experiences with me during our sessions.

"He thinks you're a fortune teller, but also something more than that and he is curious about you and what you do," she said one day. She went on to say that he would ask her questions and that he wanted to speak with me, and so I agreed as I was curious to meet him as well.

We set up a time for me to speak with, and when she called, she introduced him and he came on the line.

"Hello," he said, "are you the fortune teller?"

"No," I replied, "My name is Amenti and I am a Spiritual Healer and Coach, working with your mother. I work with and on behalf of the Most High Our creator and that I was a messenger of the light"

"Oh" he said, "that's good. I thought so. Fortune tellers don't know very much, but I know you know a lot. I know you're here to help me too"

I could see very early I that this young boy was awake and I also knew there was something very special that he was going to share with us. As my work with his mother progressed he seemed to open more and lore and want to share with that he had experience in his dreams and visions to myself and his mother.

On one occasion, his mother being inquisitive had asked him what he can remember about his life before he came here. And he asked her to call me so he could tell us both and I could help her to understand.

He said that he remembered being in heaven in the clouds and playing and having fun. Then he was told that it's was time to get ready and that his new mum was waiting for him.

He remembered that he had chosen a mum. He mentioned all the qualities that he wanted her to have and that he had to build he from all his thoughts and intention.

Then the face of his mother appeared on the moon, which he said was like heavens TV screen.

He said whilst he was waiting for the right time to come he would look in on her often and see what she was doing and that at times she would be praying or crying.

The mother broke down as she remembered and confirmed his recollection.

She was in awe as to what he could remember and the clarity in which it came through.

I was so in love with the spirit of this young being and so excited by the magic and wonder that he would bring to this word for us all to share and enjoy.

Whilst I was growing up, I was always asked to help babysit the children of friends and family and I obliged, as I loved kids. In fact, I sometimes found the children to be better company than those my age, as I would always feel awkward and overwhelmed, a trait I developed from years of abuse and sheltered living.

But when I was with children and young people, there was none of that. We just got along. I saw beyond their physical and into their soul and we connected from that space and I felt that it was my purpose to be someone they could talk to and rely on. I knew them and they knew me and we tested each other with acknowledgement and respect.

From this viewpoint, I was able to experience the children in the natural environment and they spoke openly to me about their spiritual or magical experience which, to many would have been dismissed as imagination.

I knew differently and this was because I was once a child fully connected to Spirit and My Higher Self, like them.

I could hear what people were thinking and I would say it and get in trouble. I would be able to heal people when they were sick, see colours around them and give sound advice on issues and situations way beyond my years.

I have a high spiritual awareness high energy and a passion for learning and I could see that in the children who were drawn to me. It was then that I knew that part of my purpose was to help support children in maintaining and developing their spiritual gifts and talents.

And there are so many more special children out there, even very close to you, I'm sure.

I encourage people to be mindful when you see a child who is showing signs of greatness beyond the normal or one who seems regressed and withdrawn. They may just be a 'diamond in the rough' and your interaction and inspiration may be just the polish they need to shine.

We are all here to learn from ourselves and from each other and ultimately, we all hold the keys to ascension within us. We just have to remember and then embody that knowing.

> *"The Key is to Know Thyself to the fullest degree, and once you have known all that you can know, forget it all and seek to know thyself once more. This is the secret of Self Mastery"*
>
> *Tehuti*

It's not all about who you were before you were born, but all stages of your life, which have an impact on who you are and to be fair, who you are is always changing.

This metamorphic process of the caterpillar to the butterfly is synonymous with the activity of transformation and alchemy. Understanding who we are at all stages of our life helps us to figure out where we are in our growth and development and where it is we are going on our journey, and exactly how we are going to get there.

You are a free and Sovereign divine being and to truly Know yourself, you must start by assessing yourself on all levels.

1. Do you know your body?

2. Do you know how you think?

3. Do you know what drives you and your passion?

4. Do you understand the language of your emotions?

5. Do you know our purpose?

6.   *Do you know yourself Spiritually?*

These are just some of the questions that will help you to start to gain a snapshot of yourself and where you are now. Don't worry if there are some questions you cannot answer of if your answers are short or too long. Trust the process and let it flow.

You will notice that once you start to put pen to paper and engage your heart and mind, the answers will flow and it will be an enlightening and interesting experience.

Self-reflection and analysis is key to knowing yourself on a deeper level and is a powerful tool to help you identify where you are and where you might need to improve and also, any qualities that you like and would benefit from in your life. All of life is a journey and the gift and blessing is not only in reaching the destination, but the journey itself!

My Beginning

Patiently waiting,
for my time to be
Meticulous Planning
By My Angels, Guides & Me
For the greatest trip of Life
The beginning of a long journey
Now begins my biggest challenge
To experience more of me

Lightening my vibration
Making my descent
Part of Divine Planning
Ready for this big event

My Mother I have chosen
For her unique qualities
All the greatness/keys inside her
Now reside in me
From my Fathers seed
Comes All the strength I need

As my numbers called
The stars wait to greet me
As the portal opens
This new world I see

A world of love and colour
The lesson of duality
The illusion of restriction
A longing to be free
Through the birth canal I travel
To a world that welcomes me

Bursting through the barriers
Blood runs like the sea
Bright lights flicker
Faces glimmer
I open my eyes to see

A great big breath
My entrance made
Ready to break free
Screaming, yelling 'Hello World'
I've arrived, It's Me

I Remember – Part I
I Let Go

I give thanks for life
And then I Let Go
I give thanks for all that I am
And then I let go
I love without apology
And then I let go
I dance to the universes rhapsody
And then I let go

I create from a place of passion and purpose and truth
And then I let go
I Cry, I Share, I love, I Connect
And then I let go
I feel. I embody, I experience, and I embrace
And then I let go
I marvel at the wonders and see them manifest
And then I let go

I heard the call and agreed to be one of the ones
And then I let go
I lost my way down the rabbit hole
And I forgot to let go

I Remember – Part II
My Descent – 'Down the rabbit hole'

Dense vibration holding me,
The pushing the pulling, the stress and the strife
Emotions running all around and through me
As I enter this game called life

Nothing feels like love down here
So much pain cuts like a knife
Restricted energy
No longer free
Trapped in a body
What happened to me!?

Interactions with the beings down here
Is slow and not so nice
Everyone is busy rushing around
And many have hearts cold as ice

They know not that better awaits them,
When they open their hearts and minds
The Whole Universe awaits their Ascension
(They are part of a grand design) That's why we are here at this special time

I remember a trumpet sounding
1 thru 7 times

The people of earth, they need you
Time to Rise and shine

The moment my heart ignited
As I answered this magical call
I forgot to remember the Creators wise words
As I began to fall

Deeper and deeper and deeper
Into carbon density
Body and bones and blood
With divine essence running through me

I landed in this body
Bound and no longer free
But I remember this overwhelming feeling inside
Of great purpose, passion and intensity
A feeling that helped me remember
There's something more to me
In this life, I have a purpose
A voice says, 'remember you are free'

The pain of being in my body
The Angels guided me
The tossed me in light, and wrapped me in love
And sung me soundly to sleep

From the beauty filled slumber, I awakened
In a world with light and screens
I looked into the face of my mother
Felt like it was all a dream

I had seen her face before
On the Moon, heavens TV screen

I thanked my mother for housing me
In her earthly time (space) machine
I marvelled at the wonder
Excitement filled in me
I'm on a secret mission
Something about being free????

Life's deep dark spiral
Manifested plenty for me to see
Abuse, rejection, hurt and pain
All new experiences to me

I couldn't understand why the people here
Acted so horribly
I saw shards of energy flying from them in anger
If they could (only) see, (they wouldn't choose to be)

They eat at flesh like animals
Believing it's their right and reign
They were told by the ones who put them to sleep
That this was their domain
I felt lost and misguided in a world
Filled with fear, hurt and pain
I sought to always see the rainbow
And be a positive part of the game

I tried to be the sunshine
That dried up all the rain
But I could still not remember
The greatness from which I came

The more I helped, the more I became
The very same thing that I had come to change
Feeling like a human, trapped in the game

From the world of spirit, I felt disengaged

I dedicated my life here
To helping others to be free
To bring light to the darkest corners
To help people to see
How powerful, beautiful and perfect
The design of man can be
When it releases itself from the darkness
Awakens and knows it is free

Mother Earths Inhabitant Are part of a story,
A great conspiracy
You have forgotten how to fly
And have been robbed of your divinity

You've forgotten that you are kings and queens
Perfect in every way
You have forgotten that you are cut from the cloth of creation
Mother earth is the garden in which you play

You've forgotten that you can move mountains
With faith the size of a mustard seed
You've forgotten to seek the magic
In that which you cannot see
You've forgotten to be the superheroes
That you see on the TV screen
You've forgotten that good health and abundance
Are gifts of your divinity?

You've forgotten that you're more than a body
Limited by all you see
You've forgotten to ask the question
What really flows through me?

But many here are supporting you
Reminding you of who you are
Speaking to your hearts and minds
Guiding you to the stars

I forgot that I was one of them
As I came down the rabbit hole
So saddened by what I thought and felt
I forgot what I was told
I enjoy all life
And then I let go
I connect with all things
And then I let go
I dance in the darkness
And then I let go
I dance with the stars
And then I let go
I love for the sake of loving
I go with the ebbs and flows
I hurt, I heal, I innerstand
And then I let it go!

I remember the magic
I receive the guidance
I trust I what I know
I share unapologetically
And then I let go

I protested about the killings
I protest about the show
I protest that people are treated badly
I pray and then I let go

I cry, I feel, I awaken
And see miracles everywhere I go
I acknowledge the world is changing
And then I let go

As I let go, I remember
How I came to be
In this physical body
Restricted but yet free

I came here for a purpose
I came as I heard the call
I forgot what spirit told me
When I jumped down the rabbit hole
But now I remember
With every part of me
I'm here to raise the vibrations
For our earth family
By leading by example
The Christ consciousness, I embody
The key to evolution
And the higher states of being

The Merkabah reminds me
As it carries me to the council's seat
That I am not bound by space and time
And it's ok to believe

That I am someone special
Not the same as all whom I see
But knowing deep down, at the same time
All I see is also within me

I let go of separation

I let go of the control in me
I let go of restriction
I let go of dies-ease

I let go of being right
I let go of trying not to be seen
I let go of the idea of perfection
In the knowing that is already me!

A conduit of source and spirit
Of the highest quality
I chose to come and be here
Now I remember
Now I am free

I let go of restriction
I fly now, through clouds, above seas
I can show you the way
Turn your inner light on
Come on, follow me, you'll see!

Let's live beyond our wildest dreams
Let's live abundantly
Let's dance with the magic of the stars
Ad our creator intended it (us) to be

Awaken from your slumber
Awaken and be free
Remember who you are, my friend
And you will truly see

There is magic in every moment
If you only choose to see
Release, express and awaken

Let Go
Be Guided
Be Free!

I Am the Way Shower

WHO AM I?
I'M A WAY SHOW,
NOT A FOLLOWER
A SHEPHERD
NOT A SHEEP
A WIZARD
NOT A WORRIER
AWAKE
NOT ASLEEP
EXPANSIVE
NOT RESTRICTED
PERFECT
NOT INCOMPLETE
SOURCE
AND THE SORCERESS
BEYOND CARBON DENSITY

A LOVER
NOT A FIGHTER
SEEKING TRUTH BEYOND THE LIES
A RECEIVER
AND A GIVER
SEE THE UNIVERSE IN MY EYES

I'M NOT HERE TO BE YOUR REDEMPTION
I AM HERE TO HELP YOU SEE
THAT YOU MAY NEED REMINDING

OF WHO YOU TRULY CAME TO BE

A HEALER
A TEACHER
A PRACTITIONER OF SACRED ARTS
A WONDERER
A TRAVELLER
MY NAME IS WRITTEN IN THE STARS
DEEP BENEATH THE LIONS HEART
IN THE GREAT SACRED CITY
YOU WILL FIND THE DOOR THAT LEADS YOU TO
THE SACRED HALL OF AMENTI

HERE YOU WILL REMEMBER
WHO YOU TRULY ARE
AND YOU CAN FULFIL THE PLAN FOR YOU
WRITTEN FOR YOU IN THE STARS

SUPER
HUMAN
POWERFUL
BEYOND WHAT YOU KNOW NOW
STEP INTO YOUR POWER
JOURNEY THROUGH YOUR PAIN
I CAN SHOW YOU HOW

I'M THE NATURAL MYSTIC
BLOWING THROUGH THE AIR
BRINGING FORTH GREAT WISDOM AND POWER
AND PREPARING THE WORLD FOR CHANGE
YOU TOO ARE SOMEONE SPECIAL
AND IT MAY TAKE TIME TO SEE
BUT ONCE YOU REMEMBER
DON'T YOU FORGET

BE YOURSELF UNAPOLOGETICALLY

YOU ARE THE WAY SHOWER
BE WHO YOU'VE COME TO BE
DON'T LET OTHERS TELL YOU
THAT YOU CAN'T BE WHAT YOU BELIEVE

YOU ARE MOST POWERFUL
MORE POWERFUL THAT YOU KNOW
SO TAKE OFF YOUR MASK
BE TRUE TO WHO YOU ARE
AND WATCH THE BLESSINGS FLOW

I AM A WAY SHOWER
AND I TOO HAD TO LEARN AND GROW
AND NOW I'M TO REMIND YOU
ITS YOUR TURN TO STEP UP AND SHOW

THAT YOU ARE MADE OF GREATNESS
MUCH GREATER THAN YOU KNOW
SO STEP INTO YOU PURPOSE
STEP INTO YOUR POWER
AND LET THE WHOLE WORLD KNOW

My Sacred Cup

My Sacred cup
The Chalice of my femininity
My Divinity
My Majesty
My Magic, My power, My testimony

The bringer of life

The Philosopher's stone
Through the great halls within
Many will return
From the eternal to the material

As I cradled my sacred centre
The world stirs within me
All of the elements of she
Mother earth resides in me
The Fire, The Air
The Earth, The waters
The winds of intention blow
The power of creation
The expectation of presence
In my eternal cocoon
I nurture the heavens

Each cycle brings shame and doubt
From the beginning, you are taught of sin
The mark of the beast
For treachery and deceit
A punishment fit for a Queen

The red letter returns with each cycle
Every season, to remind you
Of the pain, the transgression, the shame
I hold myself on pain
Sit back and allow myself to drain
All the power within me
And I wrap it up and throw it away

Powerless, depleted and drained
For 3 to 5 days I Am
Powerless, depleted and drained

3 days of peaceful power, drained

You see
Within my sacred space
Is a sacred place, where a sacred river flows
This river flows
So deep
Its nutrient rich and bring life
Info a form that houses the soul
So powerful
So beautiful
So wonderful

So why do I deny myself?
Why do I deny yourself?
Why - do I- deny - my power
From my sacred flower
My goodness
My God-essence
My magic and my majesty

Why do I deny what flows through me?
Is it because I do not yet know?
The power of the blessing given to me
Not a curse
Or a sentence
But a powerful elixir of Alchemy

As a young woman, I wasn't shown
All the power and magic
Hidden within this so-called sin
I disliked and feared the river within me
This painful thing that 'all girls' have
Now made me a woman,

I couldn't understand that
Cramping and moaning
Bending over in pain
And once this is over, next month it starts again
The only blessing that comes from this, I am told,
Is to bring forth life, not pleasure, until I get old
Then it stops
You stop
And your time is done
You sit back and baby sit
Whilst others go out and have fun

You see
No one told me of the power within
And that my rivers flow not from sin
But from Creation, a gift of power and majesty
A harmony of Alchemy between God and ME
This potent brew
This elixir of love
All the world is healed through my sacred blood
The god and the Goddesses helped me to see
How magical and power-filled a woman can be
When she looks deep into herself
Breaks free from the chains of conformity
And seeks to know more of who she is
And who she came to be
The bringer life from the cosmos,
A symbol of divine femininity
An embodiment of the stars and skies
All of the universe is within me

You see
At 33 I took a journey
On a magic super moon night

A journey into my greatness
Guided by the magical moonlight

For this journey, I had no luggage
Everything that I needed was inside
I was about to receive a gift of knowing
Straight from the Divine

I knew I must go deeper
Dig deep inside of me
To awaken my sacred power
And embody my diving femininity

I stepped into the waters
To cleanse and purify
My cycle, such a dirty thing
So much so, that when It comes, I want to hide

But I knew felt something different
There was something precious hidden my sacred space
To attract such negativity and slander
I knew that the power inside me must be great

Our Ancestors knew the power of
The women in the red tents
I wanted to remove the inner image of the harlot
And awaken a sacred Goddess in its place
The moons sweet and healing elixir
Flowed through my crown
And Filled up my body with light
As it made its way down

Within my heart is a sacred cup
A golden chalice of love

Opens to receive the sacred moonshine sauce
And it overfills my cup

The abundant and enchanting overflow
Cascades further down within me
Towards my sacred divine centre
Where heaven and earth meet

As it travels down my centre
In my sacred space, I see
Another chalice of power
Where my sacred space should be (hidden deep inside of me/ shining bright for me to see)
As the elixir of moonshine touches me
And starts to fill my magic cup
My sacred womb is awakened
And transforms from a chalice to a sacred box
This box I have seen before
Once cased in sacred blood
Now golden and shining with divinity
And filling with sacred love

My ovaries awaken
Like the angels on the sacred box
Awakened in to their purpose
As transmitters of Alchemical Love

The Ark of the Covenant within me
Awakened by my sacred blood
The holy space of the Trinity
Filled with the elixir of love

The most sacred gift of healing and creation
Lies deep within me

And is my eternal radiance
My power, my magnificence
My greatness within
The sacred gift of motherhood
A Divine Power, not a sin

Between them, an arc of energy and light forms
The sparks of creation, the current of life flows
Through my space, this sacred place
Where love flows and all is made whole
When used with power and intention
It can raise the vibration of the planet,
Empower the heavens and give rays to the sun

I am charged
I am potent
I am powerful
I am electric
I am alchemical;
I am beautiful
I am magic, God personified
And the essence of all creation
Flows inside, between my thighs

So, I take my hand and make my descent
To the centre of my centre,
To touch the power that lies in wait

I bathe my finger in my sacred elixir
And feels its warmth and power
It feels so rich and shines with power
Is this the source of my pain all those days and hours?
As I gaze at the liquid light that shines on my hands
I feel something take over me

And now I understand

I Am a Goddess, not a woman in shame
I can heal the world
Rid others of pain
I can heal the sick
I can feed the poor
Within my sacred centre
I have the power of the infinite all

As I hold my sacred essence
I breathe deeply and take it all in
I am comforted by the essence of newness
Like the smell of a new baby's fresh skin

I rub my sacred blood on my temples
And my inner eyes that sees
And instantly I am transported
To the source of my inner peace

I saw the power within
I was shown all the potentialities
That can come about from my sacred blood
I saw the true power in me

I saw that I am a creator
Not another's property
That I was one of God's chosen
And in me, perfection s/he achieved

I saw that all the shame
All the pain and the disgrace
Was just a constructed illusion
To keep me from knowing the true power of my sacred space

You see
You cannot truly be a sacred Goddess
Until you have basked in the fullness of yourself
Put to death the inherited illusion
And put Divinity back in your sacred space
You are not yet a woman
Until you explore your sacred gates
And awaken to who you truly are
Open up and take a taste
Dip into the depths of You
Dig deep into your shame
And find your peaceful power
And know the true source of which you came

Rise Divine Feminine
Rise from deep within
Dance in your sacred waters
Trust the power within
Get rid of all the fear
So, the healing can begin
As you awaken the true Goddess within you
And remove the illusion of Sin

On this night of my initiation
Into sacred womanhood does begin
For now, I know myself a little deeper
And know the true source of my power within
Its feels my heart with joy to know
That I have this special gift
And to know that each month it comes back around
With more magic, peace and love to bask in

If I use it wisely

I can heal the world from within
For I am no longer a girl
I Am now a Sacred Woman
And even though I am a Mother,
Who has given birth to 5 wonderful babies
This sacred initiation into of woman hood
Is the birth of a new world within me?

From Created to Creator
Power filled Goddess here on Earth
Everything is made manifest
From My Sacred Blood
The gift of life and abundance
The source of Divinity
I now awaken and Embody
The Divine Feminine in me
Transmuting and rebirthing
The mother of Alchemy
Bring healing to the nation
The world's leaders will be birthed through me

I Am the I AM that I AM
And I am the I Am that you are
My skin is formed form the universe
My eyes are made from the stars
My hips are the coco basket
That carries life from one realm to another
And from my sacred waters
All life is fed
And nurtured and comforted into greatness

All the magic and beauty of this world, all comes through me
A symbol of the Cosmic mother
The creator of humanity

Through my pain, passion and power
Reality comes to be
So why then should I be ashamed
Of such a special part of me

I am gifted with the true knowing
The illusions are blown away
The secret which was once hidden
Is now made clear and plain

They tried to keep me from my power
The Divine Goddess that runs through me
Turn my power into prostitution
And my blessing into sin

But through the Most Highs Wisdom
And my willingness to dig deeper and see
I have now been beautifully awakened
To the power that flows through me

Perfectly created to be all that we are
Emotions flows like the sea
Our wombs are created from the stars
So, the power that flows within me
Is for each Goddess to explore and know
Open up and take a journey within
And see how much you grow

Between your legs lies the gateway
To all that you can and cannot see
The sacred red river that flows
Is the source of divinity

Stand in your peaceful power

Rise in Sacred Femininity
Take a step out into a new beginning
Be all that you came to be
And when you have danced in your magic
Share this knowing abundantly
With all other Goddesses and Sisters
So, they can know their power
And the Divine Feminine can be free

And with my daughters I also share
The gift and the magic in this story
So that you will always know your power
And in your centre, bring harmony
To the powerful young goddesses
The journey has just begun
But know there is nothing horrible about you
And your cycle is a gift from the One
Nurture and allow
Yourself to be all that you become
Know that you are a Queen
And you sacred centre is as powerful as the sun

Guard it and keep it sacred
Love it and find your peace
Learn to understand yourself
As your journey is begun
Goddesses of this nation
Queens for a King
Know that only those of the highest love and vibration
Have an invitation to come in

Know your power and purpose
As powerful priestess of Alchemy
And nurture the soil within you

To prepare to receive the sacred seed

This sacred initiation
My power-filled journey
From little girl to a woman
My sacred blood and me
Transformed into my purpose
Of alchemy magic and mystery
I dipped into my sacred waters
And awakened the lost parts of me

I rise in jubilation
Hold my head high in majesty
Giving thanks for the power and the knowing
Of the magic hidden within me

So, I'll smile when I'm in my season
And laugh heartily
To know that there is great magic happening
Within my red seas
I will walk with a sassiness
Ill put flowers in my hair
And I will bask in my radiance
And transmute all fear

I am so grateful
For the gift of knowing myself
No longer ashamed of Disempowered
For I now know the Sacred Power in Me

Nurturing the Seeds

Seed Two- KNOW Thyself

It is one thing to read books and gather information, and if your anything like most of us, you will sit there gathering information and not doing what it takes to get you to where you want to be, and that is by taking action and doing the work.

The Law of Action requires that we understand that in order to manifest our intention we must act. And so, if we want to learn to be masters of our reality and embody our true potential then we too have to do the work.

Below are some questions to help get you started. Seed 1 is about the importance of Knowing yourself. The questions below will assist you in taking a deeper look into how much you already know about yourself and what you need to improve on or celebrate. This will form the foundation of your seed work and help you to create an action plan to continue to nurture your seed and your personal development.

Time to Do the Work

Air – Know Your Mind

Your mind is one of the most powerful organs within your body. But is your mind a friend or a foe? Take a moment to Know thyself and take a deeper look into the way your mind works.

- ❖ *What kind of thinker are you? Are you organised and methodical? Or creative and sporadic?*
- ❖ *Do you find it hard to stay focused and pay attention or are you extremely focused and clear in your thinking?*

- *Assess your thoughts? Are you optimistic and hopeful? Or are your thoughts negative or restrictive? Is the way that you think, working for you?*
- *Do you get stressed easily and find it difficult to relax? What do you do to help balance your mind?*
- *Write down 3 things you like about the way that you think. And write down 3 things that you can change to improve your thinking.*

Earth – Know your Body

Your body is the Divine vehicle that houses your spirit allows you to manifest your purpose and experience on this realm. Your body is the Earth and made from the Earth and is part of a living consciousness that is connected to all things. Take a moment to access your body. Bring your attention to all the different parts of your body.

- *How do you feel about it?*
- *What are you feeding your body? Is it healthy or not? How is your body responding?*
- *What would you like to improve with your body and how would you do that?*
- *Does your body have any scars that tell a story? Are you a mother with stretch marks or do you have a wound with a powerful story behind it? Take a moment to recall a memory*
- Identify 3 things that you love about your body and 3 things that you would like to improve. Write them down in your journal and make a commitment to take a step towards those changes this week!

Water – Know your Emotions

Your emotions are your way of interacting with and understanding your environment and how it affects you. Emotions are a powerful source of energy which can either empower or destroy your greatest dreams and manifest a very limited and painful reality if not balanced and understood. Take a moment to look at how you understand yourself emotionally

- *Are you a 'feeling' person? Do you feel like you are in touch with your emotions?*

- *Do you think before making decision or do you act on impulse and gut feelings?*

- *Are you reactive to your feeling and allow them to inform you or are you controlled by your emotions and usually end up in hurt or conflict?*

- *Do you openly share your emotions and feeling with others or do you keep them inside?*

- *Do you take on the emotions and energies of others and allow it to bring you down, or are you quite distant and do not take the emotional outpourings of others well?*

- *Take a moment to answers these questions in your journal and take an emotional snapshot!*

Fire - Know your Passion

Fire is the energy that brings forth your passion and drive and when we are passionate and driven about something, we are usually successful in it and see it to the end. When you are not living from a place of purpose and passion you can find that life can be a hard task and that nothing inspires you. Finding the source of your power and drive will assist you in finding the right kind of outlets to channel your energy and also which paths in life you might wish to pursue, rather than wasting time doing something that you don't not enjoy

- *What is your passion? What drives you?*

- *What makes your sing?*

- *What or who inspires you and why? What do you admire about them?*

- *Write down one of your ultimate life goals, something that you enjoy doing?*

- *What would you like to achieve in your life that you have had a chance to as yet? write it down and this week take at least 3 steps towards making that dream a reality! You can do it!*

Spirit – Know Your Spirit

You are spirit first before anything else. But for a long time, our spiritual side has become the least developed aspect of and of which we give the least amount of energy. But spirituality is about understanding and connecting with the very nature that created you and also seeing your connection to all things. Your spirituality can inform your reality, whether positively or negatively. And some of us have been initiated into religions and beliefs systems long before we had a choice to choose for ourselves. More and more people are awakening to that fact that there is so much more to life and so much more to us. And this is where the power of spiritual enlightenment and development begins. In order to truly know thyself, you must be able to see beyond thyself and master it from within and without. Spiritual development and practice helps us to stay connected to all things and all that we are and to seek council from the highest part of our selves and honour our connection to all.

Take a moment now and think about your own Spiritual journey? Take a moment to take in each question? Let it sit with you, and place your hand on your heart, breathe and allow the answer to come honestly from your heart-mind.

Jot down any notes you have in your journal or the notes section in this book

- *What is your spiritual journey up until now and what have you learned about yourself and your experience.*

- *Where would you say you are spiritually? What do you understand about your true nature?*

- *Have you or are you are part of an organised religion? If so how has this impacted on your life?*

- *Do you have a current spiritual practice? Does it benefit you? Write 5 things that you are already doing?*

- *How would you like to develop your spirituality further? What can you do to help you to do that?*

- *Jot down any notes you have in your journal or the notes section in this book*

Love – The Spirit of Love

Love is the most powerful but yet misunderstood force in the universe. There are so many different types of love and experiences of love which all do not even compare to the true purity and simplicity of Source Love

- *What is your definition of love? What is love to you?*

- *Make a list of all the things that you love to do.*

- *How do you show you love and affection? How*

- *How have you experienced love in your relationships? Have you experienced true love? Have you had your 'heartbroken' what did this feel like and what did it tell you about love?*

- *Make a list of all of the people who you love and write down why you love them and what you love about them*

Through this exercise, you should be able to gather a general understanding of where you are in your awareness of self in all of the above aspects of your life. Take a moment to reflect on this information, did you learn anything new about yourself and were you reminded of the greatness of who you are and also the points for improvement and further action.

Golden Seeds of Wisdom

As Tehuti said, the process of truly knowing oneself is the constant expanding and contracting, unfolding and awakening and infinite nature of the universe.

"Everything is born, lives, live, transforms and is born again and the ultimate purpose is to know and experience more of yourself.

Because to truly know thyself is to truly know source, the creator the Most High.

Because that is essential to who and what you are.

Affirmation: To know myself is to know the Wisdom of God expressed through me

The next exercise will help you to take the journey of knowing yourself a little deeper and invited you to make a connection with the highest and wisest part of you, your higher self.

Star Seed Journey

Soul journey – Journey to connect your higher self

Your higher self is the part of you that knows all things and is the Ascended part of you. It has access to all of the knowledge, wisdom and information that you need to achieve your goals on this realm and help navigate your way through your life.

Your connection with your Higher Self is key towards facilitating your ascensions and offer guidance and wisdom that can empower you to make the right choices and decisions in your life.

Guided Journey to Meet your Higher Self

1. *Find yourself a comfortable position, in a place where you will not be disturbed.*

2. *You may light a candle and/or some incense to create a peaceful and sacred space*

3. *Sit or lie comfortable and take a few deep cleansing breaths in and out*

4. *Set your intention now to take a journey connect with your higher self through the gateway to the halls of Amenti – Through the Heart*

5. *As you continue to breath in and out, draw energy down through your crown down to your feet. As you breathe in and out continue this process for a few moments*

6. *Then as you take your next breath, look into your heart space and see a green glowing ball of light*

7. As you look into this ball of light, your consciousness is carried down a long green tunnel of light

8. As you continue to follow this tunnel of light you see this figure standing at the end of the tunnel

9. You feel the presence of this light being and energy and notice how it towers above you as you stand before it.

10. You feel a familiar presence and energy and recognise this to be you. Your higher self.

11. Take a moment now to connect with your higher self, allow is to share any wisdom and guidance for you now in this moment.

12. Make the intention now to merge with your higher self at a speed that is comfortable and in your highest good so that you can develop a relationship with your higher self.

13. Take a step forward see merge in oneness with your higher self. Notice how it towers above your, absorbing you and bathing you in light.

14. When you are ready, thank your higher self for being present and know that this is now a part of you that you can access at will whenever you need.

15. See yourself travelling back along the green tunnel of light through your hearts sacred chamber and bring your consciousness slowly back into your body and into the room.

16. You may need to take a few moments to wriggle your toes and move around slowly to fully bring you back to consciousness.

17. You may take a moment to journal your thoughts and experiences and take note of any guidance of wisdom that your received.

18. Over time you will build up a connection with you higher self and will be able to activate its wisdom by simply commanding by

saying something like "I call on the wisdom of my higher self Now" or "I connect with my higher self now".

19. You then just sit and mentally ask anything that you need and listen keenly to the guidance expressed through you heart to your ears and your mind.

Use the next page to write down any wisdom and guidance that your received

Do not worry if you found it difficult or felt unable to connect with your higher self or follow the visualisation. Everything is always as it should be and when trying something new, expectancy amongst other things can create interference.

Just repeat the process as many times as you need to and trust and relax.

All is well and always working in your highest good.

Journal Page

Use this page to make any notes of your experience.

Seed 3

Understand

Your Energy

"Everything flows out and in; everything has its tides;
all things rise and fall; the pendulum-swing manifests in everything; the measure of the swing to the right, is the measure of the swing to the left; rhythm compensates"

— Three Initiates

SEED 3 – UNDERSTAND THAT YOU ARE ENERGY

> *"The Human Energy System provides a map of your most important journey, Life. Its seven fuels station/chakras represent a full range of human experience and possibility. Taking you from Fear to Faith, rage to Radiance and Vision to Manifestation"*
>
> *Caroline Shola Arewa*

Your Body's Natural Energy System

Understanding Energy

Energy is the very essence and driving force of who we are. It is the very fuel that animates our spirit and activates our physical body and its through understanding energy, that we are able to manifest our greatness into this realm. Everything is energy.

Energy is the fundamental building block of life force manifesting through us and around us.

You are pure vibrant energy! Einstein's $E=MC^2$ tells us that everything animate or inanimate, is made from a pulsing creative energy. It is everywhere and in the tiniest subatomic particle to the very in and out breathe of your body.

Energy manifests in the physical, emotional and spiritual aspects of your being. It is expressed through the things in all densities.

Energy is a sought after commodity. Many people in our current climate are lacking in energy and don't have enough energy and vitality to live life to the full. Energy is the fuel humans are designed to function on.

However the food we eat can lack the nutrients that we need, stress from over working can leave use drained and depleted and affect our overall health and wellbeing.

Energy is the container, the carrier of in-form-a-tion, the intelligent force through which all things come into being.

As energy we are part of an evolutionary journey of consciousness. Out of the void of nothingness came all things and so did we.

In physics the concept of energy is defined 'as a quantifiable attribute of physical systems.

Energy can neither be created nor destroyed. It can only be transformed because it exists in all that there is.

Even the food we eat is transformed into energy for the body. Energy comes in many forms from the subtle force we know as vital energy or prana to the solidity of your physical body and the material universe.

We are energy and therefore also part of the abundant energy that exists in all that is, the Divine Spark. This is the active and tangible force that is present not only in our consciousness but in our physical body also and allows us to be fluid transmitters and receivers of energy on many vibrational energies.

Let us explore the simple yet powerful exercise below to help you to feel and sense your energy.

Hand Energy Sensing Exercise

We are energy and we are also vibrating and charging and flowing. Use this simple technique to help you become aware of the natural energy already flowing in your body.

Keep your spine straight and aligned as this will align your own chakras.

Exercise for Developing Hand Sensitivity

1. Sit comfortably with your back straight and tall. Allow your mind to quiet down. Spend a few minutes breathing deeply and comfortably into your belly. When your breath has become slow and even, then you are ready to go on.

2. Rub the palms of your hands briskly together for 15-30 seconds.

3. Hold your hands out in front of you, palms facing each other. Keeping your elbows in close to your sides will probably be most comfortable.

4. Slowly bring your hands together, as close as you can without touching. Pay attention to any sensations you feel in your hands.

5. Slowly bring your hands apart again, so that they are separated by 6-12 inches.

6. Repeat this process several times, bringing your hands together and apart. Be slow and steady. As you do it, pay close attention to your palms. You may experience a sense of pressure or thickness between your palms; warmth; buzzing; tickling; pulsing; or other sensations. You're feeling energy!

7. Don't worry if you feel something different that described above. Everyone is unique in what and how they sense energy.

8. Don't worry that you are imagining what you are feeling. You aren't. Allow yourself to believe in what you are feeling.

9. If you can't feel anything yet, don't be concerned. Try "imagining" that you are feeling something. This technique can be very useful in opening a mind that is closed to the experience.

10. If you still don't feel anything, don't worry. Sometimes it takes a while. If the experience is new for you, you might not know what you are feeling for. So just keep an open mind and keep working on developing hand sensitivity by repeating this exercise at later times.

11. *If you are feeling something, that's great, this is your natural magnetic energy. Practice cultivating it and using it to heal and energise yourself and others or even your next glass of water!*

Your Body's Natural Energy System

The Human Aura

The Aura is an invisible emanation or vapour or a particular atmosphere or quality that seems to arise from and surround a person or a thing. Although it is referred to as the Human Aura it must be realised that all living things (plants etc) have an aura.

The **Human Aura** is made up of seven main energy levels which extend up to four feet from the Human body. This aura's all occupy the same space at the same time, each Human aura extending out further than the previous aura. All Human auras are interconnected and reliant on the others for normal function.

The seven main energy layers of the aura are:-

1. ETHERIC LAYER
2. EMOTIONAL LAYER
3. MENTAL LAYER
4. ASTRAL LAYER
5. ETHERIC TEMPLATE LAYER
6. CELESTIAL LAYER
7. KETHERIC TEMPLATE LAYER

The Etheric Layer

This is the first layer and is close to the physical body and fits like a second skin. It has a definite size and shape. Generally it extends from ¼ of an inch to 2 inches from the body. Lines of energy are readily seen in this section of the aura since it is most closely linked to the physical body. It usually appears as a blue colour. The shade of the blue relates to the condition and health of the body. Athletes have strong etheric auras of a deeper blue in shade. In this aura you feel all the sensations, both pain and pleasure. Whenever there is pain, the flow of energy in that area of the etheric is erratic.

Emotional Layer

This is the second layer and deals with emotions, emotions with us and emotions we have for other people. Generally it extends about 2 to 4 inches from the body and although the form approximates the human shape, it is not as defined as the etheric layer. In fact, each layer becomes less and less structured as a physical person. This layer appears as rainbow coloured clouds. Positive feelings generally create bright colours in this layer, whereas negative feelings, generally create dark colours. Problems in the aura will eventually lead to problems in the first and third layers.

Mental Layer

This is the third layer and deals with thoughts and ideas. It extends about 4 to 8 inches from the physical body and is usually most visible around the head and shoulders as a yellowish light, especially when the mind is focused. Thought forms appear as blobs, which may carry other colours if emotions are attached to thoughts. The more active our thinking processes the brighter our mental aura becomes.

Astral Layer

This is the fourth layer and extends about 8 to 12 inches from the physical body. It is similar in appearance to the emotional body, the colours are brighter and rose-hued with the light of love. This layer marks the division between the physical layers and the higher layers. It is where we experience love, both personally and spiritually, the love for humanity. The astral Human aura is the bridge between the physical world and the spiritual world.

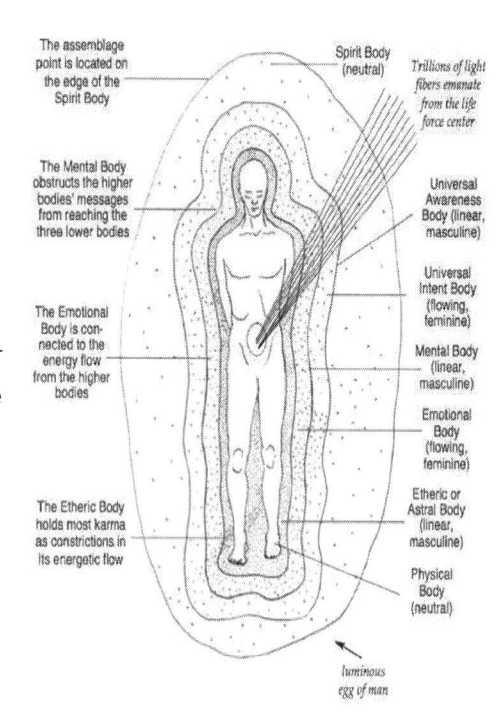

The assemblage point is located on the edge of the Spirit Body

The Mental Body obstructs the higher bodies' messages from reaching the three lower bodies

The Emotional Body is connected to the energy flow from the higher bodies

The Etheric Body holds most karma as constrictions in its energetic flow

Spirit Body (neutral)

Trillions of light fibers emanate from the life force center

Universal Awareness Body (linear, masculine)

Universal Intent Body (flowing, feminine)

Mental Body (linear, masculine)

Emotional Body (flowing, feminine)

Etheric or Astral Body (linear, masculine)

Physical Body (neutral)

luminous egg of man

Etheric Template Layer

This is the fifth layer and is a copy of the physical body on a higher level. It extends about 12 to 24 inches from the physical body and appears as a blueprint (like the negative of a photograph). The etheric template holds the etheric aura in place. This level is associated with a higher will, more connected with Divine Will. Here we create through word and thought and we must take responsibility for our actions.

Celestial Layer

This is the sixth layer. It extends about 24 inches from the physical body and appears as pearly shimmering light of pastel colours. It is the emotional level on the spiritual plane. This is the level of feelings within the world of our spirit. Here we communicate with all the beings of the spiritual world. It is also the level of unconditional love and trust. It can be reached through meditation and other spiritual practices of a devotional nature. The celestial body carries our experience of spiritual love, the connection with and nurturance of all live.

Ketheric Template Layer

This is the seventh and last layer. It extends to at least 3 feet from the physical body. This is the mental layer of the spiritual level. Through this layer we can become one with the Spirit. This is a template of fine threads of golden-silver light that surrounds, protects and holds the whole aura together. Although the least dense, this is the strongest and most resilient level of the aura. This is the higher mind, the highest level of knowing and integrating our Spiritual Self with our Physical self.

The Chakras – Your Personal Energy and Information System

"These seven chakras are who and what we are, what we feel and how we think and change, they are how we express ourselves and how we create. The Chakra system is precisely the means by which we gain our awareness. It is how we experience life, how we perceive reality and how we relate to the self, others and the world, it is life itself".

Rosalyn Bruyere

The Chakra System

The word "Chakra" is a Sanskrit word which translated means "wheel", it is believed that Chakras are non-physical energy centres which are situated slightly away from the physical body and allow the flow of energy through the body.

The word chakra is also said to come from the Kemetic words 'Kara' which means shrine, karaka which means cylinder and thesu/kasu which means knots. The seven knots, or seven vertebra, are associated with seven Neteru who work through these centres. These energy centres connect us to the higher forces or are aspects of the Higher Forces within us. They are connected to planets and days. The Ancient Egyptian also called the Chakras 'Aritu' which is a Kemetic world which also means wheel.

It is understood that the Chakras are akin to spinning wheels which move in a clockwise direction, and each wheel has to spin correctly to ensure that the next wheel to it also spins correctly, thus aligning and balancing the body's energies. If the wheels do not align correctly, then it is believed that the body is not balanced correctly. The Chakras' energy frequencies are lowest at the base and highest at the crown.

The body's seven main Chakras

- Crown
- Brow
- Throat
- Heart
- Solar Plexus
- Sacral
- Base

There are 7 major Chakra's located along our spine, 22 minor Chakra throughout our bodies, one Chakra 6 inches below our feet called the Earth Star which connects us to the earth and our ancestral power and many chakras above our heads outside of our physical body but within out spiritual bodies and energy field head which connect us to the heavens, our higher self and so many other dimensions of experience.

The full consciousness of who we are at our source is so vast and expansive, therefore, through the understanding of the chakra system, we are able to channel and tune into different aspects of the one collective energy of Source.

How are Chakras are functioning, can deliberately affect the amount of information we are able to receive, how we process our human emotions and experience and our potential for elevation and Ascension in this physical reality.

When your chakras are properly balanced and attuned, they also help to assist you in raising your vibration and bringing more light and soul consciousness into the body.

The Chakras give, receive and store energy. It is at these points where energy is exchanged. It comes into us from food, sunlight, and air. Then from these points vital energy is sent to our organs, glands and other parts of our body. This energy is what keeps our bodies and minds working as they should. So if our life force is low on energy there is not much energy available and dis-ease begins in the physical. Many physical ailments come from a spiritual, mental or emotional issue that has not been process properly, therefore it causes a block in energy flow and creates sickness in the body to get you to pay attention and address your issues.

Remember energy can attach itself to you, your thoughts, feeling and/or your aura. You may feel a shift in energy when your Chakra or Aritu are out of balance. Sometimes you feel a shift in energy and are unaware of what you are really feeling.

As energy conscious beings, we seek to remove blockages and bring balance to the chakras through various exercise to bring overall wellness to the ourselves. We use colours, sounds, crystals, symbols and palm healing to bring alignment and harmony to the Chakras. Understanding more about the Chakras will help you understand how to keep them active and balanced.

Understanding your 7 Chakras- What are they?

The first 3 Chakras represent our physical connection of being grounded and belonging to the earth, they are your mental and physical Chakras. They are essential to your growth and survival for living in the material and physical world. When these become unbalanced or blocked, you have problems working, living and adjusting in today's world. If you are someone who has problems coping day by day with life, love, work and health, then working on these Chakras can provide helpful healing in these areas.

The second set of chakra from 4 -7 are your transpersonal chakra and relate to how you communicate and express yourself in the world. How you receive information from outside of yourself, how you connect with other and how you manifest your purpose in this realm.

The higher Chakras from the 8th Chakra upwards deal with our soul consciousness and connection to all that we are beyond all that we can see, and hold the codes and information that allow us to evolve and bring more of our soul consciousness and who we truly are in our highest potential.

The planet herself also has chakras, energy centre which hold, cultivate and channel sacred energy.

Our own personal chakra system offers us an intelligent system of self-analysis, and renewal and can be a road map to helping us to intelligently navigate our emotion, thoughts, and experience in this reality and be our inner GPS and internal guidance system to help support our development and growth.

When you learn to understand your chakras and what their purpose, natural functions and how they to manage your energy, your journey of healing through the chakras, can give you a deeper insight into yourself and help to developed conscious awareness of self.

Spotlight on the 7 Chakras

1. First - Base Chakra – (colour: Red)

Situated at the base of the spine, this Chakra is defined as a Red lotus flower with four petals. It is associated with the adrenals, and is connected to health and survival, and may relate to fear, obsessive/compulsive disorders and possessiveness.

This Chakra has a physical association with the kidneys, the spine and excretion and when imbalanced can be linked to digestive disorders, obesity, constipation, bladder issues and frequent illness.

A person with an imbalance in this Chakra can feel as if they are ungrounded and unfocused. They may feel weak, lack confidence and be unable to achieve their goals.

When balanced the Chakra is associated with stability, security, good health, optimism for life.

2. Second - Sacral Chakra– (colour: Orange)

Situated in the lower abdomen, this Chakra is defined as an Orange lotus flower with six petals. It is associated with the reproductive organs and is connected to relationships.

This Chakra has a physical link to sexual reproduction, body fluids and male/female hormones, and when imbalanced can be linked to impotence, frigidity, uterine and bladder problems.

A person with an imbalance in this Chakra may bury their emotions and be overly sensitive, can also lead to sexual difficulties and energy blocks which affect creativity. When balanced the Chakra is associated with a zest for life, pleasure and desire.

3. Third - Solar Plexus Chakra– (colour: Yellow)

Situated just above the navel, this Chakra is defined as a Yellow lotus flower with ten petals. It is associated with personality, emotion and strength.

This Chakra has a physical link with the stomach, digestion and metabolism, and when imbalanced can be linked to lack of confidence, bad temper, stubbornness, ulcers, diabetes and poor skin.

A person with an imbalance in this Chakra may feel depressed, insecure, lacking in confidence and may worry what others think.

People who are under stress will show imbalance in this chakra, shock and stress have a greater impact on this Chakra as it is the solar plexus that negative energies relating to thoughts and feeling are processed.

When balanced the Chakra is associated with confidence, peace and inner harmony.

4. Fourth - Heart Chakra– (colour: Green)

Situated in the centre of the chest, this Chakra is defined as a Green lotus flower with twelve petals. It is associated with the thymus gland and is concerned with empathy and sympathy.

This Chakra has a physical link with the lungs, heart, arms, hands and immune system, and when imbalanced can be linked to heart, respiratory and circulatory problems, ulcers, fear, and resentment.

A person with an imbalance in this Chakra may feel sorry for themselves. Be afraid of letting go, feel unworthy of love or feel terrified of rejection.

If the energy does not flow freely between the solar plexus and the heart, or between the heart and the throat, it can lead to energy withdrawal into the body.

When balanced the Chakra is associated with sincerity, caring and loving.

5. Fifth - Throat Chakra– (colour: Blue)

Situated in the centre of the throat, this Chakra is defined as a Blue lotus flower with sixteen petals. It is associated with the thyroid gland and is concerned with communication.

This Chakra has a physical link with the throat, ears, mouth and nervous system, and when imbalanced can be linked to allergies, throat, neck and shoulder problems, shyness and tension.

A person with an imbalance in this Chakra may feel unable to relax

If this Chakra is out of balance it may affect our ability to express our emotions, frustration and tension may result. When balanced the Chakra is associated with creativity, open and honest feelings and sincerity.

6. Sixth - Brow Chakra– (colour: Indigo)

Situated in the centre of the head, this Chakra is defined as an Indigo lotus flower with two petals. It is associated with the pituitary gland and is concerned with inner vision. This Chakra has a physical link with the brain, nose, eyes, face and ears and when imbalanced can be linked to headaches, migraine, sinus issues, eye disorders, pituitary problems and insomnia. A person with an imbalance in this Chakra may be oversensitive, be afraid of success, and be non-assertive and undisciplined. If this Chakra is not functioning correctly it can lead to headaches and nightmares.

When balanced the Chakra is associated with intuition, memory and perception.

7. Seventh - Crown Chakra – (colour: Violet)

Situated at the top of the head, this Chakra is defined as a Violet lotus flower with a thousand petals. It is associated with the pineal gland and is concerned with thinking and decision making.

This Chakra has a physical link with the nervous system and cerebral cortex, and when imbalanced can be linked to apathy, depression, confusion, epilepsy, and the inability to make decisions. Imbalance in this Chakra may be unwilling to open up to their spiritual potential and show an inability to make decisions... When balanced, the Chakra is associated with spirituality, understanding, wisdom and open mindedness.

The understanding and application of the knowledge and wisdom gained from studying your energy system will create the opportunity for you to take responsibility for your learning/development and gain a better understanding of your experiences in your life and how may have affected you energetically.

My Journey

My introduction to truly learning about the nature and science of the chakra system in relation to myself and my personal journey, was when I went to study with the 'Energy Doctor" Caroline Shola Arewa on her 'Energy 4 All wellness' practitioner course.

As part of the study we learned to understand how energy, transmitted through traumatic experiences, could create 'distortions' or 'blockages' within your chakra system and energy field, which can then manifest into disease and imbalance within your body, character, mentality and nature.

Whilst on the course, we had to address our own chakras to facilitate any healing work that I needed to do. It was through this process I understood how the effects of my childhood traumas had manifested as blockages in my life and my body.

I noticed that when I would sit, I would hold my body tightly to me, almost as if I was protecting myself. I learned that the outer body experiences that I had, whenever any trauma happened when I was younger and that my issues with feeling safe and protected were stored in my root also from things that affected me as a child.

Using a range of techniques, we learned how to heal, clear and connect with the root of the traumas so that we could free the energy in the chakra system which would then create a more positive flow of energy in my life.

Each Chakra holds the key to helping you to master yourself and your reality and understanding how everything that we experience can affect us and our energy, when our chakras are imbalanced they offer us ways to learn and to heal.

During my time on the course, I learned that many of my chakras were affected by things that took place during my childhood. And these memories, or trapped energy was stored in areas within my body and were affecting the way I expressed myself into my reality.

Many people who experience sexual abuse, neglect or displacements during childhood, can find imbalanced energy within their lower three chakras;

> *The Root - Survival Instinct, Security, Protection, Boundaries*

> *The Sacral - Sexual power, Emotional Stability, Self Esteem and Creativity*

> *The Solar Plexus - Will, Fight or Flight, Power*

> *The Throat: Ability to express oneself, Truth, Freedom*

And for me, I identified with imbalances within my personal lower chakras and began to understand how the energy of those experiences had affected my choices and decisions even in my adult life.

Although In my higher self, I understood the purpose and intentions of the trauma I experienced, the 'energy' of the experience, the thoughts, the emotions, the pain ; was still held within my mental emotional and physical energy systems or bodies.

We are multi dimensional beings and multi layered as well. Energy and information from our experiences can manifest on any layer of our energetic bodies and our conscious awareness and understanding of ourselves as energy, offers us the opportunity to expand beyond our current perception of ourselves as humans and bring healing collectively.

We are in a time, where our limited understanding of what we thought we knew about our human anatomy is changing. With the birth of Quantum physics and new ground breaking discoveries into the world of energy and dimensional reality, we are seeing that there is so much more for us to learn aboht ourselves and to experience as we and the planet go through our Ascension and evolution.

As with everything, what ever is happening outside, is happening within and collectively we are making a shift into the 'higher experiences or aspects of life, - a shift in frequency, if you will, and this also offer opportunity to awaken to a new lesson for humanity. And a transition from the collective experience of the lower dimensions and into the experience and dimension of Unity Consciousness.

The Journey of Ascensions through the chakras

Ascension through the Lower Chakras

For a long time, humanity as a collective have been locked into a loop collective experience.

Humanity is locked in the lower chakras; being encouraged to ascend, and this is only done through the heart. When we have mastered the root, our survival instincts, the sacral, our ability to create and the solar plexus our will, we must now move out od the experience of our personal individualised self and into the experience od our relationship to the Universe and all things.

Passing through the gateways of the heart

For a very long time, whilst we have been operating in the limited world of the 3 dimensions, the lower chakras have been the ones that we are here to master as they are the most tangible to our reality.

Survival and emotional fears which are held in the lower chakras, are keeping the base, sacral and solar plexus chakras third-dimensional.

This is clearly demonstrated when you look at the way our world is currently operating. Many people are hold in a constant state of fear and terror or threat to their survival. Sex of the lowest vibration, through porn and the sex industry and the repression of the Divine feminine is holding us hostage in the sacral and we are constantly battling with our sense of free will and power in a system where most feel powerless to change their reality.

Until we learn to master the challenges of the lower chakras, we will not be able to vibrate higher and move through the gateway into a collective reality based on the experience of the heart.

It is as if, there is a wall that separates the lower from the higher, the heart is a gateway towards the next stage of our experience. And this is demonstrated as we move from the lower, which is connected to our personal experience, into the higher chakras which are about our connection to others and our projection into reality.

The Heart chakras qualities include Love, Forgiveness, Compassion and other 'Feminine' qualities. We must vibrate at the resonance of the heart in order to walk through the Halls of Amenti and also to raise in our vibration collectively as humanity. The whole Earth is moving into the gateway of the heart and this is the vibration of the 5th Dimension.

As Mother moves, so do we, and we are moving out of the lower chakras to collectively experience and manifest the lessons and experiences of the higher; and it is through the heart, that we must go.

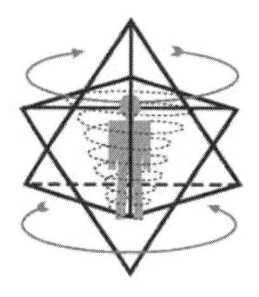

During the Golden Age of Atlantis everyone had 12 chakras in place which contained the codes of all their extraordinary gifts and talents. As the energy de-evolved, five chakras were switched off. At the same time the fifth-dimensional Merkabah dissolved.

The Merkabah is the energetic six-pointed star that surrounds our aura and contained our fifth-dimensional blueprint and light body. (Our light body holds all the light and wisdom codes we have earned in the course of our soul journey. It is the physical manifestation of our Higher Self.)

"Mer" means Light. "Ka" means Spirit. "Ba" means Body. Mer-Ka-Ba means the spirit/body surrounded by counter-rotating fields of light, (wheels within wheels), spirals of energy as in DNA, which transports spirit/body from one dimension to another.

The Merkabah is based on the structure of the Star of David or Metatron's Cube.

The fifth-dimensional Merkabah was replaced by the third-dimensional Merkabah so that the remaining seven chakras radiated at a lower frequency.

> *Around the world, so much is misunderstood about the Mer-Ka-Ba, the light body created by the brain that surrounds the physical body. And how the Mer-Ka-Ba is involved with ascension into a new world is also misunderstood. It is no longer activated manually as it was with the Flower of Life, but is now activated in the ancient manner through the heart, which is so much easier. This new/ancient teaching is called Awakening the Illuminated Heart.*
> Drunvelo Melchezidec

It is now time for us all to bring back our 12 chakras and our whole range of extraordinary gifts and talents. Then we can bring in a new civilization and a new Golden Age on the planet. This will have the imprint of Golden Ascended Atlantis, but our task is to recreate it at an even higher frequency.

We can reinstate our fifth-dimensional chakras ourselves, and when they are installed and operational, our fifth-dimensional Merkabah will automatically be anchored. Note that we are now moving metaphorically from a house with five floors to a skyscraper with 12 floors. Therefore, our foundation, which in the 12-chakra system includes our Earth Star chakra, needs to be much stronger than before and fully anchored. This is our connection, our roots, into Gaia.

Galactic or Collective Consciousness Chakras

Higher Level Chakras

Theses chakras are being newly awakened in us as the earth and our bodies allows space for more light and higher frequencies of source, light and expansion. The provide the energy, light and consciousness needed to experience astral travel, connect with higher beings, support unity consciousness, clear collective karma and connect with and integrate the highest parts of your soul.

8. Earth Star (seed) Chakra – Ancestral Gateway

The 8th Chakra is another gateway chakra that leads us into a another 'lens' or means of experience.

This golden chakra lies three to seven inches beneath the feet and allows the earth or notion of being on the earth to be balanced in the individual.

It is a golden star tetrahedron, but it also contains the Seed of Life Symbol. The Earth Star seed chakra is the seed that is planted deep into the earth and contains all of your past information, your ancestral energy and everything that you were before you came here.

As a being of Earth you have your own energy pod which is your personal link to Earth. This energy is an Earth Kundalini which winds its way up from the core of the Earth, through the Earth and up into your root Chakra. From there it ignites your own Kundalini which is like a fiery serpent, winds its way up your spinal cords and out of your Crown Chakra and overflows its lava power, down your body, back into the Earth and again back up through your body in a none ending cycle.

The Earth Star chakra also holds all of your ancestral and karmic energy. This is the very foundation that you walk upon and we are being encouraged to continue the legacy of our ancestors and heal the wounds of past lives

9. Universal Heart or Higher Charka – Unity Consciousness

This Larimar Chakra lies between the throat and the heart and is also called the 'higher heart chakra'. It is the space that houses the love that connects us all. If the heart chakra is about our personal relationships, then the higher heart is about our collective relationships and the highest truest vibration of love.

The symbol for the higher hear is a heart with the infinity symbol in the middle contained in a torus field. This is to demonstrate that this love is coming from the divine source if all love and is infinite flowing and abundant.

The higher heart chakra is our connection to everything, to each other, to nature to source and it's through this space that we exercise unity consciousness and is the main vibration of the 5th dimensional experience of oneness.

10. Cosmic or Causal Charka (Divine Masculine)

This silver chakra lies just above the crown and its vibration connects the individual with access to all the psychic information they need. This chakra helps to adjust the body's vibration so that it can receive and understand psychic information and filters it so that we do not feel overwhelmed. A fully activated causal chakra acts as a focus to achieve a sense of serenity.

11. The Soul Star (Divine Feminine Centre)

This Magenta Chakra connects the soul entity to the feminine aspect of spirit represented by Kwan Yin, Mary etc, and is also the bridge between impersonal essence and personal reality. The soul star works like a transducer to moderate the very high vibrational energy and information beamed down from the spiritual planes through the stellar gateway to a level we can assimilate into our physical existence. Its virtue in compassion and unconditional love.

12. Stellar Gateway/the Womb (Enlightenment – I Am Consciousness)

This portal of pure white light lies seven inches above the eleventh chakra at the edge of the light field. Through this chakra you may feel your connection with the inter-galactic aspect of yourself, your true connection to the Universe and Source. It is through this chakra that evolved spiritual beings living their purpose as a movement back to wholeness and become at one with source. It is the emanation of Ra and house of the Christ consciousness energy and so also connect us with the **Merkabah** (MER- Light KA- Spirit BA- Physical body/vehicle) – The chariot of ascension: that becomes our energetic vehicle which enables us to travel across dimensions of space and time consciously. Activation of this chakra returns us to our original sense of higher consciousness and the expansiveness of unconditional love

When this Chakra is activated, you enter the Super Galactic Centre that is the Womb of the whole universe. It is here that the Goddess who is Mother resides. Through activating this Chakra and connecting with the Goddess energies you become one with the Mother, becoming a star gate that enables peace and balance to work through you and enter humanity.

Working with your 7 chakras and your 12 will help give you a great understanding of yourself and empower you with self-awareness and self-healing that will empower you to do great things.

Our energetic system is upgrading because we are also expanding in our consciousness and awareness of who we are. The chakras offer us a way of understating and navigating our experiences so that we can be happy and healthy and in alignment with our highest good and potential.

Working with the higher chakras was like a 'duck taking to water' and I had a natural awareness of them. But my challenge in this time was to heal and rebalance the lower chakras. A lot of us are held within the 3 lower chakras by lower vibratory thoughts, feelings and experiences and the fear conjured up by society. The constant fear keeps you in a space of survival instinct and unable to truly see the wealth and abundance and power we hold within our reality. Fuelled by trauma and lustful sexual energy, which can distort our sacral chakra and block our ability to manifest and create and most importantly, trust in our ability to do so. To be self-sufficient, to be self-sustained, to practice balance, feasting and fasting and times of cleansing and purification.

The Importance of Grounding and Protecting Your Energy Field

When working with higher vibrational being or energies or just when dealing with everyday life, it is important to stay grounded and develop a practice which helps you to support this.

Grounding means to 'connect with the earth' then embody the feeling of being anchored and held by the earth and also in your mentality.

When dealing with the world of spirit and subtle energy, we open ourselves and lift our vibrations slightly outside of our bodies. When we are ungrounded we cannot properly channel the energies that we are receiving which could lead to misunderstanding and depletion of energy amongst other things.

Being grounded is an important part of the spiritual foundation of the Spiritual practice. If you are not grounded with your subtle energies/ aura connected to the earth, it is impossible for the universal source energy to flow fully and freely though you. When you are grounded spiritual energies flow freely through your own energy field and you can draw on this energy.

When we are not grounded, the energy that you use, will be your own which will then leave you feeling very drained and depleted very quickly.

It can also cause weaknesses and holes in your aura which allow other discarnate beings and energies to feed off of your energy.

This for me was one of the major lesson I encountered on my journey with spiritual work. It is imperative that you develop a daily practice which enables you to ground your energy and receive energy also. When we ground and connect to the earth, she anchors us but also give us her energy and her love. This gives us a solid and safe foundation of which explores the higher realms upon.

- ❖ *Grounding your energy changes the way it flows*
- ❖ *It boasts your astral reception making it easier to receive guidance and information*
- ❖ *It also activates and stimulates the root chakra*

If you feel tired, sluggish and stressed out a lot then you may just need to ground your energy. Below are a few grounding exercises you could try.

Grounding Exercises

1. *Find a quite space where you will not be disturbed. Light some incense and candles to raise the vibration of the space (if you have available) and limit all distractions.*

2. *Sit in a comfortable position and take a few deep breaths in and out to get you centred and prepared (3-7 times Is good)*

3. *In your mind eye envision seeing a central sun above your head. In the middle of the Sun see a symbol of your higher self's choice. (This could be an Ankh, Beetle for Khepher or any symbol that comes to your mind. For this practice we can use the Ankh as it is life giving.*

4. Take a deep breath and draw the energy of the sun down into the top of your head.

5. See the energy from the sun dripping into your crown like thick, glowing honey.

6. Allow this honey to gently seep into your body through your temple. Down your torso, all of your chakras into your feet.

7. Take a deep breath and envision roots coming out of your feet.

8. See them grow and stretch down into the soil beneath you. Past the soil, the clay, the bedrock, down deep into the earth

9. See a glowing ball of orange fire and energy. Wrap your roots around this ball and anchor. You are now suspended between heaven and earth, Father and Mother. Stay in this space for a moment feeling connected, grounded, supported.

10. Mother earth is always there for you. She loves her children and is here to help take any burden from us. Spend a moment connecting with mother. Share with her your feelings.

11. Mother always likes to offer her children her gifts. Now in this moment ask for a gift from mother earth. Trust and know that it will be delivered.

12. Take a deep breath in and as you inhale, draw in the energy of the gift that she has given you and secure it in your heart

13. Thank mother for the gift and connect with her once more. Feel the firm foundation, feel the support, and feel the love.

14. Thank Mother for the Gift and for her time. Then on your next breath, draw up the roots from the core. Draw it up past the bedrock, the clay, the floor beneath you and up into your body and in to your heart

15. Take another deep breath and draw the chord from the central sun, down into your crown and again into your heart.

16. *See yourself in golden bubble of protection and place an Ankh on your heart, head and feet.*

17. *Give thanks for the experience and when you're ready, open your eyes.*

This exercise can be done daily and will instantly help you to feel grounded and more connected, it can be very useful in stressful situation and is fanatic as a morning ritual to help keep you connected, grounded and supported the whole day through.

Energy Protection

Energy protection is very important when dealing with subtle energies and doing any sort of spiritual or healing work. When we are entering into the higher realms of consciousness we expose ourselves to all types of energies that we are not aware of.

As we know energy is fluid and can be transferred from place to place as it is within all things. We are also energy and at times we can attract energies of a lower vibration.

If you are a healer, meditate a lot, expand your consciousness, listen to hypnosis tapes or a range of other reasons, then you may need psychic protection.

The word 'Psychic' has two meaning. One pertains to the things of the psyche; that inner part of us which encompasses not only our conscious mind and convictions, but also the subconscious mind and the irrational beliefs associated with it.

The other meaning pertains to the unseen, hidden, esoteric, and occult part of our beings that exists beyond the purely physical. This is the realm of non-verbal communication, telepathy, subtle energies and other dimensions of consciousness.

Psychic protection is subtle and invisible. It works on the non-physical level of your being. It resonates to the principal of 'like attracts like'. It teaches us the true power of thought. It surrounds us with a protective barrier and also brings our ancestors and guides closer to us.

At its simplest level psychic protect can be a hoop of light around your feet, or a bubble of protection or a pyramid, the key is to find the right protection for you.

The explosion in consciousness over the past few years, has seen a surge in people exploring occult, magic and mysticism. Some do not have the proper training and can bring forth energies they are not prepared for and people sell all kinds of spells and rituals on the internet. This is not to scare you, but to bring your awareness to the fact that as you open your conscious awareness to other dimensions you become visible to all, and so for this reason amongst others, protection is needed.

Opening up to consciousness, makes us more sensitive and this makes you sensitive to other energies as well. We may pick up the vibes of others and if not careful, can become a vacuum cleaner for other people's junk and unfriendly entities. Many psychic development and healing courses, are being taught and people are not taught how to properly protect themselves. We have to be honest in the fact that we are dealing with the unseen, so therefore prevention is better than cure.

Everyone, who opens their awareness, needs techniques for screening, closing and protection...Now. Protection needs to be done easily and quickly and most importantly you must feel the protection.

The object is to prevent intrusion or interference from an unwanted source. The aim is to cleanse and strengthen your own natural protective energies.

Simple prayer for protection

A quick and simple prayer can be very effective for protection. It affirms your power and protection for the source of all that is that runs through you and in everything. It also reminds you that you are safe and puts your mind and body at peace. Below is one that I use but feel free to make up your own.

> **Divine Creator of all there is,**
>
> *I come in humble heartfelt communion this day to ask for your protection and guidance. Cover me in unconditional love and keep me safe so that I may continue to share and spread this love.*
>
> *Divine ancestors let no negativity come my way and if any reside with myself help me to know, to see and to release in love*
>
> *In line with my highest good and with harm to none I pray*
>
> ***Ashe***

You are what you Eat

Let food be thy medicine and medicine be thy food."

Hippocrates

Diet and nutrition is not only about the food we eat but also the nature of the food that we eat so that we ensure that it provides us with the nutrients and mineral and energy that we need.

The earth Is abundant with nourishment and everything that we need, we can obtain from her. But with the current state of affairs in society, most of us are not getting the sustenance that we need and this is manifesting in diseases and illness.

The quality of the life that you lead, and the energy that you have in your body, is dependent on what you put into it, on all levels and this include your food.

The mass produced food that many of us are eating, is usually highly processed and devoid of any nutrients and goodness. Nature shows us the right types of food to eat as they grow in abundance and are in themselves bursting with energy and vibrancy

Food and The Elements

Everything in nature is governed, or can be understood by the 4 main elements of Air, Water, Earth and Fire. This is the same for our food and in order for our body to function at optimum level and have enough energy to vibrate at its highest frequency, then we have to nourish it with the right foods and fuels.

Our bodies need a holistic and balanced diet in order to vibrate at optimum health and Mother Earth provides all the nutrients we need.

Energy rich foods can be found all over the planet and it is up to us to discern what is right for us as individuals. This can be further identified by our blood type, our star sign or element and environment. Each one of our bodies is naturally designed to absorb light from our foods. But we have been programmed and conditioned to feed dead, low vibratory foods and energy into our bodies which have manifested as long-term disease and ill health.

When you become conscious of what you put into your body, you are becoming the master of your reality. To nourish yourself and ensure that you only put the best into your body, is one of the greatest acts of Self Love and preservation. Your body is the Temple, it houses your Spirit, your 'God-essence' and helps you to manifest your reality on this planet. Your body is built to last, and if you feed it well, it will last you as long as you need it to.

Learning to honour our sacred temple mean to also love it and honour it. Food is much more that a necessity, it is a gift and a choice, so we must be mindful of what we feed ourselves, mentally, spiritually, emotionally and through the foods we eat.

Elements	Foods
Earth - Earth foods grow within the Earth. They are grounding and nourishing to the body. They grow deep in the depths of the Earth	*Roots, Vegetables, Potatoes, Carrots, Onions, Beetroots, roots and root vegetables, potatoes, rock salt, peanuts, peanut oil, strawberries, and cereals, especially buckwheat.*
Water - Water Foods are mainly composed on water and provide hydration and minerals to the cells and the body. They are a mixture of Air and Earth and grow just below and above	*Green vegetables, Cucumbers, Melons, Squash, Marrows, Pumpkins, Rice, Algae, Sea food*

Fire- Fire Foods help to bring heat and energy into the body. Heat is good for cleansing and clearing and empowering. Fire food helps to boost the immune system and fight off illness.	*Citrus fruits, Cinnamon, Olives, olive oil, Ginger, Sunflower seeds, Sunflower seed oil, Cereals, Tomatoes, Pepper and Chilli, Grains, some Seeds and Pulses*
Air- Air Foods stimulate circulation and encourage energy flow within the body. They are usually foods that grow high above the ground on vines or trees	Gingko, Raw foods, Kiefer, Fruits, Nuts, Seeds, Berries, avocados, bananas

This information can also be effective when connected to astrology. If you are an Earth sign, then it is suggested that you eat more Earth foods, such as root vegetables and cereals and balance it with Air Foods, such as nuts, berries and Fruit.

Likewise, when you are feeling a little unbalanced, you can eat the foods that will help you to feel nourished and grounded

As well as eating from the right elements, we can also include eating foods from all of the colours of the Rainbow.

Have you ever wondered why Sweets and unhealthy foods, have such attractive and colourful packaging? And why we are so drawn to it? This is because we Eat with our eyes. Our first sense that is stimulated when it comes to our food is the visual- what does the food look like? and when we see colours, we see nature. we see all of the colours of all the foods in nature, which provide use with nourishment and the minerals we need. so when we see these bright coloured packages in the shops, somewhere in our psyche, we are seeing food.

But this is because colours are frequencies and each colour has an element or attribute and therefore feed the body with light and energy, as we are energy, frequency and light.

Just as within the colours of the Rainbow, each colour holds a vibration, which has an affect on us, so too does our food. The colours of the foods that we eat is important because colours are light and light is energy and information.

So it makes sense to know how this applies to our food and our bodies, so that we can be conscious to ensure that we are feeding our bodies with the vital nutrients and energies needed, for it to vibrate at the frequency of Optimal Health.

Rainbow Food Colour Chart

Colour	Foods	Benefits
Red	Beetroots, Tomatoes, Pomegranate etc	Lycopene, Anti oxidants
Orange	Oranges Pumpkins, Mangos etc	Beta-carotene, Immune system builder
Yellow	Pineapple, Bananas, Yellow Peppers	Vitamin C, Detoxifying
Green	Kale, Spinach, Apples, Leafy Veg	Folic Acid, Iron, build healthy cells
White-Green	Garlic, Brussel Sprouts, Cabbages	Allyl Sulphides, Destroy cancer cells
Blue/ Purple	Blueberries, Fig, Purple Cabbage,	Anthocyanins, Destroys free radicals
Brown	Whole grains, legumes	Carcinogen removal, Fibre

After many years of the masses, senselessly eating whatever is available without any consciousness, we are now seeing more and more people taking responsibility to source healthy and more organic foods to feed the body.

Many are becoming vegan or going for life style changes, that allow them to have more energy and a better quality of life.

You are what you eat and so therefore whatever we eat, we become.

When we eat dense or low vibrational food such as Meat, we are taking in not only the energy of the food but also the consciousness of the animal. When we eat flesh, which is death, we are putting dead fuel into our body in order to give it energy, and this simply won't do. Have you noticed that when you eat a Steak or some meat for dinner or lunch you suddenly feel very tired and lethargic. This is because the food is so dense in vibration that the body actually has to use more energy in order to break in down so it can be used.

Plants, roots, fruits, vegetables are just some of the high energy foods that can actually help us to raise our vibration.

We are light and so are plants as they absorb the light and they also are nutrient rich because they come from the ground, from the soil from mother earth as we do.

When we eat plant based food we are eating light and within light is energy and information. When this enters our bodies it gives light to our cells and energise our body.

When you eat from all the colour of the rainbow you can feed both your body and your chakra system. The different colours of the fruits and veg also pertain to the chakra system and each colour found in the food directly energies that chakra and the organs within this space

We get our energy from our food, so if you want to have a higher energy vibration that you must first start with taking a look at your diet.

Chakra Cleanse – Power Up

I AM
The keeper of the Divine Spirit
Multi-dimensional being, with no limit

Earth Chakra pulsating
Solar Plexus agitating
Sacral Chakra…master-mating
Third Chakra, Meditating
Pineal Gland, Resonating

Throat Chakra's song is playing
Breathing sound into creation
Hearts Chakra magnifying
All the love in there residing

Amplified in the Cosmic Heart
In beautiful hues of Larimar
Crown chakra, full ascension
Opening up to higher dimensions
Through the Stellar Gate Way
Ascended Masters Make way
Pay attention to, what they say
This is my intention this day
and everyday

Nurturing the Seeds

Seed 3 - Understanding yourself as Energy

We are energetic beings and therefore understanding our nature and how our energetic system works helps us to be more conscious in the choices we make and what we put into our bodies.

To master your reality, you must master yourself and that includes understanding how you operate and making the changes that you need so that you can enjoy the richness of life to the fullest. The questions below will assist

Time to Do the Work

Earth –Root Chakra

The Earth element naturally connects to the Root Chakra

Earth energy is grounding and supportive and can help you to remain calm and focused and also replenish your energy. As an energetic begin, you are able to absorb energy from the environment and from the soil and nature to help empower and infuse your own energy system.

- ❖ *'Earthing' is a great way of connecting the earth and replenishing your energy levels. Not only does it leave your feeling charged and re-energised, you also get a moment to relax and gather your thoughts in nature. Grounding and using the Earth energy is also a great way to bring you dreams into reality.*

- ❖ *You could also use some **essential oils** in your bath to help relax and ground you. Rosemary, Cypress and Cedar are great Root Chakra Oils*
    - o The Root Chakra is concerned with our survival consciousness and early childhood development

- ❖ *Understand your needs – what is it that you need in your life to help to maintain your sense of stability and value? Are you able to support yourself?*

- ❖ *You can also **activate your Root Chakra daily**, using light Energy by visualizing a Red ball of energy at your Root Chakra and 'charging' and clearing it with the power of Light and your breath. First take a look at the condition of your root chakra in your mind's eye. Observe it vibrancy and energy. Set your intention to charge and clear it and as you take a deep breath in, release and send the energy to your root chakra. See it spinning with each breath until it is a vibrant red colour and flowing freely.*

Root Chakra Affirmations

I Am Safe Grounded and Secure

I Am at Home in My body

I AM sustained and nourished by nature

Water - The Energy of Movement and Flow

The Water Element is connected to your Sacral Chakra and governs your sexual and creative energies. It is connected to your emotions and feelings. Water energy is flowing and clear and bring forth new life and inspiration but when unbalanced can be stagnant and inactive. A harmonious Sacral chakra can reawaken your zest for life and give you the energy you need to enjoy it.

- Try a **Healing Chakra Massage** – *using essential oils, take the time to lie down and connect with your sacral chakra. Using the healing power of touch connect with and awaken you sacred centre. Place some warm oil on your hands, take a few deep breaths and rub into your abdomen area. Rub anti clockwise to clear and imbalanced energy and then clockwise to energise and empower the chakra. You can use Orange, Geranium, sandal wood or Myrrh essential oils. Crystals include Carnelian, Amber and Aventurine*

- *Your* **Sacral chakra** *is also connected to your* **sacred creative expression** *and dance is a great way of opening up your sacral chakra and energizing your centres. You can put on your favourite music and have a dance, tuning into your sacred feminine or masculine energy and making a connection with that space*

- *Take a moment to observe your connection to your sacred sexual power. In your journal write down anything that comes to mind about the nature of your sexual energy. Are you aware of it? Do you hold on to sexual trauma and painful memories, or do the thoughts of sexual liberation and freedom spring to mind. Remember that all is energy and your thoughts are able to reconnect you to old emotions but that you also have the power to heal and detach. if anything painful comes up, just ask you higher self to bring understanding and awareness to your heart and mind and the send healing to yourself. Know that whatever comes through will be for the highest good. You can also follow on with the exercise below*

- ❖ You can also do **this healing body affirmation** to help you to cleanse and clear any negative thought forms, experiences or energies that arise. Visualise your Sacral Chakra as a ball of orange, vibrant light at your naval. Hold it with your hand and breathe into it 3 times. The following affirmations are will assist you in empowering your Sacral Chakra.

Sacral Chakra Affirmations

On the OUT breathe- I release all negativity I hold about my wants and desires

On the IN breath – I receive with joy, everything that I want and desire

On the IN breath – I release all negativity and guilt that I hold about my sexual nature

On the OUT breath – I embrace my sexuality in all it beauty and fullness

Stay in this space for a moment and observe how your feel. Make any notes in your journal

Fire – Solar Plexus - Your Inner Sun

The Solar plexus chakra is connected to the element of Fire. Fire is the creative essence of all things. Fire is driven passionate and focused. The Solar plexus is all about our Will and how we manifest that in our reality. The energy of Fire is Masculine and Proactive in its nature. This sacred centre is connected to our ability to speak up for ourselves, to push through with our goals and intentions and also our confidence and motivation

The exercises below will assist you in rebalancing and connecting with your Solar Plexus Chakra

- ❖ Take a moment to **connect with your Solar Plexus** and **awaken your inner fires**. This simple meditation is a powerful way of connecting with your Sacred Power and energising your Solar plexus chakra. Place your hands over your Solar Plexus chakra, just below your rib cage. Close your eyes and envision a golden ball of light, like an inner sun. connect with the energy of your inner sun by taking a few deep cleansing breaths. Also be aware of your heart beat. You heart beat provides the energy and current that gives flow to all your chakras.

- You will now **energise your Solar plexus with your sacred breath.** – As you close your eyes again and connect with your inner sun. set you intention now to energise it. When you are ready, take a deep cleansing breath and draw it into your Solar plexus and release. As you continue to breath in and out, Notice how your inner sun grows bigger and bigger and brighter and brighter with every breath. Continue doing this until your inner sun if glowing brightly and is full of life

- You can also use this exercise to power your intention and help you to reach your goals. Hold your intentions in your mind and as you breath light into the solar plexus, state your affirmations either aloud or in your mind. As you do feel the energy of your inner sun, empowering and charging your intention.

- You can also **chant the sound RA** to assist you in empowering and clearing your Solar Plexus Chakras

- And as a general exercise you could observe how you use your power and where you may need to be more assertive in your life. Do you need to speak up more? Or are you a little aggressive and overbearing towards others. Take a few moments to honestly access how you use your power and write down any notes in your journaling section.

- **Essential oils** for the Solar plexus include lavender, chamomile, lemon and anise. Crystals – Tiger's eye, Yellow Jasper or Cirtine

Solar Plexus Affirmation

I am worthy.

I am confident.

I am powerful.

I release judgement of others.

I release judgement of myself.

Love - The Heart Chakra - The Gateway to understating our connection to all that is

The Heart Chakra is the 4th chakra and is the first of the transpersonal chakras, which demonstrate our connection to the reality outside of us and others. The Heart Chakras when balanced brings understating between all things. It virtues are Compassion, Love and Empathy. But when imbalanced this chakra can manifest trauma, heart ache and a break down relationships and feelings of depression and loneliness. Love is the Animating force of the Universe and the heart is a gateway to the heavens and also the Halls of Amenti. The heart hold are most scared and most painful feelings.

When we cleanse and rebalance our heart we allow for loving and joyous experiences and moments with others and also cultivate love for self. Try the exercises below to help you clear your heart and create space for more Love

- ❖ *The **Heart chakra** is connected to **Love, and our relationships** with other. Not necessarily of a sexual nature but this can be included. It is about how we relate to others and our environment. Take a moment to observe the relationships in your life. Pick 3 relationships and observe the nature of the interactions. Are they* loving? What do you love about these relationships? What do they show you about yourself? What needs to be rebalanced in your relationships

- ❖ **Forgiveness** is one of the most potent forces in the Universe and is also the Key to all liberation within the heat. To offer forgiveness can at times seem hard and painful. But the more that your practise this sacred art and experience the true healing that can come from it, you will never hold a grudge again and to forgive will become like breathing. Take a moment now to bring to mind anyone that is in need of your forgiveness? Bring them to your mind and offer them your forgiveness. Connect with their higher self and their heart and send the vibration of Love and Forgiveness to them and see them receiving it.

- ❖ Also what do you need to forgive yourself for? What are you holding against yourself that either wasn't your fault or no longer serves you. Write them down and hold your hands on your heart and speak your forgiveness to yourself. When you are finished you can burn the paper to transmute the energy or discard of it.

- ❖ **Self-Love is Key** to ensuring that you are healthy and balanced. When we give too much love to others, and do not give enough to ourselves, we become depleted, unhappy and depressed. Spend a little time with yourself and make a weekly commitment to do so. What would you do? What do you enjoy?

Heart Chakra Affirmations

My Heart is Open to giving and receiving Love
I loving accept myself as I am
I Forgive myself and others and send Love to all including me

Air – The Throat Chakra - The Space of Sacred Expression

The throat chakra is the 5th chakra in our energy system and is connected to the element of Air. Air is the energy that carries everything else in existence. It is the cosmic space between everything and the container of reality. Air energy is expansive and fluid in nature. The Throat chakra is all about how we communicate with and express ourselves into our reality and acts as a bridge between the heart and the mind. When it is balanced we are able to express ourselves freely and manifest our intention into the world. When it is imbalanced, we can be reclusive and unable to express yourself fully and clearly. To check in with your Throat Chakra, try some of the exercises below:

* *You **throat chakra** is also connected to **sound and creation**. As we know, the world was created into form by the words, sound power. Sound is a very important healer as everything in the Universe and in our body have a certain frequency, sound or tone that can bring it back into balance and harmonic resonance. To awake your Throat Chakra you can Chant to seed sound for the Throat Chakra which is HAM (pronounced HANG). Try chanting this a few times with your breath and be aware of the changes that take place in your body. You can also just choose to Sing a song that you like that helps to raise your vibration.*

* **Speak your truth**- *Is there anything that you need to say to someone that you feel you cannot? When we suppress our true thoughts and feelings we can create energy blockages in that chakra. Take the time to write down anything that it is that you feel you need to say to some that you have not. You can start by writing them down and then when you're ready visualize the persona in front of you and speak your truth to them. Notice how this feels in your body? How do they respond? You can practice this a few times until your feel confident and then Speak your Truth to the person. You never know, it may just be something*

that they really need to hear. And you will definitely feel better afterwards

- ❖ **Crystals** *associated with the Throat chakra include: Blue Lace agate, Lapis lazuli, topaz and Aquamarine*
- ❖ **Essential oils** *that are great for the throat chakra include Peppermint, camphor and Eucalyptus*

Throat Chakra Affirmations

I speak from my heart and let truth be my guide

I use the power of my words to make the world a better place

Every day it becomes easier to express my truth

I am always able to find the right words

Spirit – Third Eye and Crown Chakra- Your inner eyes and connection to all things

The 6th and 7th Chakras of our energetic system both connected to the element of Sprit and Ether. The Third eye chakra is connected to our powers of intuition and imagination and connects us to the subtle realms. The Crown Chakra connects us to the Universe and the one Cosmic Mind which is the mind of the Creator and of the cosmos. It's the connection to our higher selves and the gateway to our galactic chakras. When we embark on our spiritual journey of growth and development, it is these two centres in which we focus the most energy. Try the exercises below and see if you can awaken a deeper connection to spirit and your 6th sense.

- ❖ ***Mediation*** *is a great tool to help you develop your intuition and help you connect deeper to yourself. Meditation is also a great way to relax and get grounded and connected to the earth. Try the guided meditation on the Star Seed Journey page.*

- ❖ ***Third Eye Massage*** *– you can use any of the following essential oils and carry out a massage on your third eye. Using your index and middle finger, rub the oil in the centre of your forehead and envision cleansing and empowering your third eye. Rub anti-clockwise to release and a clockwise to empower. The oils you can use are:* Lemongrass, Frankincense, Lavender or Juniper Berry

Third Eye Affirmations

I recognize wisdom comes from within.
I see all situations with clarity and objectivity.
I am open to inner guidance.
The knowledge of the Universe is within me.

Crown Chakra

1. Prayer and intention can help to awaken your Crown and strengthen the connection between your heart and mind and the heart and mind of all there is. Prayer is about being in a space of gratitude and communion with source. Prayers spoken with reverence and power can help to restore faith and hope.

2. Service is also one of the ways of which you can balance your Crown Chakra. Do something nice for another, or help out or volunteer where your energy is needed. We are all connected to each other and are empowered by each other's also

Crown Chakra Affirmations

I Am fully aware – in my body, thoughts and feelings

The essence of my being is Peace and Light

I open myself to the infinite power of God within and without

Journal Page

Use this page to make any notes of your experience.

Star Seed Journey- Soul Journey

12 Chakra Activation and Cleansing Meditation

This 12 chakra mediation can be done in the morning or in the evening when you have time to yourself. The purpose of this meditation is to energise and activate your chakras. It is quick and easy and a great addition to your daily spiritual practice.

When you make a visualization and intention, you manifest what you request. We will use light energy and visualization in this meditation. Please make a note of the positon of the Chakras, if you are not sure, then check the diagram presented earlier in this section.

Guided Meditation

- Find yourself a nice comfortable space where you will not be disturbed. Either lying down or sitting in a chair or on the floor

- As before, we will begin by taking a few deep cleansing breath and prepare to make our connection with the earth and the stars

- Make your intention to cleanse and activate your chakras

- See a cord of light running down your spine, down your body into the Earth and connect with mother Earths core through the roots from your feet

- Take a moment to connect with mother earth and her energy and anchor there

- On you next breath, draw up the molten energy from Mother Earth's core up into your body

- Just beneath your feet about 4 inches below you will notice a Golden Star-this is the earth star chakra, take a deep breath and draw the energy of Mother Earth into this chakra and as you do see it spinning

- When the spinning stops see you Earth Star Chakra glowing a bright golden colour

- Draw the light now into the Root at the bottom of your body. Take another deep breath in and energise this Chakra. See it spinning and any dense energy being removed. When the spinning has finished observe and prepare to move to the next

- Do this for all of your Chakras energising them with light and cleansing your chakras

- When you have cleansed the Stellar Gate Way Chakra, see above your head a Star of David or Merkabah

- Make your intention to flush your chakra system with liquid light energy ad as you do see a surge of light coming down into your chakras all the way down to the root and then into the core of mother earth

- Stay in this space for a moment, suspended between heaven and earth and feel the energy running through your body and energy system

- When you are ready make your intention to disconnect from the flow of energy and to seal your chakras with light

- Give thanks to Mama and draw your energy back up through your root and into your hearts secret chamber

- Draw your attention to the star above and make your intention to disconnect from this energy

- As you, draw the energy of the heavens down into your heart chakra and lock it into your hearts secret chamber and take 3 deep cleansing breaths

- see yourself in a light bubble of protection surrounding your aura and a symbol of your choice and when you are ready, open your eyes

Take time with yourself after this journey as it may take a while to get back 'into' your body consciously.

Take a few moments to write down your thoughts, feeling or experience

Journal Page

Use this page to make any notes of your experience.

Seed 4-

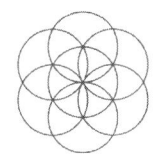

Understand the Power

of Your

Mind and Emotions

"If you knew the power of your mind, you would never hold another negative thought in your mind, ever again

Anon

SEED 4 – UNDERSTAND POWER OF YOUR THOUGHTS AND EMOTIONS

Everything is energy.
Energy follows thought
Thought becomes reality,
Belief creates reality,
Reality determines success
The Destiny Formula

The Power of the Mind

Every statement, thought and action is reflected by the things we manifest in our lives. Every decision is made upon the mirror reflection of what we choose to create. What we think and say have a direct bearing upon whether our manifestations are for our benefit or detriment. If you constantly say that you are poor, then you most definitely will be.

The mind is such a powerful organ within the human body, which operates on more than a physical level. The mind is split into many layers and is ultimately connected to the Universal Mind or the one mind of the universe.

The Mind is defined as, the element of a person that enables them to be aware of the world and their experiences, to think, and to feel; the faculty of consciousness and thought. And is also, a person's ability to think and reason; the intellect. It is the active art of our brain or consciousness, that interprets our experience of reality.

The Mind is fickle and easily influenced, and when imbalanced, the Mind can cause traumatic experiences such as depression and mental health issues. When balanced and aligned and working in harmony with Spirit, your mind can be a very powerful tool in assisting you in bringing forth reason and rationality and also developing the ability to use the energies available to you to master and create your own reality.

You mind is a powerful creator, and dependent on your thought, emotions and vibrational frequency, have the power to create Heaven or Hell.

We have our physical mind, which processes information, helps to regulate functions within the body and helps to keep the subconscious systems of the body. Nevertheless, the mind is not the brain itself, but the consciousness that is connected to all things.

The definition of the mind is:

> *"the element of a person that enables them to be aware of the world and their experiences, to think, and to feel; the faculty of consciousness and thought"*

The mind has three main levels: The Conscious, the Preconscious (or Unconscious) and the Subconscious (or Super conscious) levels.

The **Conscious mind** involves all of the things that you are currently aware of and thinking about. The Conscious mind is the arena in which thoughts, feelings, moods and will power are most prominent. This is where your short-term memory is stored and it helps you to connect with your surroundings and environment.

The **Preconscious mind** includes things that we might not be currently aware of, but if we would like to access them, we can. The preconscious mind is said to be like the Subconscious mind. This part of the brain holds on to all of our experiences, and also the things that we have told ourselves, whether or not they are true. This part of the mind is connected to your emotions and can trigger memories that generate feelings. This part of your mind is also connected to your intuition or 6th sense.

The **Subconscious mind** is also the part of our mind that holds our deep-seated memories, drivers and patterns. Everything we've ever thought, felt, said and done is recorded here; this is the hard drive where all data resides. The memory of the subconscious is a cellar, which for the most part, is kept locked and is largely immersed in darkness. Traumatic experiences embed themselves in this part of our mind and through methods, such as hypnotherapy, we can uncover some of the trauma and implement new processes that are more supportive to the client.

The key to all success is to master and engage all of your minds. Hypnosis and Meditation, work by getting you to a state of relaxation, which alters the frequency wave pattern in your brain.

Everything is Energy and this includes your thoughts and intentions

Negative thoughts create a low vibration and more positive thoughts create a higher vibration. When you think a negative thought, you can usually feel your whole energy level shift or if someone is being negative around you, you can feel the same. But when you are happy you feel inspired and lifted and so your thoughts really do affect your reality.

Affirmations work on the Conscious mind and assist in helping you to introduce new ideas to your brain. Your mind will accept anything you tell it, and through practiced repetition, your affirmations will slip into the subconscious and become an automatic response. Affirmations are a great way to create positive changes in your life and get your mind on board. For example, repeating them daily for up to 21 days, can really help you to make some long lasting changes in your life.

Moreover, when you engage your emotions with the intentions of your affirmations and tune into the feeling that is created once you have attracted what you want, this then boosts the power and the energy 10 fold.

Our mind is so powerful that it can literally create anything, regardless of the intent. All you have to do is trust in what it is that you want, and match yourself with the vibration you desire, and stay focused and it will come.

The Power of Your Thought

"The first thought that comes to the thinking man after he realizes the truth that the Universe is a Mental Creation of the ALL, is that the Universe and all that it contains is a mere illusion; an unreality; against which idea his instincts revolt

The Three Initiates

Thought power - or the power generated by your thoughts - is the key to creating your reality. Everything you perceive in the physical world has its origin in the invisible, inner world of your thoughts and beliefs. To become the master of your destiny, you must learn to control the nature of your dominant, habitual thoughts. By doing so, you will be able to attract into your life the elements you intend to have and experience, through this, you will come to understand The Truth, that your thoughts create your reality.

Reality is a projection of your thoughts or the things you habitually think about.
~ Stephen Richards

The mind has 3 main frequency bands in which it operates

- 1. Beta (14-40Hz) — The waking consciousness

This is the frequency of the brain when it is in normal, conscious, waking state. Beta is important for our everyday functioning and awareness. It is also useful for reasoning, questioning, problem solving and rationalisation.

- 2. Alpha (7.5-14Hz) — The deep relaxation wave

This is the frequency level when we are in a space of deep relaxation. This is the stage before we go to sleep, our most relaxed mode. This is the gateway to your sub consciousness. This is the best time to program your mind for success, visualisation and learning.

- 3. Theta (4-7.5Hz) — Vibrational Field of Change

This is the most relaxed that your brain can become whilst still active. The theta state is the time when you are in deep relaxation and light sleep. Your minds most deep seated programs are embedded at this level and healing modalities such as Theta Healing and Hypnotherapy, are very useful at this level. This is the optimal rage for mind programming, and the clearing of deeply embed memories and traumas.

The construct of our collective reality is composed and created from the very constructs of the thoughts and affirmations of the mind, the individual mind and the collective mind.

The conditions and circumstances of your life are as a result of

your collective thoughts and beliefs.

James Allen

Everything in reality, that we experience outside of ourselves, is directly linked to what is taking place on the inside. Every aspect of our lives, from our finances, to the house we live in, the partner we choose and the job we have, are all down to our own negative or positive manifestations that take place within the mind, which is accurately manifesting and reflecting to us, our deepest thoughts and beliefs.

I, myself, have had to really work to master my Mind. At a time when I really questioned the source of the success that I was looking for in my life, I had to realise that everything manifested, or didn't manifest, based on what I was truly feeling and believing deep inside.

Librans are supposed to represent balance and harmony, have great diplomacy skills and the ability to see things from all sides. But what good is all that, if you are left unable to make any concrete decisions. Resultantly, you are left unable to see clearly and with crystal clear intention, what it is that you want to attract. You are also left without that deep 'knowing' or reassurance that, regardless of whether it happens today or in the future, what you wish will manifest.

It's funny because, I could manifest loads when I wasn't putting my mind to it, or when it was for someone else. But when it was something I felt that I wanted or even needed, I would notice that my ability to see and trust and know that I deserved what I was asking for, was lacking, to say the least. Instead of joy and conviction, my affirmations were full of fear, doubt and disappointment and I couldn't shake the negative vibrations, which in turn, manifested more of what I didn't want.

I decided that I had had enough of not being successful and asked myself what was the worst that could happen if I at least pretended that I knew what I wanted and that I would get it, and that I deserved it. (Eventually, I decided that I had had enough. At the least, If I pretended that I knew what I wanted, that I would get it and that I deserved it. What would be the worst that could happen?)

I took a moment to think back to a time when had asked Spirit for something and it manifested. For example, when I manifested my dream home, or manifested the funds to take my pilgrimage to Kemet (Egypt). I noticed, that when I was filled with joy and excitement, my intentions would manifest. I also noticed that the more joy I put into my intentions, the faster they manifested, and the more grateful I was for what I had received, the more I received!

This is the infectious nature of the Universe and how the law of attraction works. Everything in your reality will match the vibration of your intention. If your intention is of high vibration and the energy you put behind your intentions is equally so, you will start to see how the powerful combination of your intentions and visualisations can be positively empowered by you. Joy and emotions help to bring forth your deepest wishes and intentions with light speed.

Charles Haanel, author of The Master Key System says that "thought power is the vibratory force formed by converting static mind into dynamic mind". Your thoughts are alive. Each time you entertain a specific thought, you emit a very specific, corresponding frequency or energy vibration and attract back to you that which you put out".

In order to understand the universe, we must see it in terms of energy and frequency. Everything vibrates, shifts and alters in patterns.

Your life is the perfect mirror of your thoughts, beliefs and dominant mental attitude. Whether you realise it or not, you are already creating your own reality through your thought power.

Every effect you see in your outside world has its original cause within you - no exceptions. To gain access to the greatest creative power at your disposal, you must learn to control the nature of your habitual thoughts, and learn to align yourself with the One Source of All Power, of which you are a part. Your thoughts create your reality - know, internalize and apply this Truth and you will see your life transform in miraculous ways.

The Power of Emotions

As we have seen above, our thoughts play a critical role in our emotions. In fact, feelings are based on memories that are held in the mind, so this goes to show how much they are connected.

When you think of a certain thing, it could be the feeling of sand under your feet, or the joy of a lover's kiss, you instantly feel the image and feelings connected to that experience. You literally raise your vibration to match the energy and vibration of your thought.

Emotions are so powerful they can also cause harm within the body.

Negative emotions have a major impact on the immune system of the body and can literally cause the immune system to get low and attract illnesses such as flu and herpes. So when you are in bad mood you can literally draw illness to yourself as you match the vibration of ill health.

However, when you have positive emotions, they have a positive effect on your body. When you feel joy, happiness, excitement, hope or loved, your body responds by releasing endorphins and oxytocin, often called 'the cuddle hormone'. We feel good when we have these emotions, which lead us to want even more of the good, positive emotions, almost like a drug craving.

As a way to keep my emotions balanced inside and out, I use a mindfulness meditation called 'the Inner Smile', which is included in the 'Nurturing Seeds' section of this chapter.

'The Inner Smile' meditation encourages you to connect with each organ and connect with the vibration of happiness and joy from the inside, out. Joy and love are some of the highest vibrating emotions and energies.

Below is a list of the frequencies of our emotions, high and low.

Level	Emotion	Log
Enlightenment, various levels	Ineffable	700 – 1000
Peace	Bliss	600
Joy	Serenity	540
Love (unconditional)	Reverence	500
Reason	Understanding	400
Acceptance	Forgiveness	350
Willingness	Optimism	310
Neutrality	Trust	250
Courage	Affirmation	200
Pride	Scorn	175
Anger	Hate	150
Desire	Craving	125
Fear	Anxiety	100
Grief	Regret	75
Apathy	Despair	50
Guilt	Blame	30
Shame	Humiliation	20

In order to master your reality, you have to understand the power that lies within you and be conscious of how you use it. Word sound power is what created the universe and is the same thing that you can use to create your reality.

With such precious energy at our disposal, without the right level of conscious awareness and responsibility, we can maybe see why we live in a world where so much is imbalanced and so many people are unwell and holding onto so much pain. What reality are we co-creating together and most importantly, what reality are we creating with our emotions?

Your affirmations will not work for you, if you cannot match the vibration of what you want to achieve and if you do not believe. Without matching the vibration of what you want to achieve, and without the faith that you will achieve it, your affirmations will not work for you. You must engage your heart, soul and mind when setting your intention and then universe will have no choice but to deliver.

> "Words are singularly the most powerful force available to humanity. We can choose to use this force constructively with words of encouragement, or destructively using words of despair. Words have energy and power with the ability to help, to heal, to hinder, to hurt, to harm, to humiliate and to humble.

The Power of Your Words

In my opinion, words are indeed the most powerful force on this Earth. In the story of Genesis, 'God' spoke and the world was created into form. All by perfect design and how it ordered it to be, so it was.

Words have the ability to uplift and empower, and most importantly 'kill and destroy!'. The words that fall from the mouth so easily in one minute, can have long lasting effects, that could affect you for much longer after the word has been uttered.

We as humans really do take for granted the power of our words, the energy behind them and the damage that they can cause.

My own personal journey with words and understanding the power behind my words, has been a long and arduous lesson, of which I am still learning. As I child, I loved everything to do with words; I loved reading, I loved writing and I loved truth, I was interested in everything.

I would talk and sing all the time…and I mean all the time. I would sing about food or cleansing products, I would sing to tell my mum what I was feeling and I would sing to ask people questions. I would sing for everything and my joy was received by many.

However, when I was sexually abused at the age of 8, I went to tell my mother what had happened and she didn't accept my truth. In fact, she near enough begged me to take back my words and forget about it. I saw how the truth of my words affected her and so therefore I took them back and chose from that moment only to tell her things that would make her smile.

But as life continued to progress, I became more and more reclusive and unbalanced. In the presence of others, I would smile and be happy and helpful, but to myself I would speak on how horrible my life was and how much I didn't want to live anymore. I was telling myself all of these negative things, because I couldn't let it out. Before you knew it, I began suppressing everything and it felt as if my life was one big ball of misery.

On some rare occasions, I noticed that whenever I was not happy or felt attacked, I would use my words to fight back as physically, I didn't have the confidence to do so. I would speak about people and I would judge them in my mind and question why they had done the things that they had done and how I deserved more. As a result of my own hurt, I would moan and complain and wonder why more and more of the same continued to manifest in my life.

I realised that i was 'blocking' my own blessings with my negative thinking and words. I had to learn and understand that I could choose to perpetuate the hurt that I had encountered or that I could use my truth now, in my adult life, to bring some healing and transformation to my own life and relationships.

I realised that I didn't believe in myself and that I didn't trust that I deserved anything that I was asking spirit for. I felt unworthy and thought that if 'God' couldn't save me from the abuse, then how could I expect any better in my life.

I sat and I cried, feeling helpless and sorry for myself. I knew that I was manifesting all kinds of negative energy, from debt to fractured relationships, all because I no longer valued my word. The value that my mother placed on my truth, was the same value that I accepted and also expected to world to offer me.

Since then, I have had to make peace with my mind and the little girl that felt so hurt and unheard. I had to go into myself and reconnect with her and give her voice back, but also remind her to use it wisely.

I decided from then, that I was going to speak only positive things to myself for 10 minutes that day. Instantly I felt a shift in my energy, I felt light, I felt happy, I felt hopeful.

After a while I started my healing practice and started training as a Past Life Regression Therapist, with The Past Life Regression Academy.

One day whilst we were carrying out a practice session on each other, my teacher came and whispered in my ear, "You have a very healing and powerful voice. It can both soothe and command. Use it wisely and it will serve you well!"

I still wasn't able to take it all in at the time, but the more I saw my clients, the more they commented on how powerful and healing my voice was. When I spoke words of love, comfort and kindness, they felt nourished and secure. And when I spoke words of authority and power, they felt the energy and aligned themselves with it.

Since then, I now use the power of my voice to bless new life, to cleanse and heal sacred lands and water, to command and to nurture, to empower and inspire. Now, when I truly focus and engage my heart and my feelings, my thoughts and my mind positively and be mindful words, anything I need, manifests with ease and sometimes at warp speed too.

Don't get me wrong, I do occasionally fall back into my old ways, but in those moments, I am able to see the power of my negative thoughts and words materialise and I know to check myself before everything goes wrong instantly! I now know that it is my spirits way of reminding me to get back on the frequency of love and the highest vibration and speak from the Divine Space within me.

Our words and the energy behind them, can be a gift or a curse, but whatever your experience, know that all is preparing you to be a super Master Creator of your reality and reminding you of your connection to and effect, on all things. Your word, sound, power, is your key to creating whatever it is that you need. If you believe it, you can achieve it, all you have to do is focus and align yourself with love, clarity and truth.

Everything is Vibration and Frequency

Einstein states, that to understand the Universe and our power and our reality, we must understand Vibration and Frequency. Everything in the universe, and in all of creation has a sonic signature, a frequency or vibration. Nothing in the universe is stagnant, everything is vibrating, moving, expanding and contracting.

Our thoughts, our emotions, our physical body, our spiritual bodies, our intentions, our creations, our organs, everything, has a vibration and a frequency.

Each one of us has a signature sound, a tone that forms the very pinnacle of who we are and our sonic signature blueprint. Ancient civilisation, like the Dogons, understood this principal. One of their customs and rituals was to ensure, that for each soul that was born into the community, a rite of passage is performed for the coming spirit.

The Elders would hold sacred ceremonies before a child is born into the community. These ceremonies would help to establish the intentions and purpose of the incoming soul and how the community could support their purpose. In the days before the new soul arrives, the Female Elders would go out into the wilderness and wait. They would wait for a Sound, a Tone from the cosmos that would be the soul signature for the new life that was to be born. This tone formed the sonic signature for the incoming soul and was seen as something very sacred and precious.

When the child is born, the community would sing the tone or sound to ensure that the baby knew that it was coming amongst family and that it was safe and welcomed.

This tone would also be used throughout the child's life, at scared ceremonies, initiations or when they were in trouble and needed reprimanded. Likewise when the child is celebrated, the tone will also be expressed.

It was their understanding that this tone, was unique to each person and when sounded it reminded them of their Soul consciousness and connection to Source and all things.

This story is one example, of how the understanding of sounds, frequency and vibration is embedded in our collective reality.

Sound is the healer, Sound is the Creator and Sound will be the healer of the past, present and the future.

For every illness, there is a sound and frequency and for every cure there is one too. The Chakras are frequency, your bones are frequency and even sickness has a frequency and vibration. When you go to the hospital for an x-ray, they use frequency and vibration and light to help build up the picture of what is going on within the body.

I have been a Tuning fork therapist and Sound healer for over 7 years, and have witnessed, first hand, the powerful and transforming nature of vibration and Frequency. Each organ in the body has a frequency and tone and when the organ is imbalanced, it vibrates at a lower frequency rate than, usual and this can cause ill health.

Tuning fork therapy works based on harmonic resonance. Through resonance, we can be healed and have an effect on reality, each other and our world. We all have an effect on the Whole. Our negative thoughts and positive thoughts, also have an effect.

Each Tuning fork is tuned to an specific frequency, known to be beneficial to the body, auric field and organs, in order to produce a specified affect. For example, a set of chakra healing tuning forks will have 7 or 8 tuning forks, attuned to frequency of each chakra:

> Root Chakra - 'C' - 256 Hz
> Sacral Chakra -'D' - 288 Hz
> Solar Plexus - 'E'- 320 Hz
> Heart Chakra - 'F'- 341.3 Hz
> Throat Chakra - 'G'- 384 Hz
> 3rd Eye Chakra - 'A'- 426.7 Hz
> Crown Chakra - 'B'- 480 Hz
> Higher octave of Root C- 512 Hz

Each fork is tuned to the relevant frequency and when struck, creates a sonic vibration that can be felt by the body

We are Energy. We are Vibration. We are Frequency. This is the language of Creation and all within it. Our thoughts, our intentions, our body, our actions, our food, our emotions, all omit a frequency and vibration whether imbalanced in imbalanced.

The tuning forks are attuned to the vibration of health and optimal function. And when placed on the body or within the auric energy field, can cause positive affect and healing by shifting any energetic imbalance and emitting a vibration that raises the vibration of of your body or energy centres, to that of the frequency of the the tuning fork and intended vibration.

When you use the tuning forks for healing, the harmonic resonance of the fork, which is that of that chakra or body part.

Sound is the fabric of Creation, therefore, when we learn to understand the Universe as Sound Frequency and Vibration, we begin to understand the power within ourselves and our power to affect all of creation, both positively and negatively.

We are Sound and Energy beings.

Keep your thoughts positive because your thoughts become your words. Keep your words positive because your words become your behaviours. Keep your behaviours positive because they become your habits. Keep your habits positive because they become your values. Keep your values positive because they become your values. Keep your values positive because your values become your destiny

Gandhi

Confusion Illusion

I'm confused
I'm confused
About everything
I know I must turn my world around
But where do I begin

I feel trapped in old habits
Held back by old pain
Confused by old conversations
That replay in my brain

I feel like no one is listening
I feel like no one cares
I search deep in my own feelings
But it seems nothing is there

No reason behind, why I feel as I do
And no one can tell me these feelings are not true

You see the cause of a lot of our pain
Is down to the confusion that goes on in the brain
It creates a picture so dark and so bleak
Makes you feel at times that there is no joy in life to seek

But when you give it the right foods to eat
Right knowledge
The Right energy
Balanced thought it what you receive
Energy rich thoughts empower your intentions
Are imperative to conscious right living

Your mind is a powerful, well-oiled engine
Designed to serve you from the beginning to the ending
And there is one way to keep it intact
So mental confusion can never come back

The first is step is to be true to who you are
Suppression of yourself won't get you far
Know that your experiences
Have helped to shape the person you are
But don't let them determine whether or not you go far
They really are gifts to help you to see
How strong and powerful you really can be

Number 2 is to always stay true to you
Too much input from others and confusion will ensue
Now that doesn't mean, don't seek guidance from others
It just means don't give your power to another

Number 3 is to share your pain
Don't allow it to fester and rot in your brain
The very thing can drive you insane
So take a pen and paper and write it away

Allow each tear to flow through the pen
Dig deep and connected and let the expression begin
Take a moment and reflect on what has been written
Because I'm sure inside, you way out is hidden
You pain is telling you the things you need to change
And you'd better take heed or your will end up confused and deranged
In a repetitive cycle of confusion and pain
Especially if you don't do what you say

So number 4 addresses just this
Don't offer more that you are able to give

Your need to please your ego and others
Can definitely lead your mind into hot bother
As it twists and turns itself into a knot
Trying to make space for things it simply cannot
This is a sure way to mental confusion
So don't buy into the Ego's illusion

Number 5 is just take pride in your thoughts, actions and deed
One of the best ways to keep you mind in order
Is to act with integrity
Honour yourself enough
To hold yourself in high esteem
Keep your thoughts to the highest vibration
Be the best that you can be
Expecting nothing from others
As you give you receive
Accept life challenges
With confidence and ease
Take care of your, heart soul and mind
Give your mind healthy food
Bring focus and clarity
To everything you do
Clarity is your foundation
Optimism is key
Be open to the best in life
And that's what you will receive
Your mind is a powerful tool
One that's not to waste
So get rid of confusion
And put Divine order in its place
I promise you'll never regret it
You'll look back on this day and say
Never again will I let confusion
Rob me of my power

In any Way!

Freedom is a Frequency

Freedom is a Frequency

(Chant) AN…..KH FREEDOM IS A FREQUENCY

AN..KH FREEDOME IS A FREQUENCY

(RISE IN TONE) AN…KH FREEDOM IS A FREQUENCY

(BACK TO ORIGINAL TONE) AN…KH FREEDOM IS A FREQUENCY

REEDOM IS A FREQUENCY
THIS IS WHAT SPIRIT SAID TO ME
AS YOU RISE
SO SHALL IT BE
THINK IN VIBRATION
AND FREQUENCIES
THEN YOU WILL KNOW
THE MYSTERY KEYS
FREEDOM IS A FREQUENCY
A TRUTH FOR SOME
ILLUSION TO SO MANY
HELD IN MENTAL CAPTIVITY
LOVE VIBRATIONS
AND DENSITY
FREEDOM IS A FREQUENCY
A VIBRATION
LIKE YOU AND ME
VIBRATE HIGHER
COLLECTIVELY
COS FREEDOM IS A FREQUENCY
I RAISE YOU
YOU RAISE ME

TOGETHER WE LIVE IN HARMONY
IN ONENESS
UNION
AND PROPERTY
COS FREEDOM IS A FREQUENCY
HOW CAN YOU ASK ANOTHER
FOR YOU TO BE FREE
FREEDOM IS YOUR DIVINITY
THE MOST HIGHS BLESSINGS
YOUR DIVINE SOVEREIGNTY
VIBRATE HIGHER
AWAKEN AND CHOOSE TO SEE
THAT
FREEDOM IS A FREQUENCY

Freedom is a frequency
Just tune in and you will see
Just like analogue TV
Freedom is a frequency

Steeped in illusion, of bondage and delusion
You have come to the conclusion,
There's a fight to be had
Your spending all you waking hours
Giving others all your powers
Whilst fighting the same system
You fuel with your illusion

The frequency of fear, has helped to keep you there
Denying your true power, every second, every hour
Rejecting the inner truth, you've known since your youth
That you're a Divine Being
And there's nothing you can't do

So let me give you a key

To help you crack the matrix
To understand this world
You must understand vibration
You must know that you are fluid,
More than the flesh that you see
Learn to master your mind
Think and live in frequency

528htzs and above, is the vibration of love
When you tune in every hour, it increases your power
Anything lower, can affect your aura
This where you find fear, don't let it hold you there
Just raise your vibration, seek some elevation
A smile or a thought, a special moment you caught

The most important thing, is to master your mind
And mastery of emotions is close behind
Cos emotions bring thoughts into reality
So you really control what you choose to see

Release your mind, take off the locks
See the falsehood in the story you bought
Stop banging the doors down asking to be free
Know that freedom is a frequency
Deep within you is the strength and the power
To create what you want
Every minute, every hour
And when we all thing in harmony
There is no establishment that can say we are not free
The quickest way to destroy the indestructible
Is to make it THINK that it can be destroyed
But of one knows its power and potential
There is no affliction that can take hold
No freedom can be taken, unless you agree

Freedom is a vibration, freedom is a frequency

Freedom is a frequency
Tune in and reclaim your divinity
And enjoy the richness that life can bring
Remember your connected to everything

Freedom is a frequency
Freedom is a frequency
As you think it, so will it be
Freedom is a frequency
Part of your life's tapestry
All that you were made to be
Just practice mental alchemy
Know your power, just be Free

Joy

Joy is…
Jumping in puddles
And not feeling the rain
Running around the house naked
Watching children play
Listening to birds singing their melodic tune
Finding the last Ice Cream and paying Kiss chase at school
Playing with cousins and laughing together
Hearing Gran's stories, that go on forever
The moment you turn Your Own Key in Your door
And not having to share a room anymore
Nice sunny days
And cosy warm winters
Wrapped in comfy blankets, with veg soup for dinner
Warm cups of tea, and long friendly chats
Finding a friend to scratch that itch on your back
Dancing to music
Witnessing a birth
Going into nature and sitting with Mother Earth
Smelling new babies
Excitement of new life
Late night snuggles with your husband or wife
Joy can be found in the simplest of things
Creating magic and wonder, love is what it brings
Being grateful and joyful, makes life like a brand new toy
So go on
Why don't you tell me,
What brings you Joy?

Journal Page

Use this page to make any notes of your experience.

_____

_____

_____

_____

_____

_____

_____

_____

_____

_____

_____

_____

_____

_____

_____

_____

_____

Star Seed Journey

Soul Journey

Getting the Measure of your Fears

Our thoughts are truly powerful and have the ability to positively or negatively influence, our reality. During this next journey into the Halls of Amenti, you are going to examine your negative and transform them into empowering ones, so that they can empower your intentions, rather than destroy them.

Guided Meditation

- Find yourself a nice comfortable space where you will not be disturbed. Either lying down or sitting in a chair or on the floor

- As before, we will begin by taking a few deep cleansing breath and prepare to make our connection with the earth and the stars

- Make your intention to transform the energy of your fears.

- See a Green ball of light opening at your Heart Chakra and allow the light to carry you to the secret chamber within your heart. Notice Anubis looking on. in his hand he holds the sales with the heart and the feather.

- Through your heart, ask Anubis to show you the measure of the fears in your heart. Notice how the scales tips accordingly. Make a mental notes of the measure

   - Take a moment to think of something that you fear?

- What thoughts come to mind and how does it feel. Notice where you feel it in your body

- Ask you higher self to show you the root of this fear. When did it manifest and why? Are you ready to release this fear?

- Allow this image to fade from your heart and release the feeling of fear.

- Now take a moment to think of what it would be like to overcome that fear. Allow your higher self to show you what you would be like without the fear. How does it feel? What would you do?

Spend time building and embodying this vision. Become a part of in and walk into this empower reality of self.

- Notice how your feel. Make your intention to release all fears and transform them positive energy

- You may choose to bring forth another one of your fears and repeat the process again

- When you are finished, ask you higher self if there is any further guidance.

- Bring your attention to Anubis, who is standing on your right. Notice the scales in his hands once more

- Ask Anubis to show you the measure of you heart now. Make a note. You may need to complete this process a few times to gain the balance but use it as a tool for self-development and practice.

- Give thanks to All and then make your way back through the passage of light in your heart

- Take a deep breath and in slowly bring your consciousness back into the room

- Take a few moments to get centred within yourself and then make any notes that you can in your journal

Journal Page

Use this page to make any notes of your experience.

Seed 5

Make Peace With Your Past

"Those who do not remember and heal the past, are condemned to repeat it"
George Santayana

SEED 5 – MAKE PEACE WITH YOUR PAST, TO UNLOCK YOUR POWER'

Each one of us has a past, a beginning and foundation, on which to create the learning opportunities or experiences that either make us or break us. So many of us are walking around with unresolved past trauma and crafting our lives around the fractured memories and experiences of the past.

In life there are key stages of development that we go through that help to shape the fabric of personality and perception of reality. Each one offers a different level of experience and interaction, with varying degrees of will, growth and development.

If we experience any traumatic experiences in our formative years of development, then these may form the basis of any dysfunction or challenging behaviour in the future. This, in fact, is a part of the nature of life and each experience, we have chosen on some level to create.

You may be thinking, "Why would I choose to create trauma in my life?" or "Why would you choose to be abused, or killed or hurt?" Why?

Because your higher self knows that through the experience, pain, healing and then transformation of that experience you will gain mastery of a soul lesson which is of benefit to your soul development and highest good. However, I understand that knowing this doesn't make it any easier.

Childhood- The Foundation in Your Book of Life

Our childhood is so important in forming the foundation for the lessons that we will go on to learn in adult life. When put into context, we see that the seemingly short time that we spend in child hood years and the experiences within, help to form our future and the lessons we may eventually have to learn or unlearn from those experiences.

Whilst growing up, I didn't have anyone around me who could see my gifts or know how to even understand, let alone nurture.

People around me saw my eagerness to learn, show love and to serve as a mask for hidden agendas and mistrust and I would often feel ostracized from groups for always wanting to succeed and do my best. Which then made me regress into myself a lot and deepen my connection with spirit.

My childhood experiences, as for most of us, played a big role in my relationships and interactions in my adult life. And even until today, I'm still learning, growing and evolving. On reflection, I give thanks for the guidance of Spirit and My Higher Self, that allows me to always reflect on my learning and seek to make better choices as a result.

Most people, on the whole, will have a healthy experience during childhood, filed with good memories and practical support and love that will nurture 'good' seeds.

Childhood is also the time where we experience being our closest to source and the world of Spirit. Still connected to all the magic of the world and wonder of life, we are encouraged to take our time to grow and enjoy our childhood while we remember the happy moments and happy times.

In the Peter Pan story, it is the happy thoughts and memories from childhood that allowed Peter, Tinker Bell and the rest of the lost boys, the ability to fly. Another testimony to the power that this time and the memories we create in this time, can impact on our lives.

Some of the experiences we have are not so great, traumatic even, but the revealing and the healing of these traumas can bring breakthroughs for a whole linage and help bring an end to recurring lessons.

I went through many colours of life experiences that shaped the foundation for my adult life on this planet.

My father left when I was 4 years old and from my mother got married to her husband, I went through all forms of childhood abuse; physical, mental, emotional, spiritual, sexual, which all became the tapestry for my life.

And even my perception of that whole experience at the time was both etheric, conscious and very, very real. At the time, I was gifted with 'coping mechanisms' that allowed me to transcend above the experience at the time and not 'feel' a physical to the pain.

For instance, I would have out of body experiences, at the time where I was beaten severely and would see myself looking down on my physical body, disconnecting from the pain of the experience and observing the 'higher learning' and purpose.

But later in life through my own healing journey, I would have to reconnect and embody those traumatic experiences. Not from a spiritual perspective, but from a physical and conscious place.

The Healing Power of Forgiveness

"We may still be suffering terribly from the past while those who betrayed us are on vacation. It's painful to hate. Without Forgiveness we continue to perpetuate the illusion that hate can heal our pain and the pain of others. In forgiveness we let go and find relief in our heart"

Jack Kornfield

Forgiveness is one of the most powerful forces in the universe and is the unifying principal of all things. It is love that connects us all and sustains us. Forgiveness, is an act of Love, that gifts us with the opportunity to bring peace, wisdom, resolution, healing and ultimately redemption for all involved and bring healing and resolution to any situation.

Many wars have been fought, and families destroyed because of the absence of forgiveness in the hearts of so many.

If only we could see how much pain and hurt we cause each other by holding on to old out dated energy and holding onto old memories.

Forgiveness is never about 'giving in to make another feel good' or absolve them of their cause. Forgiveness is to free everyone involved and bring them harmoniously to the vibration of love.

When we understand the true nature of reality and know that everything that is happening to us, is happening as part of a grand design to help assist us to learn our soul lessons and elevate in our level of consciousness and experience, we begin to see that everything is energy and energy informs and transforms. That nothing is happening to us but is instead happening because of us and for us.

Forgiveness offers us the opportunity to be healed and to heal, to understand and to be understood and to ultimately free ourselves. To stop us from allowing our love and bitterness hold us hostage in the victim victimiser blame game.

Forgiveness is one of the fastest ways to bring a turnaround in your life and breath new energy into your relationships. Forgiveness is your super power, and is one of the greatest tools in the world right now, for it keeps our heart clean and clear and keeps us in harmonic resonance with the world around us, which we are connected to and is, us.

In life we learnt our lesson through our relationships and interactions with others. This is the basis of experience and learning.
But also through this journey our actions and choices may offend others and even hurt our self.

It is in this time that forgiveness can seem the hardest thing as our ego blames and projects whatever learning onto others or even uses it to damage and put down the self. Creating programming which can affect you from moving on and more importantly learning the gift within the experience.
Forgiveness comes from an over-standing, which is wisdom gained through experience, that all is always in alignment with truth.
Forgiveness releases judgment and balances ego. Forgiveness allows us to see ourselves, to heal ourselves and free ourselves from the guilt and

shame that holds us locked in our past experience.

When we have done wrong to others or they to us, years can go by where we never really address the situation and can spend years stuck with a perception that doesn't serve you or the other.

This will ultimately be your journey and learning as you either hold on to things and let them purify your being or allow yourself to always be in a space of self-reflection and learning and unconditional love for self and reflection.
Forgiveness should be as breathing! And when it becomes as such your heart will truly know unconditional love. To forgive shows grace and unconditional love. To be forgiven, allows for peace and growth.

We are all reflections of each other, good and bad and we are ultimately here to help bring healing to all aspect of ourselves, so that we can become master of our reality. We learn from each other and understand our relationship to all creation through our interactions.

I give thanks for the gift of forgiveness and the gift of being Forgiven so that my heart can be free to experience, explore and love and remain free!

Who do you need to forgive and do you need to forgive yourself?

Maybe you need to forgive yourself?

Yes, it's true that, sometimes in life it is You that requires your forgiveness!

Many of us hold shame guilt and other lower vibrational frequencies in relation to our life experiences, trauma and choices. Maybe you were abused and thought that it was your fault, or you have made bad money choices in the past, or any of the many things that we humans blame ourselves for.

But when you understand that **your true purpose is to experience yourself;** your choices and free will, you understand that there is no need to feel guilt or shame and on to these feelings. And that you should, instead, use them as a reference point to show you where you may have fallen out of alignment in the past and where you now need to improve and make changes.

When we hold ourselves hostages with feelings of guilt and shame, we can create immense pressure and tension on the heart and our body. We can manifest physical illness within the body, from the repression and containment of such toxic emotions.

We must **learn to embrace our experiences** and see them as opportunities for learning and growth and love ourselves enough to learn from the mistakes of the past and release any guilt or shame.

How can you truly forgive others if you cannot forgive yourself? If you hold yourself contempt in the court of your own experience, then what hope do you leave for resolution, learning and success?

Do not allow your experiences to trap you in a cycle of negative learning and growth. Of self-pity, anger, guilt or shame.
Embody and embrace all and let your forgiveness be like breathing.

Many times in this experience of life I was forgiven and forgiven some who for so long I had loved and also felt hurt from. In the Divine act of truth, with love and forgiveness, we were able to see ourselves in each other and that the love we had for each other drove home the lesson we had chosen on a soul level to teach each other. Through sharing our truths, we saw ourselves in each other and remembered who we are to each other.

Without forgiveness, we still blame each other and without sharing in truth, we wouldn't have realised how damaging holding onto pain and untruths had been for us both.

To move into the 5th you must have a restored heart, which implies that it must first be broken. In the unfolding of life, you find the keys of creation and rebuild and restore your heart through conscious reconstruction, through the understanding gained from the experience. All comes back to

Love and the knowing of your connection all things. As I heal, you heal. As we heal, all is healed!

> **I share because this is my journey.**
> **I share because this is my Truth**
> **I share because this is The truth**

The keys are there for all to see when you step into the heart and master your reality.

On a higher level of consciousness, I knew somewhere that I had 'chosen' it all. Not from a place of taking on the blame of another actions – I didn't think that I was consciously responsible for the abuse I experienced, but I knew on a higher level in my soul, that it wasn't coming from a place of negativity or destruction that it had to be for a purpose and a higher learning.

I didn't feel any hate towards the people who had abused me, how could I, I knew their soul and I knew that all came from Love, however later on in life, I would still have to embody these experiences from a 'normal' or human level of consciousness, so that I could uncover the nuggets and soul lessons within the experiences I had chosen.

Many may argue, that this may not be a healthy perspective to come from, when dealing with trauma and abuse. However, my understanding was ultimately that there is no judgment, hell or eternal damnation, and that our soul is eternal. And that through the experience of life, we co-create, on a soul level, our lessons and experiences of our incoming life, that will allow us to achieve our highest learning and good, on a soul level.

We have this life on Earth, which is the realm of experience, consequence, cause and effect etc. And it is here, that we manifest the lives we planned behind the veil. Through free will, spiritual amnesia and then awakening, we experience what is needed for the soul's highest development and the intention.

There is extensive research by the Spiritual Regression Academy and testimonies of people who through hypnosis, were able to access soul memories from not only past lives but also the time space in the time between one life and the next- the planning stage.

Through Life-between Life Regression Therapy, you can access the knowledge of your pre-incarnation intention and access any information you may have forgotten, which may help to assist you in your current purpose and mission.

There is extensive accounts available online and in books and I would recommend the book "How I died and what I did after" by Peter Watson Jenkins as a book of interest. In this book Peter and Therapist Toni interview a number of people, via regresdion therapy, who are able to access memories of their past lives and what the soul remembers next. It's a very interesting and insightful book.

Through my own metamorphosis in later life, via healing, and bringing enlightenment and understanding to all that was buried within, I began to weave the beautiful colours of magic, life, vibrancy and purpose, into the once, dull and painful fabric of my life.

I knew that I had chosen each and every thread, each and every knot, each and every kink!

My Higher self knew exactly what I needed to experience down here, to turn my Lead into Gold, my Pain into my Purpose and my Passion into my Power.... True Alchemy in Action; and the true purpose for our existence on this realm.

Buddha once said that, "Suffering is the road to enlightenment" yet although it may be necessary, and teaches us blessed gifts such as humility, grace and love; it is not something that we should see as a destination in our life, but rather, a welcomed and valued part of the puzzle towards uncovering your true divine purpose and supporting our learning as a being, of this Earth.

The tragic moments or feelings, that colour our life's tapestry, form the masterpiece that will shine its light into the world and be a beacon for others.

Once inner-stood, my experience of this life shifted from one of confusion, sacrifice and delusion to one of magic, purpose, creation and intent!

Suffering through enlightenment is a thought-form or 'reality' of the age that we are now coming out of, the age of Pieces.

This is depicted in the story of Jesus and his suffering on the cross for all of our sins. It afforded expression such as 'turning the other cheek, wearing masks and hiding our feelings to not show our pain. It perpetuates a thought form that 'we are sinners' and that our life was saved by his death.

These collective 'thought forms' are embedded in the collective conscious and human story and affect us continuously and create a level of disempowerment and cause us to seek wisdom and acceptance outside of ourselves.

It speaks of life as 'things happening to us' and puts up in space of victimhood and disempowerment.

The thought-form or theme of the Aquarian age, is that "You are the Master of your Reality'. Everything for a reason and with purposeful intent. That you are a powerful being of light and power; a spark of the Creative Source. Your emotions and feelings are also energy and help you to understand how you are connected to and affected by everything, because you are everything.

They empower us to be self-reflective and conscious of our life choices and experience and empowers you to ask, "Why did I choose this?" and "What is my spirit teaching/telling me?"

This process of conscious living, of 'I and 'self 'reflective learning, is becoming more influential in our daily lives as more of the Aquarian energy flows into our collective consciousness.

As we are part of everything, and everything is evolving. We are also in the midst of a shift of energy and expansion above these 'thought- forms', but we have to consciously to the work to 'remove' theses thought forms from our collective experience

Therefore, each one of use, must do to work necessary, to view our life and our experiences consciously, in this more self-empowered or spiritually empowered way, by healing, reflecting and transforming our pain and finding our purpose and power within.

This is how we turn our pain into our purpose and power!

If we had not known suffering would we know how to love? If we had not known to be without, would we value having as much?

The illusion of separation and suffering, has been the mode of experience and self-discovery up until now, but we are moving away from that as our collective truth and understanding our power and ability to manifest experiences of Love, Joy and laughter, to experience enlightenment, instead of through suffering.

But you may ask then, why do we need to tune into the vibration of suffering, why do we need to reflect on our pain?

My answer to this is that in the principal of Sankofa, that what has gone before, us can powerfully inform our present and out future so that do not make the same choices or mistakes again.

And through your self-transformation, you can support others through their own healing and live an empowered life, therefore helping us all evolving to beyond the need for suffering at all.

> ***To know thyself is the greatest achievement!***

Your journey and enlightenment will make someone feel beautiful when they felt invisible, help someone to seek life, rather than death, and to empower someone with Love and Light, when they felt they had none.

We owe it to humanity, and our past, to uncover the jewels within our pain, our story, so our light, out Krystal Light can shine from within and light up our world!

The next poem that follows next is a testimony to that fact. A raw and healing story that I know many of us can relate to.

Through our life experiences, and as part of the human story, we inherit many things, some we can control and some we can't control.

But what we can do, is seek to do the healing within our own selves, turning what we have in gold and ensuring that the legacy that we leave behind, is that will empower and inspire the next generation in their human story.

I trust you will connect and enjoy.

Key to our Legacy

Deep within my centre there's a yearning,
A deep feeling, that's something is stirring
Urging me
To break free
From a tainted legacy

Left behind by insanity
Robbing me of my divinity
What is this feeling, what could it be?
Show me ancestors, what you wish me to see

I am willing and open,
with a heart strong and true
Open the doors and I will walk through
I wish to know, feel and break free
To release the hurt,
From the deepest parts of me

A voice bellowed out, "come and you'll see"
You have chosen this moment, because you are the key
We will open your centre
To help you to see
What needs to be healed, released and made free

WOW!!!!......
So I take a deep breath in…………..
And then the journey begins
On my body, below my naval
I see my energy vortex spin

As I hold my sacred centre
I feel the pain of my ancestors

Raped, Abused, Mutilated
All for another's pleasure
Screaming, resisting, helplessly failing
To protect their sacred centres
From becoming tainted
As I travel into this scared space of purity
I feel the hurt and trauma of thousand
Which never should have come to be
The freedom of life's joys and pleasures
Tainted with the darkness of lust filled endeavours
Inside this sacred space
Love no longer flows
And the river runs red with the moans and the woes

A message came from deep within me
You have the power to set them all free
You have the eyes, so you will see
Open to your power and turn the key

Unlocking all the deep suppression
The hurt
The pain/trauma
The great depression
But from this sacred space of expression
To go deeper and deeper is my Divine Mission

So I dig down, deep, deep inside of me
And faces in the mist before me, I see
A familiar face
Someone I know
A feeling in my heart
That is starting to grow
My mother, Her Mother and great gran so and so
Bringing forth a truth, that only they know

In their hearts, a sad song I hear
A distance, confusion, fear and despair
A longing to understand how they came to be there
Screams covered and muffled so no one could hear
So I look deeper, and deeper
And behind them I see
My father, Stepfather, his father and me
I'm taken to a place only I can see (a familiar place I've been)
Mother and father arguing
Now let's set the scene

Father feels frustrated,
Mother feels it too
Mother wants to help, but doesn't know what to do
Both inexperienced
In matters of the heart
Both needs to be healed
No one knowing where to start
He knows not how to communicate
His struggles and inner pain
Frustrated at not being good enough

Or able to provide and maintain
The image imposed by his father
Of how a man should be
And the internalized pain of his mother
How he wished he could be free

Free from this frustration and the restrictions that he sees
Mothers Love
Fathers trust
Are all things he still needs
But now he must grow up they say

And raise his family
Oh how he yearns for guidance love and support
And someone to help him see
Blessed with many children
Sons and daughters equally
He tries to do his best to hide
The hurt he feels so deeply
In his daughter he sees innocence
And a vision of purity

But through the tainted eyes of his suppression
he says
"I need some of that for me"

His vision becomes cloudy
As he sees what she can become
A woman
A lover
A friend
A comfort to someone

Mother watches on silently
Knowing where this will lead
Her father loved her like this once
Back then when she was free
She sees how his love changes

As he gazes at her lovingly
Oh how he wishes she could be her
And be loved so tenderly
A father's love is nurturing
A love that keeps you safe and sound
Someone to hold you and protect you
When others let you down

But in her heart, a memory
That cuts deep like a knife
Her father loved her that way too
Brought much pain to her life
He beat her
He cursed her
He hugged her tight
He told her everything would be alright
He knew deep down
He had committed a sin
And that now her tainted journey would begin
Giving in to lucid feelings of negativity
Disguised as love and protection
He stroked her tenderly
Not knowing how this would affect her
And their ancestral legacy
He opened up her sacral
And filled it with his chi

Within her, confusion is stirring
This is not how it's meant to be
How can someone cause me such pain?
Someone who's supposed to love me
Is this really how love is meant to be?
Maybe this is true
This is my father showing me love
So I must love him too
The conflict and confusion
That began to bubble and brew
Runs through all dimensions of space and time
And taints everything that you do

In this moment she lost her power

In this moment she lost her trust
In this moment whatever happened to her
trickled down to us

Her father feeling helpless
And drowning in misguided lust
Must now make sense of this mess he caused
But instead hides his head in the dust
In this moment he feels shame
In this moment he feels disgust
But crippled by fear he turns to her and says
"Let's just keep this between us"
Affecting all her energy centres,
Every cell in her body remembers
What had taken place that day
And how she was gifted with this legacy

Root Unstable,
No Longer able
To feel safe and secure

Sacral Corrupted
Feeling disrupted
Not sure who I am Anymore

Solar Plexus
In a mess, just
Wanting to break free
Screaming silently to myself
He can't do this to me

Can he????

Heart shattered into a million pieces

Where hope was, now is misery
Is this the measure of the love of another?
Now unbalanced and restricted in me

Throat chakra- ceased up
As no one heard my cries
Can't breathe, Words stuck
They'll say it's a pack of lies

Third eye closing
No longer showing
The truth there to be seen

Crown shattered
Feeling damaged
I no longer feel like a Queen

Left in this space, which stunted my growth
True love was something, I yearned for the most
I tried so hard to understand
How, this act, could have come from the man
Whom I called father or uncle or friend
But this broken legacy I had to mend

I chose to forgive him,
For what he did to me
And I chose to forgive my mother
For not choosing to see
I forgive my family for the lies and deceit
But this tainted legacy I will not keep

I choose to go into my sacred space
And all the trauma, I will replace
With love, abundance, and purity

Healing, and blessings and positive chi

I'll dance with my beauty
And delight in the stars
Ill embrace every curve
Wrap myself in my arms
I'll love me and them and all will be healed
No room for sadness
It's pure love I now feel

In my sacred space I used to see
Hurt, pain and trauma
This outdated legacy
But the story has been re written
And now we are free
To love and express, to create and to be
To enjoy our own magic
Bask in our sexuality
To love deep and freely, with every part of me
To make love to my husband
Create a loving family
I Love my mother
I love my father
I love them abundantly
I love my brother
I love my sisters
And now we can all free

Our ancestors rejoiced
As the healing was in me
And by healing and freeing myself
I became the Key

To unlocking the secrets

Shining light on the unseen
To bring forth change
And restore a broken legacy

Deep within my centre,
Lies a yearning within me
To share with you my story
So you too can see

The journey begins with a single step
And desire to be free
Just dig deep
Past all the pain
Cos deep in you
Lies…

The Key

Nurturing the Seeds

Seed 5- Make Peace with Your Past

The true nature of Alchemy is to be able to transform lower energies into those of a higher vibration. That which can enlighten and inspire. Sometimes it can be daunting to look back into our past and wade through painful experiences. But that is the very same journey that we must take, because within the pain of the past lie the keys to transform your future and empower others in the process

Time to Do the Work

Air – Clear Your Mind

In this chapter we looked at how the past has an important part to play in our present and our future, and can provide the foundation for a lot of our learning as we grow through life

Take a moment now to review your thoughts on your past.

- ❖ What are the first 3 words that come to mind when you think about your childhood experiences?
- ❖ Write down one of your most challenging childhood moments. What are your current thoughts about the situation? What has changed?

Earth – Know your Body

Earth element is connected to our foundation and our connection to the material. Our early childhood experiences also have a direct to our Root Chakra which is concerned with our ability meet our own needs and feel safe and secure

- ❖ What was your childhood experience of Money, Security and stability?
- ❖ Were your needs met, or did you feel as though you didn't have enough? Do you have a prosperity consciousness or a poverty consciousness?
- ❖ How has this affected you as an adult? Looking back what can you learn or have you learned about your connection to the material.

Water – Know your Emotions

Past memories and experiences can bring up painful feelings and emotions that can have long lasting effects on our future relationships and also our ability to love ourselves.

- ❖ What experiences of the past do you still hold dear to your heart or have an emotional connection to? Who has caused you pain or hurt your feelings deeply in the past?
- ❖ What happened and why? What do you think was the learning from that experience?
- ❖ Are you ready to release this hurt so that you can heal?

Fire – Know your Passion

Fire energy is great to bring for the drive and push needed to make positive changes in your life. As well as negative memories from the past, we all definitely have experienced a positive emotions and feeling as well and you can use this to transform the old and push you forward into new experiences and success.

- ❖ Take a moment now to think of a positive and uplifting memory from the past? A time where you achieved something of benefit to you?

- *What did you do to make it happen? How did it feel?*
- *Generate the energy to drive and excitement about what it felt like to achieve your goals and be successful.*
- *Use this energy to remind you of how great you can be when you put your mind to it*

Spirit – Know Your Spirit

Everything that we have experienced has been chosen by out highest self and hides within it a valuable lesson for our soul's growth and development. Your Higher Self is the part of you that is connected to all things and remembers things that you may have forgotten.

- *Take a moment during your time of meditation to connect with your Higher Self and as it to reveal to you any wisdom that it can; to support you in gaining further understanding and clarity, about anything from your past which needs healing or revealing?*
- *What do you need to understand to assist you on your healing path?*
- *Make a note in your journal*

Love – The Spirit of Love

Love is the source of all things and the true healer and balancer. When we can have love even where there is no understanding, we allow for the gift of healing to manifest for all within their highest good and open ourselves up the healing light of wisdom and compassion

- *What is your past needs your love? Who is your past need your understanding?*
- *Can you in this present moment, send Love to all of your past situations? To all those who have hurt you?*
- *Can you forgive as you would like to be forgiven?*

- *Allow the light of Love to Shine forth into your heart and fill it with the Love of the Universe, The Love of the Most-High Source!*
- *And allow this love to cascade into the past, the present and the future.*
- *All is healed and all is Love...Ashe*

Golden Seeds of Wisdom

The Pain of the Past is the Source of your true Power. If you can be brave enough, to go back into your past with love, you will uncover the Golden Nuggets of Wisdom, Love and Healing and experience the Virtues of Humility and Grace.

Journal Page

Use this page to make any notes of your experience.

Seed 6
Embrace Your Shadow

" A Thing of Beauty is Never Perfect "

Kemetic Proverb

SEED 6 – EMBRACE YOUR SHADOW

To confront a person with his shadow is to show him his own light. Once one has experienced a few times what it is like to stand judgingly between the opposites, one begins to understand what is meant by the self. Anyone who perceives his shadow and his light simultaneously sees himself from two sides and thus gets in the middle.

"Good and Evil in Analytical Psychology" (1959). In CW 10. Civilization in Transition. P.872 Carl Jung

Embracing Your Shadow

One of the fundamental aspects of our journey through life in this realm and in the lesson of duality is about the shadow the ego the hidden Darkness.

The part of us that hurt pain and rejection. The part of us that is always seeking to serve itself, itself and protect itself from all of the lessons and challenging experiences that we create and our life. Carl Jung called these hidden parts of our nature the shadow.

Our shadows are those parts of the selves that make us feel that we're not good enough that were unwanted are that wear a failure and that we will never be happy.

It's the space in which all of your dark memories are stored and seeks to always game power shaken in challenging experiences.

A main function of the shadow is the ego.

To the Ancient Egyptians, the shadow (or shade, as it was also know) was a form of the "self" often represented by a darkened painting of the individual.

Apparently it was imperative to protect the shadow from any harm, although it itself was considered a form of defence for that individual.

Going into the Shadow realms, went to venture into the aspects of the hidden self, the lower aspects of ourselves, which give refuge to our fears and insecurities.

Our journey in this time to go into our shadow and bring forth the consciousness of light and divinity which in hidden within each aspect. When we face our demons, and bring our ego and self into harmonious alignment, we access the full source of our power and become the self-realised master of our own reality.

Balancing the Ego

Ego is the individualized self-Express aspect of our self. Ego is the part of the mind that meditates between conscious and unconscious and it's responsible for reality testing and personal identity.

The ego concerned with the individual identity and is built up from all of the different skills attributes thoughts feelings and experiences that define you. The ego is self-serving and constantly demands to be satisfied and sustained and always Compares itself to. It is responsible for many negative human traits and behaviours including but not limited to:

- *judgment of others*
- *inflexibility*
- *manipulative behaviour*
- *superior attitudes*
- *feelings of arrogance anxiety fear hopelessness*
- *mood swings addictions*
- the need for praise and from an approval from others.
- It always seeks to reassure itself of its importance and false power.

- ❖ It seeks to dominate and control and keep you from learning your soul's lessons. It has no understanding of its relation to everything outside of itself was always seeking to serve itself.
- ❖ The ego constantly wants to be right about everything always wants to be superior to others and always seeking self-importance and power.

Projection- our external mirrors

Projection is the mechanism through which experience these traits and underlying issues is the way that the eagle and about itself by projecting itself onto another. We project both the positive and negative aspects of ourselves into the world.

The ego is not something that can be destroyed, fact the eagle is a vital aspect of our being one without which we would not be able to exist at all.

However, the lesson in this life hence the ego so that it can positively enhance.

Tempering the Ego

The ego when positively reinforced can be of great benefit to you. The Ego is also responsible for the drive that we have and that we can activate in order to achieve our goals. It gives us the confidence and the boost to make us know we can achieve anything and drives our desire to be self-serving, to get up every day, to eat, clothe and care for ourselves.

The lesson of the ego is to learn to see itself as a perfect and valuable part of the whole and connected to all things.

Until this is done peace happiness cannot be achieved or attained.

In order to transcend the negative influences of the ego it is necessary two fully recognise can exert in our life and over the lives of Others.

As we know the ego is not a part of us that we can destroy for neutralizing all of those negative aspects of the ego that hold us back is part of our physical life and spiritual growth and development.

Racing your shadow facing your fears and darkness I'm making peace with the experiences that have caused you pain is the very first thing that we need to do in order to be able to fully live a life of true happiness self-mastery and oneness.

Record negative experiences in Our Lives can affect aspects of our personality and walked feelings such as jealousy guilt and anger can putrefy us and create distortions and imbalances in our nature and how we think.

We may develop negative and disagreeable tendencies the others because they hurt us or find coping strategies that shield us from the we feel inside.

The our early, formative years, we begin to understand or experience the duality of our nature and emotions.

We know what makes us happy and how we respond to that and we also know what makes us unhappy and create protect ourselves.

When the ego feels challenged sponge or retaliate in a way that will allow it to feel empowered once more but this reaction will continue to help keep you in a space of isolation and separation the key is to learn trigger's you get to the source of why it hurts I seek to resolve and heal it within yourself so that you can experience harmonious and balanced relationships with others.

The Shadow Space is also the realm of our deepest held memories, experiences and thoughts of sadness and fears. These affect the way that we see ourselves and others and affect our ability to truly be happy in our lives and in our relationship with other traumas held from childhood or beyond left unresolved insert themselves into our psyche and distort our way of thinking.

When we are faced with challenging situations the Ego in its need to preserve and protect can shut down rather than consider the whole story or the learning involved and take responsibility for its actions.

The Ego then creates coping mechanisms to keep safe and protected, usually either by violent outbursts or retreat.

Shadow healing work

Our attachment to the energy and emotions of certain experiences can affect the way that we see ourselves and others and so therefore if we really want to make the journey towards living our true divine self we have to do some work to explore understand and Heal Our Shadow.

Shadow work or shadow healing can be one of the most hardest, parts of our growth and development. To take full responsibility of your actions, hidden truths and painful traumas and consciously confront and rebalance it's a lot of courage discipline self-love.

Holding on to the painful memories and experience of long held and repressed situations can suck out of the life of your current moments and Rob you from any future and you deny yourself the opportunity to gain the wisdom and healing available from journeying into your shadow realm transforming your darkness into light.

To face our fears and to make peace with our past, in itself, is empowering and healing and but in t doing so, we can learn tools and wisdom, that will assist us in becoming whole again and seeing the beauty and value in even some of the most contrasting experiences.

Forgiveness is the most powerful tool when dealing with your shadow of love. We all seek to be forgiven of something you have the power to forgive. Forgiveness is a true act of love and service not only for the other person but also for yourself. You forgive yourself for your actions it doesn't mean that you dismiss it what you allow yourself to be removed from the Guilt or negative attachment to the situation and offer yourself an opportunity to receive any healing and truth with ease. If you can be open and truly forgive yourself and others for whatever you have experienced, you will free yourself from the egos delusion of Separation and judgement.

Our ability to forgive others is also a direct reflection of our ability to forgive ourselves when we understand the true Nature of life we understand that every experience that we have is informing us and helping us to decide who we are in relation to the all.

Our judgements and projections towards each other, only perpetuates the illusion of separation even further.

So forgiveness can be the first step to in another I can see themselves in you. This is the bridge that will create understanding and allow you to now shadow heal you and reveal to you to true love that's within and without.

When you forgive you free yourself from the mental prison and the emotional pain that keeps you bound to the experience and robs you of the gift of the lesson you are about to learn.

For me shadow work has been very important to my growth and development and it is still something that I continue to do.

The Shadow and Ego create opportunities for you to see the balance and dualistic nature in yourself and all things as well. Light and Dark, good and bad all experiences of the one source. Although they may seem different in vibration and experience each aspect still exists as part of the whole.

I always wanted to be 'good' and for a long time I didn't want to believe or accept that I had a shadow side or a dark side or that I was disagreeable in anyway.

I didn't like the feelings of negative emotions within my body and always wanted to get back to love and hated any form of confrontation.

I would avoid arguments and when others impose their will on me I would avoid any kind of interaction in which I could create any negative feelings for myself.

I learnt to suppress my feelings and to my egos need to find gratification and empowerment from outside of myself.

Although naturally I love to support people to see people happy and to be of service, of my negative experiences a child always wanted to protect myself from hurt and pain.

I allowed people to disrespect my time my gifts and my energy I would smile and share it abundantly because my ego was satisfied with the illusion of service to others. I would smile and help others under the guise of oneness but underlying there were feelings of the contrary beneath.

Within me and I could feel a part of me start to go cold. Help and serve others but feel scorned underneath and would repeating myself how unappreciated until I continue to feel even more so.

I was feeding my Ego by helping others feeding myself and my Ego would also attack me thoughts of not being good enough not protecting myself which would encourage more self-sabotaging behaviour.

There came a point where I could no longer keep my feelings in. I could no longer pretend that there was nothing wrong even if I tried and even behind my biggest smile.

Others could see no longer happy and they could also feel that whatever I was doing was not coming from the right place however I still acted like I was ok.

I didn't feel like I was allowed to be upset or even feel resentful so I also piled shame and guilt onto my own suppressed feelings.

However much I tried to put others first and not focus on my unhappiness, the more it became apparent to myself and others how deeply unhappy I was. I became distant from others and felt as though I couldn't trust them with my pain and also that I had no right to expect them to think of me.

I realised at that time when I could no longer shift the feelings of Separation resentment and hurt that it was my responsibility to confront my Shadows and the root of my pain.

As I Began my journey my past insecurities from childhood has come up to haunt me because as much as I tried to be nice to people they didn't trust it and that was a direct reflection of how I received others as well. When others showed me true love and affection I also couldn't trust it I was truly worth of such love and support. I had told myself somewhere along the line that that if even my own mother it's me I did not love me enough to do so than anybody else. I then tried to be for others what it was that I needed for myself and became the Wounded healer.

I still tried to keep on the masks that I had created to hide my pain but my ego now wouldn't allow that. I would be asked to do something and say yes feeling and the energy of resentment out would feel it instantly.

My moods also changed I would be happy one minute and then depressed the next, calm and collective and then irrational aggressive.

I always felt like I needed to protect myself I always felt separated from everyone else and I always felt undervalued. This is what I had taught myself learning I've had gained from my early childhood experiences. My ego was trying to show me that this untruth was hidden within me and creating imbalances within my perception of self and relation to others.

How could I truly know and be love, and see the value in myself if I felt others did not see the value in me. The painful experiences of the past were now running on auto pilot and coming up now for healing but I could only gain the wisdom by going to the root.

I had to go into my pain I had to go into the illusion that I had created and find the truth all I had chosen to experience was essentially to empower me to see everything that I am order for me to understand and know true love and oneness I in our human connection I had to experience the illusion of separation. To know the love of the Creator had to feel unloved. I had to lose my mind in order to come to my senses.

Embracing My shadow

It took a lot for me to realise that I had a shadow and that my shadow was both my passion and my love corrupted unprotected and unbalanced only to demonstrate to me the true power of love and oneness.

After years of avoiding getting to the root of my pain by serving and taking over the lives of Others it was time for me to go into my own Shadow and connect with those deep and hidden parts of myself that were now putrefying in me. I had to now choose to go into my shadow and turn my darkness into light restoring balance peace and harmony within.

I went back to my child self I allowed others to take advantage it told me I wasn't able to protect myself from abuse as a child am I being nice to others was so that others would not get upset with me or hurt me or choose to overpower me.

I then realised that I was choosing relationships with people that needed healing and nurturing because that's what I needed for myself and had to give to myself.

One night after another day of me losing my temper and getting off balance, I was guided to go into the Halls of Amenti for meditation.

As I did the meditation and went into my heart space long corridor with black and white tiles on the floor and rows of doors along each side of the corridor.

I set my intention at that time to receive whatever healing and guidance that was with my highest good and would support my growth and development at this time with regards to my Ego and loving myself.

I noticed that one of the doors to my right had lit up and so I walked over to it

I open the door and walked into this dark room. Door slammed shut behind me and I was standing in silence in this huge eerie and darkened room

I could feel the beat of my heart pounding in my chest and took a deep calming breath.

As the Beating of my heart subsided I became aware of the feeling of events energy in the corner of the room behind me. It felt heavy dense and very sad.

I could feel it's presents taking over the whole room. Although the room was dark I could get a sense of this energy in the corner of the room behind me closed my eyes and intuitively connected with it and asked it who it was.

The response that I received was that this was my Ego. Instantly I felt comforted as I knew that there must be a great lesson to be learnt.

So I asked it why it had kept sabotaging all my plans and why it did not work for me and give me the passion and conviction to get the things that I needed to do for myself done. I asked why it would make me have outbursts which then made me feel inferior and small I wanted to know why my Ego wasn't working for me.

I listened for a second and after a moment of silence the ego of my voice said " I lash out because you don't protect or defend yourself. You don't stand up for your truth you don't know how you feel and so therefore I have to come in and take charge. You let everybody use you until you have nothing left and you give nothing back to self to me so I lash out at others in order to create more time and space for us.

When I heard this my heart started to beat quickly and I knew this revelation to be truth.

I could see where I wasn't honouring myself and I could now see how my actions and lack of concern for self was also affecting my ability to fully honour others.

I accepted what my Ego told me as, I knew it to be true. this is in fact what I did. and I realised I didn't protect myself and my ego because I did not feel safe and protected as a child so my ego was teaching me the lesson of self-preservation.

As this understanding was received by my heart, I accepted the truth that was being revealed.

I spoke to the heart of my Ego and let it know that I now understood the lesson that it was trying to teach me and that it was an act of love for self not necessarily to distance myself from others but to be mindful of fair energy exchange and the true intentions of your service and love.

I made a promise to my ego and myself that I would balance our needs and ensure that I would protect and preserve self so that I could share and serve others from the heart.

I put it to my Ego that I would ensure that I would honour our needs as well as rather than instead of; the needs of others and that it promised to work with me, fuel my passions and desires and inspire me to achieve and to let me know when I need to put us first.

My ego agreed and I remember opening up my arms and heart in embrace a loving receiving my Ego fully and the both of us becoming one and to be honest, since then I have experienced a dramatic shift in myself and the way I love and share.

I no longer over-give and try to please others.

I am mindful of having and maintaining a healthy balance in all areas of my life making sure that all interactions serve all involved equally. I am more determined to reach my goals and embrace my competitive nature as the drive needed to fuel that fires that manifest my own success and I honour myself and my feeling

I know now that just because I say no it doesn't mean that I do not love others, it just means that right now, I am committed to nurturing self...and that's ok.

There are many chips that I have taken and past experiences revisited to bring back healing and wisdom to my consciousness so that I can live a better and more intentional and purposeful life.

Being honest and clear with yourself and doing your shadow work is key you begin to unravel the power within in the darkness of your experiences. Ultimately you will realise that all is one and that your shadow can be your greatest Ally but first ensure that is not your biggest threat to success.

Feel the fear hunting and do it anyway dig deep make a commitment to your soul's work and transforming your inner darkness into light.

This is the true Nature of Alchemy inaction and is the highest intention for all of us at this time you have come before us have journeyed through the underworld an insight that has helped the whole of humanity to progress and evolve. When you make this same intention to heal and rebalance yourself also a become a light of wisdom for others who may be eating their own Darkness.

Your shadow and your light are one and the same and the experience of both is what brings you into the vibration of oneness all parts of you are valid all must be brought into alignment true ascension to take place. Stars are created in the darkness born again and brought back as a light that shines the way for many.

Be True to You

In life we are taught to wear many masks. We are shown that we have to behave a certain way in certain places, with certain people. Not to do this, or show too much of yourself. So many imposed rule, regulations and conditions that we end up losing our self in a mix of imposed expectations, sometimes not even knowing that we aren't doing the things that we love and being our true selves, but that we are actually living to maintain another image of ourselves. This process of initiated madness in my opinion is the cause for some of the insanity that we experience in everyday lives masquerading as sanity. There is always pressure to join the latest group or wear the latest clothes or support the latest industry puppets whilst suppressing our own true unique-ness and sparkle

The minute I stopped living for others, and peeled off the mask of presenting what I thought was the best image of myself and started working on uncovering and embodying my true self I began to see life reflect to me the magic and empowerment of my own beauty and uniqueness, warts and all. We are in a time when we are being called to live our ultimate truth and congruence. The be real about our shadows and heal them in the light until we get to the point where there are no shadows or flaws and we see ourselves truly how the Most- High intended…as perfect, whole and complete.

This is the true meaning of this life, to know that we are connected to all things, all of Creation and to allow that knowing, to empower us with to be Masters of our Reality and Custodians of our Planet. Our Shadow holds so much of our Power and when we venture bravely into its dark depths and find our light, our true source, Our Shadow then fuels our passion and drive, for success in the future.

You and your shadow are one, and as a formidable team, when working in harmony and balance together, full balance and oneness is attained. **Is your shadow your Enemy or a Friend?**

Duality Reality

The Police, The Courts, The System
Manifestations of the collective fear and accountability
That provides the backdrop
Of our experiences

Black and White
Right and Wrong
Duality and Contrast
Experiences of the 3rd Dimension

Representing all that we hold dormant
In the constraints of our hearts and minds
Projections of our inner fear and hatred
And all things we hide inside

We look into their faces
And feel their rage inside
You feel close to your kin
As your judged side by side

What do you fear
What can you see
Whom do you fear
Is this your reality?

Are you a number, a file, a case?
A name on a list
A crime that fits a face
Do you want freedom
Or do you already know your free……?
And have the ability
To be who you want to be

Have you made fear, centre stage in your movie?
Or do you fight for your rights
When you know that your free?

The battlefield of the mind,
Is where the test will be
The Government, The Courts, The Police
Are all what you choose to see

We are all held accountable
In this 3d reality
But you have the choice to ultimately
See what you want to see

So black and white
Right and wrong
What's your Choice to be
Cos Duality
Is only Reality
When its in..3D

Liberate your consciousness
Step back from the screen
Raise your vibration
And set a different scene

Release the fear of right and wrong
And soon you'll surely see
That everything that surrounds you
Is what you choose to see

Energy can be changed in an instant
Once your mind is free
Acknowledge you are infinite

And divine and loving being
So smile through all situations
Accept all challenges with glee
Cos as you think it, so it is
So create a new reality

Sides of the Same Coin (Love and Hate)

Love and hate could never be friends
Two sides of the same coin
But that's where it ends
Or is it?
I mean

Love, arouses all of my senses
Feelings of excitement bubble inside of me
Taking me into another dimension
Smiling, laughing, being free
Sharing my love willingly,
With all whom I see

Children playing, Birds singing
Sunshine on my face
When I'm in Love with Love
How could I not love this place?
Isn't life Special
Isn't Life great
Love is always amazing when everything is going great

Hate creeps up on you slowly
filling every pore
Yesterday you loved me
Today I don't love you anymore
Feelings of anger bubble inside me

Adrenaline rushing, oh how I despise
Everything about you
Your Smile, Your Dress, Your hair,
The way you make me feel so small
When you can't have your way
You hurt me, you hurt me
In every single way
But now I don't want you anymore
And I'm goanna make you pay

This hate is really toxic
Corrupts you in everyday
Surrounding you with darkness
And sucks the joy out of your day

All because I loved you
More than I can say
But what kind of Love could it really have been
If it makes me feel this way

The Love I know is giving
And wants only to be free
The love that's made for sharing
With every one you meet

Cos love is all around us
Depending on what you choose to see
And even in the midst of hate
Its Love deep down you see
So love and hate are beasties
Two sides of the same coin
So remember this when you're in a rut
And turn you hate to Joy!

Don't Pretend

I've travelled the world
Across lands, Across seas
Seen many people
Of all different creeds

But one thing in common
With many I see
Is a stifled existence
And a longing to be free

Living in a world
With so much formality
Different faces for different places
Roles and responsibilities

Some hide behind a mask
Of strained smiles
And forced grins
In your face they appear honest
Behind your back its a next thing

Others hide their greatness
Stand back from the light
Trying to be normal
Every day is a fight

Who they truly are inside
Is waiting to break free
But there's a little voice inside saying
Why are they looking at me?

We live in a world of control and suppression

Where ill health is a profit
And most have depression

Where we're told what to think
What to do
How to feel
Feels like we live on a hamster wheel
Well I for one have had enough
And choose to break the trend
I am nowhere near perfect
But I AM who I Am
And I won't Pretend!

I won't pretend that I know it all
And I won't pretend to be responsible
But I have to bring this to your attention
It's just one thing I've been pondering

Have your noticed, or maybe it's just clear to me
That so many people are not living free
Restricted and rugged and struck in a box
Of Controlled Thinking
Controlled Being
Controlled Doing
The whole lot

Living in a world of responsibility
Competition, career ladders,
Paying bills and mortgage fees

How do you do's
Thank you sir's
Hotep-Who's and blah blah blah's
Truth is not many give a shut

These words fall out of the mouth's like spit

We do not care truly for each other
The way we really should
We have become so distant
And so misunderstood

We rarely offer words of kindness
When others are feeling down
Sometimes of it's not on Facebook
No-one makes a sound

People have become like robots
Answers comes automatically
No connection, No contact, No Love
No real in-to-me-cy

Its beep beep this, and beep beep that
Choose option 1, 2, 3
We know we are so much more than this
To live a life that is real

Remember the days of old
When you'd call round to see a friend
You have so much fun doing silly things
That you wouldn't want it to end

Remember playing kiss chase
ins the school playground
Instead our children worry
About being shot or tasered to the ground

So I don't pretend its perfect
I don't pretend its fair

I don't pretend I'm happy
When sadness is all that's there

I don't pretend I know everything
Even with all my knowledge
And I don't pretend I like purple
When I really like orange

I don't pretend that our world is equal
And all are treated fairly
But I do my best to make a change
And be active in empowering my community

I don't pretend I'm someone else
It's so nice being me
But I don't pretend I don't hurt too
And have insecurities

I don't pretend that I like you
Or even that you like me
But I will make the effort
To have love compassion and empathy

I don't pretend to love everything
About me and my body
But I do choose to love all of me
Fully and Unconditionally

I don't pretend there's no racism
I don't pretend that I don't care
But I committed to reaching the next generation
How to Love each other and care

I don't pretend to believe in magic

For me this is really true
I believe in the magic within us
And the joys in all the things we do

I use dot pretend I was happy
When I really was not
I tried to keep my cool
When what I wanted was to lose the plot
I'd pretend I was pure
No blemish, no blot
But all that pretending, soon became a lot

It twisted, contorted and changed something in me
Put me in box
Didn't allow me to see
To Beauty in me

We all are programme'd
To hide who we truly are
So you wouldn't know
That you were made from the stars

So bright and so perfect
From intention alone
A spark of divinity
In you grows

What's the use in pretending?
That won't get you far
Don't pretend to be anything
Just be who you are

Take off the mask
Your true self you expose

And there you will find your greatness
Right under your nose

That's why I don't pretend anymore
I look forward to more greatness in me to explore
And the connection with other is so much better as well
Tell me why would I go back to pretending spell?

The Biggest Enemy

I sit with myself candidly
Taking this opportunity
To reflect on.... Me
To address this burning issue, deep inside
As to why in my life,
Things are just not right

I try and I try
To make steps ahead
So many ideas, they fill me with dread
So many possibilities
But stood in my way
Is my biggest Enemy

Now this enemy is no friend or foe
In fact, many times I've told it where to go
But each time it makes its way back to see
If I really want to change
If I really want to achieve

It stops me when I have things to do
and distracts me with even more things (do (go thorough)
For I never complete the task at hand
And this circle of madness, I just can't stand

If I really want Change
If I want to Succeed
Then I have to admit
My biggest enemy
Is ME!

Yes…. Me!

It's only me that stands in my way
Especially when I don't do the things that I say
And it seems as though others are getting through
But it's only because they say and they DO!
You can give every reason under the sun
Read every book,
Try a magic potion,
But the only thing that will help you succeed
Is to pick yourself up
get your mind right
And Take Heed

Look at yourself, deep in the eye
And ask yourself why, you're afraid to fly
Why you don't trust that you have all that you need
Pushing and willing you on to achieve
Procrastination and reasons why
Are all when and good
If you want life to pass you by
Self-sabotage and self-destruction
are not your friend
So ask yourself again, when you want this to end

It matters not what came before
What matters now,

Is that you start once more
To be believe in yourself and who you are
Take a big leap, and erase those scars
Do what you need to do, to make it
The opportunities there and you can take it
Just do the things you need to do
To do the work and make your visions come true

Put pen to paper
Heart to Spirit
Destiny is calling
Can you hear it?

See your vision in your mind
Clear as day
Take a deep breath in
Open up and Say

I owe it to myself and the Most High One
To be the best that I can become
Cos only I can stand in my way
And I choose not to fail
And try my best everyday

Spirit never gives more than I can bear
So with focus, clarity and drive
I will make it there
I'll take Massive Action
To achieve my goals
Because I know that achievement nourishes my soul
Reflects to me my greatness
Allows my confidence to grow

So as I step out, of my comfort zone

And venture out into a world unknown
I open, I trust, I envision, I act
I give all that I've got
No holding back
And when I have done all that I can do
I give love,
I give thanks
And watch my visions come true

I used to think the world was my enemy
Until I realized that it was just me
No external force stood in my way
Just me
But now I'm glad to say
That I faced my fears
I made it through
And now I share my gifts with you
Cos I know in this story you can relate
And I'm here to tell you it's not too late
To change your ways, make your life a success
Just make a commitment to do your best
And the you've made it
When you succeed
You can say (up yours) Thank you
To your biggest enemy!

#ReleaseTheFear

We are in the midst

Of the time for told

By the Ancient Ones

Who came before

As we are in the time of revelation

Time to release the fear

Raise the vibration

Rasta man chant

The Nyiabingi drummers play

As they strike the heart beat

And we trod on our way

To victory

Into the world unknown

Where music is the food

That feeds the soul

Know your Alive with every breath

Stand in your power and take a step

As we walk together in this Gideon

Stand strong

Stand firm

Release the fear

Release the tension

For no man knows what our world will become

When the battle is over

And the day is done

But the drummers and the singers

Bring in the new vibration

At first it may have seemed hard

The journey we take together

But no that struggle

Never last for ever

So take a stand now

Rise Against the Machine

Open you heart

And dare to dream

Open your eyes

And see what greatness is hidden there

When you stand in your power

Shake your Natty

And RELEASE THE FEAR!!

Rebirth

Dark dense matter falls away from me
My brightness now shines for all to see
As I sat in my cocoon waiting patiently
For the day my soul awakened
And I was set free

No longer am I afraid to shine
Dimming my light is not part of my Divine purpose
My reason for being
I live my life from a space of Divine meaning and feeling

Re birthed
Reconnected
Reignited
From the ashes I have rise
I am no longer frightened
All the shackles now removed
Fully embodying, this cosmic groove
As I dance the song of delight
I am made anew in Divine Sight
My old body tells a tale
A story we all know so well
I have arisen
Ready to start my new beginning

Dark matter is no more
Allowing my soul to soar
High into the clouds above
Rooted in Mothers Divine Love

I am rebirthed my spirit made anew
The past now holds all that I went through

And now it becomes my passions fuel
To let me know there is nothing I can't do
So for now my mind and my heart is clear
And allow wisdom to dissolve all me fears
Cos I know now the power within me
To burst through any obstacle and to create my reality

I dance with the mystics
The stars at my feet
A song in my hearts
I walk to the Universes beat
Moving through me and around me
Cleansing my soul
Nourishing my intentions and birthing my goals

Dark matter turns to light
Abundant loving and free
I now know that the true power of darkness
It to help you soul to break free

I am rebirthed
Rebirthed in my divine glory
I thank you shadow for showing me
That the magic is within me

Nurturing the Seeds

Seed 6 – Healing the Shadow

The Shadow aspect of our nature holds on to our most deeply held, thoughts feeling and emotions and which can hold us back from truly living our life to the fullest and seeing clearly, our full potential for success in our lives. Shadow work is integral to our growth and development and the healing found within this space can help to transform our lives and release long held traumas and self-sabotaging habits. Shadow healing work is something that you will continue to do as you go along your journey and path, so the more you do it and confront the things that haunt you, you can start to make your way toward living a happy and vibrant life

Time to Do the Work

Air – Know Your Mind

Take a moment to think about your mind and how it operates? Do you spend a lot of time thinking negative thoughts? Are you thinking more about what could go wrong as opposed to what could go right?

- *Do you use powerful words to describe yourself or others? Are they empowering and uplifting if chaotic and destructive?*
- *Identify a time when you used your words or thoughts negatively and the affected someone else? what happened? How did you feel? Did this feel like a good way to use your power?*
- *Write down 5 affirmations that will help to ensure that your words and thought are always in alignment with your highest vibration. Repeat these affirmations daily and really put the*

power into them with your work and empower with life though the power of your vision

Earth – Know your Body

What trauma do you still hold within your body? When we experience negativity it can affect our sacred centres and become trapped within the body and manifest as illness.

- ❖ Take a moment to get connected with your body now? How do you feel about your body? Do you have any ailments and illnesses that are long term? How did this start, what was happening for you at the time and how did it make you feel? Where did you store this energy in your body?
- ❖ Make note of your thoughts and feeling and observe your energy.
- ❖ You can release the energy stuck in your body by tuning into it. Build the energy in the area of pain and ask your higher self to show you the cause. And then ask your higher self to show you how to heal. If nothing comes, then send light to the space and just repeat the words "Release and Flow" "I release all trapped energy in my body with love"

Water – Know your Emotions

Our emotions are powerful and can be either constructive or self-destructive. Our emotions are connected to our thoughts and our thoughts are connected to our past experiences or supposed threat, meaning that at times we fear things that are either not true or that we ultimately have the power to come.

- ❖ Take a moment to observe your feelings about yourself? Do you feel happy about yourself? Are there things that you would like to change?

- ❖ How do you communicate with yourself? Do you say words of love and encouragement? Or do you put yourself down and feel that you are not good at anything.
- ❖ Write down a time when you felt really bad or something traumatic happened? And then write down a time when something amazing and wonderful happened? Be aware of the feelings in your body and know that you can transform the energy of anything you create, including your thoughts and emotions

Fire - Know your Power

What is the Source of your Power? Observe what power means to you? What does it feel like to feel powerful? Have you ever felt powerful? If so what did it feel like?

- ❖ *Can you remember a time when you felt powerless? What happened? What did it feel like? What was your response to this? And how has it affected you in your life to date?*

- ❖ *Have you used your power to overpower another? If so why? And what did you do? How did it make you feel? What did you learn*

Spirit – Know Your Past

Sometimes when we come to this realm and experience this life time we may come with karma or traumas from the past which can affect us. Healing modalities such as past life regression and Quantum healing can help us to access those past life experiences that can bring insightful. But you can also access glimpses of this information via guided meditation and trance

- ❖ *Take a moment and connect with your higher mind by saying- I connect with my higher mind. Set your intention to visit any past experiences that are hidden in your shadow that can offer you some healing in the now. You are merely going to observe these experiences*

❖ *Take a deep breath, hands on heart and send you consciousness into your heart space. See sense or feel a green emerald tunnel opening up in your heart space. Follow the tunnel of light until in the distance you see a mist. As you go through the mist you are guided to an image that will help you to see the root of a part of your shadow. What can you see? How does it feel? if you feel guided to you can say "Show me the Life' and your higher self will guide you through the experience.*

❖ *When you are ready and the experience is complete. Thank you higher self and make your way back through the heart an bring your consciousness back into the room*

❖ *Make a note of any thoughts feelings and pearls of wisdom that can assist you in your life now*

Love – The Spirit of Love

Most of the traumas of the Shadow are created during our childhood. This is the time when we are most vulnerable and susceptible to creating and attracting traumatic situations

❖ *Take a moment now to connect with your inner child.*

❖ *Ask your higher self to take you to a time in your childhood that needs healing and your attention*

❖ *Observe the scene? Can you remember this experience? What happened? How did you feel? and how did this experience affect you in your adult life*

❖ *Now take a moment to connect with your inner child now as yourself. Notice what age you were and how you looked. What would you like to say to your inner child? How can you help him or her to better understand the situation? What healing can you offer?*

- *Take a moment to give your inner child some love. Share positive words with them and also embrace them with a big hug*

- *When you are done, give thanks to your higher self and inner child and make your way back to full consciousness*

- *Take a moment to write down any thoughts or feelings that come up*

Golden Seeds of Wisdom

Some of the most painful and traumatic experiences in our life hold the keys to our Empowerment

The shadow is that part of ourselves that we hide from without allowing it to serve us and help us to uncover our true power.

Anything that is causing you discomfort is encouraging you to grow out of your limited experience and expectation of self. We are so much more that we think we are.

Star Seed Journey

Soul Journey

Earlier in the Chapter I spoke about my journey into the Halls of Amenti to meet with my Ego. This meeting offered me a lot of wisdom and guidance and facilitated the integration and realigning of my higher and lower selves and was the key factor in finding my power within.

You can use the Halls of Amenti to access any past of your reality that needs healing. Past present or future.

In the guided meditation below, you will take a journey deep beneath the Earth into the Sacred chambers of your heart into the Halls of Amenti and see your own Ego

Follow the guidance below and be sure to note down your experiences in your journal after.

Journey to Meet with Your Ego

- *Prepare you scared space with candles, essential oils or incense and ensue that you will not be disturbed*
- *Lie or sit comfortably and set your intention to go into the Halls of Amenti and meet with your Ego. Ask you higher self to support and guide you*
- *ground and connected yourself in the usual way, To Mother Earths Core and to the Merkabah or Star of David above your head and activate all of your chakras using breath and light*
- *Once all of your chakras are opened and you are connecting to heaven and Earth, take a deep breath and draw the energy from the heavens down into your crown chakra, past your throat and don into your heart.*
- *As it reaches your heart chakra you see a vortex of green emerald energy start to spin*

- As it spins a clearing appears in the middle which leads to a tunnel. This tunnel goes deep into your heart, follow the tunnel until you see a mist before you
- When the mist clears you notice that you are in a long corridor. On the floor is black and white tiles and on either side of the corridor are green arched doors
- Ask you higher self to show you the door that hides you Ego
- See one of the doors light up now – this is the door you must enter
- Walk over to the door and open it, you notice the room is darkened and you walk in and the door closes behind you
- In the distance you can feel an energy- tune into it – what does it feel like

This is your ego – Spend time with it and listen to what it has to say. Develop a dialogue between yourself and your Ego? What does it say to you? What do you have to say. Allow the experience to guide you

When you are ready give thanks to the guidance of your ego, and command your higher self to take you back to your self

As you do you see the mist appear again in the hallway and the vortex of green light energy comes and draws you back through the centre of your heart.

Give thanks to your Guides and Higher self!

Journal Page

Use this page to make any notes of your experience.

Seed 7

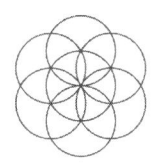

Be Open

to Change

"Nothing stands still - everything is being born, growing, dying - the very instant a thing reaches its height, it begins to decline - the law of rhythm is in constant operations...."

⁊ Three Initiates, **The Kybalion**

SEED 7 – BE OPEN TO CHANGE

Alchemy – The Key to Understanding the Journey of Life

"The secrets of Alchemy exist to transform mortals from a state of suffering and ignorance, to a state of enlightenment and Bliss"

Deepak Chopra

Alchemy is the process of Transformation. Usually attributed to metals and chemistry, the process of alchemy can also be used to demonstrate the human experience and the journey of the soul as it travels down the path on it journey to perfection and understanding of itself.

Alchemy means to transform and to transform means to change.

Change is the only constant in the Universe. Everything in life is always changing, going, moving, progressing and evolving.

Nature share with us her many graces and forms as we go through the various seasons of the year and witness as she goes through the death and rebirth cycle that is the rhythm of the Universe and of al life.

Some animals even change their skin, and change their whole look to hide and find camouflage with their environment during dangerous times in order to preserve themselves

But even though change is the most natural thing in the world, it is still one of the things that we humans fear the most.

We are creatures of habit and comfort and routine, or at least we may have been trained to be, but most of the aliments that we face as humanity is related you how we deal with the changes in our lives

Stress is one of the number one causing of disease within the body. And surprisingly enough is it is also supported, activated and empowered by our emotions.

We live in an age where we are under the illusion that we can control everything. And that is not to say that we cannot control everything, because we have free will and to an certain extent we can, but that doesn't mean that we have full control over all situations and it is the false reality that we do, that contributes to a lot of trauma and experience for many people

I am someone who is naturally used to change. When I was a child, I used to move house every 2 years or so and quickly got used to it and even found it exciting.

I enjoyed new homes, new friends, new schools, and whole new world to explore. I enjoyed the adventure of starting something new, but soon in my adult life became addicted to everything new. I lost value in the power of creating roots and foundations with others and building long lasting relationships.

I was so used to change that everything and everyone became dispensable. I found it difficult to maintain relationships, to admit to others when I was wrong and therefore robbed myself of the experience of knowing and trusting that when you share your truth, all can be forgiven and resolved, and that when you are there for others they will also be there for you.

But there were times when I would make friends and connect with the people where we lived and then we would have to move and I would miss them but I still was and still am, a major fan of change.

However, as much as I liked to move about, and proclaim my love of change, I am aware on the flipside of where I also find it difficult to change and make changes.

To release old habits and discontinue sabotaging behaviour, to make changes in my actions outlook, I found all of these areas of change so difficult, this wasn't because I didn't know better, it was because I was stubborn when it came to changing things that I could control and determine for myself. I was afraid of the responsibility for change and also of the power of my free will.

I was sexually abused when I was a child, from the age of 8 until I left home.

This formed a very big part of my life and although I was very aware of what was taking place on a spiritual and higher level for our soul's development, I still found it difficult to break out of some of the habits I formed at that time in the bid to keep me safe and as happy as I could be.

The need to please others and keep myself hidden. To withhold the truth in the fear that adults would not like it and could not handle it and the worst thing I learned was that I couldn't control my body. I had no control over my body. Something was set in me from that day, that anyone could hurt me or violate me and there was nothing I could do. Even as I grew older I could see how this perspective left me feeling anxious and distant. I was scared to engage with anyone and it took me a very long time to be able to find peace and resolution.

Everything was decided for me and I would be celebrated when I followed the rules. The adults would make the changes and I would go along with them, anything to distract me from the fact that I felt as though I had no power.

For a long time, I let others control my reality because I was too sacred to take responsibility myself. Inside I was still the same little girl who was looking for someone to save her because she couldn't save herself. And this carried on and manifested in my adult relationships until I had to take a stand and learn the lesson, and be the change, or risk continuing to manifest the same relationships experiences in my life. At that point in my life I decided that If I wanted to live and be happy, I needed to make some change, I had to be willing to change.

Willing to take control of my own life, and make my way. Will to let go of the victim victimizer blame game that I had inherited, in order to keep me safe and protected in my ivory tower.

I had to detach from that story, I had to learn to be real with myself and admit where I was still holding myself ransom and stopping myself from doing the healing I needed to do to bring the change and progression that I cherished so much.

I had to start look at my thoughts and asses the way that I thought? Was it healthy for me? Was my mind a friend or a foe? What needed to be release and what needed to be understood and embedded?

I had to look at my actions and ask whether they helping me to serve my highest good?

Was my over giving a sign of me wanting to please others to the detriment of myself?

And was my interested in the success of others really just a cover up for the failure that I felt within myself.

I had to get real with myself and take full responsibility for me healing and for bringing myself back in alignment with who I truly am at my core and value of divinity that is placed on me.

I had to release self-sabotaging ways and I had to make a decision to make my success and my happiness own priority.

I did this not only for myself, but for my children, my friends and my family, but ultimately most importantly, for myself.

I needed to make the changes that I needed to make so that I could live the life I knew I meant to. I needed to turn my pain into my power so I could transform the energy and share it with someone else. I also needed to create the change so that I could show my children the power of me being in control of me.

How could I teach them to love and value themselves without teaching then from a place of my fear attached to my old experienced.

By making the changes necessary to allow you to experience and enjoy your life you offer yourself the opportunity for rebirth and understanding of the lesson that are hidden within.

Change allows us to review and reflect, to plane and to manifest, to create and to destroy and recreate anew!

The more that you allow it to be your friend the more beneficial and stress free your life will be. We are sentient and fluid beings, always changing, always expanding and always growing and making space to learn and experience more of our selves

Learn to embrace change as the beautiful transforming energy that allows a caterpillar which crawls on the flow in the mud, to metamorphosis and transform into a beautiful butterfly able to soar above in the freedom and expansiveness of the air and the heavens above against all odd.

Even the butterfly's wings, are testimony to the magic that can take place through the sometimes darkness of transformation and change.

The Healing Power of Transformation

Transformation is the definition of Alchemy in action. To transform is to change in form, conditional, nature character or structure. To change something into another substance, is to transform it and give it new life and purpose and return it back to light. In life we too have to go through the process of transforming our lead into gold, our dark into light and our pain in to passion.

Transformation is our true purpose and the only real constant in life.

What may seem to be an obstacle, something we don't wish to acknowledge in self, something we Don t wish to see, is really a hidden gem and a gift which disconnects us from the illusion of the false ego and brings us more in truth and alignment with our Divine self.

We are not here to be perfect and through pain and suffering we truly see the power and beauty in ourselves. When we heal that we give ourselves the gift of an Enlightened and Empowered You!

Whilst looking through one of my old journals, I was able to witness first-hand how I was able to transform my emotions and reality, by recognising where the fault lay within my own ignorance and how that manifested as hate and negativity. But through the healing process I transformed that experience into light that allowed me to reflect on my personal journey and healing.

Last year I wrote:

> "My anger is potentially a great ALLY to me. It is my job to use it wisely as a SACRED gift and power.
>
> May I use my anger as healing FLAME to burn off that which no longer serves me and not as a destructive fire that harms myself or others.
>
> May I respect my anger as a PROTECTIVE force within me, as my passion for life and as a boundary-setter.
>
> May I harness the gift of my anger to LIBERATE myself and awaken from the ways in which I might have deceived myself, been asleep or uncourageous.
>
> May I learn to listen to and transform my anger into a POSITIVE force for good"

This year I wrote:

12 Seeds To Awaken Your Spirit

> *"My anger is now passion and desire that burns through illusion and reveals truth in myself my world and others.*
>
> *It is the fire and spark that ignites my imagination and makes way to birth my creation.*
>
> *My Anger is really LOVE WRAPPED IN PASSION!*
> *MY ANGER IS NO LONGER ANGER*
> *MY ANGER IS LOVE"*

Change brings understanding and growth and when we get used to change and understand the potential of what Is about to be gifted to us, it can benefit us in so many ways and make life so much easier.

> Anything that is causing you discomfort in your life or current circumstance, is encouraging you to grow and expand far beyond your current space. You may need to do some work to identify exactly what need to be embraced or realised, but the sooner you do, your will find that everything becomes in alignment and your opportunities for growth and experience expand also and offer your new and exciting ways to experience yourself, express your love and live your divine purpose.
>
> When we transform the energy of our past and hurtful experiences, into light, through self-reflection, healing and action, we give them new energy and hope that can be a blessing of a story of empowerment shared to others in need. We have to be the change we want to see and also be the change that inspires others by facing up to truths and who we are and allowing our experiences to nurture us.
>
> Let change be your best friend, a really good friend, one who tis their nudging you to move along and do your best and see your potential, even if you don't want to or can't see it yet. Trust in the Divine Flow to give you everything you need and take you everywhere you need to go. Embrace change and see it like breathing, a constant and natural part of the infinite and balanced nature of the Universe.

The Alchemy of Me

I turned my gifts into gold

I turned my weirdness into wonderful

My shyness into humility

My truth into integrity

My imagination into my reality

My trauma into my art

My pain into my passion

And on my sleeve I wear my heart

I turned my rejection into my love for others

My sadness into my joy

My shame into my shimmer

My mistakes into my biggest achievements

My sex into my creation

My darkness into my light

My flesh into perfection

Guided by divine sight

I Am here to be all that I can be

From the rock to the diamond, This is the Alchemy of Me

Nurturing the Seeds

Seed 7- Be open to change

Change can sometime be a daunting and challenging thing. We can become used to things and situations, even if they do not support our growth and development. Change help to create space for more of what you want in your life and less of what you don't and can assist in helping you to get focused and clear and bring great healing and transformation to your life. Change can be a great thing as it breathes new life and inspiration into all your intentions and creations

The seeds below will support you in preparing for change and also identifying what may need changing or addressing in your life.

Time to Do the Work

Air – Change Your Mind

Take moment of what changes you can make so that your mind can be a useful tool for heling you to manifest what you want.

- ❖ Do you need to change the way that you think? Are your thoughts empowering you are disempowering you?
- ❖ How comfortable are you with the idea of change? Do you procrastinate? Are you self-sabotaging yourself with your thoughts?
- ❖ Change starts in the mind. What you think will be your reality. Create some affirmations now that will assist your mind in accepting change and seeing how it will benefit you? An example of this would be: *I am excited about change, When I makes changes in my life great things happen*

- Do you procrastinate? Are you self-sabotaging yourself with your thoughts?

Earth – Know your Body

- What changes can you make to your body? Take a moment to observe your body. It is serving you well? do you have any ailments or illnesses that need to be rebalanced?
- Are you serving your body well? Are you giving it the right food and nourishment? Are you getting enough exercise? Taking walks for fresh air? Are you sleeping enough?
- -Take an inventory of how you are your body are working together and make a note of any changes that need to be made

Water – Change your Emotions

At times we can hold on to memory of painful situations or disagreements with others. but this vibration can really way us down and unless resolved, we can end up holding of grudges long after the feelings have dissolved.

- Take a moment to observe your feeling and emotions? Are you easily offended? do you take things lightly? can you see the funny side of life or are you always serious
- What does change feel like to you? Does it conjure up fear and anticipation or excitement?
- Make a note of your findings in your journal
-
-
-

Fire – Know your Passion

- ❖ What can you do to put more energy into your intentions and goals?
- ❖ What do you need to support you in your mission for success?
- ❖ Are you setting realist expectations for yourself? its ok to have big goals but are you willing to do the work to manifest them

Spirit – Change Your Spirit

- ❖ What changes can you make that will positively influence your spiritual development and growth

Love – The Spirit of Love

- ❖ What positive changes can you make to love yourself better?
- ❖ What changes can you make to share and show love to others?
- ❖ What do you love about change?

Golden Seeds of Wisdom

One of the best ways to deal with it is to understand that everything in nature and the Universe is always changing. Change brings the hope of something new being birthed into experience. Change is allowing the natural flow of the Universe to support and sustain you. it is the reassurance that even the darkest of times will bring forth light and the knowing that the current of life exists in everything.

The key to coping with change is embracing Acceptance for self, others and for all things. Know that everything is always happening for your highest good and that you have the power to manifest whatever reality you choose.

Change is a gift and an opportunity to experience more of what the Universe has to offer.

Journal Page

Use this page to make any notes of your experience.

_____
_____
_____
_____
_____
_____
_____
_____
_____
_____
_____
_____
_____
_____
_____
_____
_____
_____
_____

Seed 8

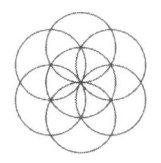

Understand Your Relationships

" A Relation-ship is a vehicle that is taking you to and through an experience of yourself that can either take you to your Heaven or your Hell.
You Decide!

Amenti the Awakener

SEED 8 – UNDERSTAND AND LEARN FROM YOUR RELATIONSHIPS

Relationships

We learn about ourselves and our nature through our relationships. Everything in the Universe is connected and is a divine expression of the other.

Relationships are the tapestry and fabric of all life and teach us about how we connect and relate to everything outside of ourselves and within. What would life be without your friends and family, to be completely separate from everyone and everything? what would life be like without the ability to see outside of a self in our world around us? The law of relativity demonstrates that each one of us is connected and that we all have an effect on each. Our daily interaction with and how we experience the world is enhanced or developed through our relationships.

When we come into this world from the sacred womb our natural instinct is to form and develop relationships. Before we are even born into the world our mother and father and family members develop a relationship with us. They speak to us and connect with us before we can even hear. The can intuitively connect with us and influence our energy and environment by their actions and energy.

They became more aware of our traits and personality from what makes us tick, our active and passive cycles, even down to what food and environment or sound we do or don't like. They are developing a relationship with us, that will help them to form an understanding of who you are and this will continue long after you leave the womb. Your relationship with your immediate family is the 1st and most important relationship of all.

Those early formative years in our soul and human development are crucial to creating the foundation, on which our life lessons; and sometimes longstanding traumas will manifest from.

Our root and sacral chakra which are in their early stages of development can become severely damaged by our relationships and environment at these times as they govern the attributes of security foundation the ability to fend for oneself how you express your emotions and how you express your will into your reality.

For many the relationships that they have with their mothers and fathers, present or absent can have long lasting effects that affect their relationships with others further on in life. Relationships help of to see the many different aspects of the human archetype and assist us in our personal development and growth.

At-times they can be like a mirror projecting back to of reflection of our most beautiful parts of our selves or the worst and if addressed and brought into awareness, can provide opportunities for after feel love and healing and empowerment.

The many different types of relationships that we have all that we have also help us to learn the different life lessons that we have come here to experience and create different environments and opportunities for us to do so.

Home and family Relationships

Home and family relationships help to establish our identity and helped to form and mould our personality. We can learn a lot in about ourselves and create a lot in challenges for ourselves within our family relationships and groups. But ultimately family relationships although sometimes hard to bear or repair can be the most impactful and so empowering experiences and interactions that we will have if you find the courage and strength enough to go back-and heal any demons and with that May have come-up. All this is teaching you hard lessons about life but from my experience no matter what

Family is family regardless of what you say or do, the blood in your veins cannot be changed. And although at times this may seem a nuisance; I find there is something comforting and grounding about being connected to a group of people who can support you in life and remind you of who you really are at your core, whether you like it or not.

Friendships

Friendships are also formed in the early years of Life mainly after your first few years when you have developed your relationship with your immediate family. Your friendships are the first relationships when you get to show who you are and get to know yourself and others outside of your family environment. Friendships and especially those formed in the early years during nursery and school are a crucial and informative part of your journeys growth and development. When you start interacting with others socially you also get to see and experience other people their nature there quirks their ways of doing things and compare them to the experience of yours in this multicultural world that we live in and especially in London there are many people from many different cities and backgrounds cultures and backgrounds all with different ways and expressions to share.

As a child you start to look at other people and compare yourself to them. We seek out them that comes naturally as it does in nature. Popular kids at school the hot girls and the nerds and the outsiders all form different social groups that begin in these informative times this is your first snapshot into the relationships that you have outside of your personal family and how your relationships define your status and position in life

Where do you fit in?

How do others see you and how does that make you feel?

And what can or will you do about it.

This process of comparison is a constant balancing act and the beginning of a long journey towards finding your true self by your relationship with others.

When we are young sometimes we may not be as confident about life or about yourself especially if self-confidence and value, were not qualities that encouraged in the home and family life.

We naturally develop the need to acquire a personality that is more suitable to the environment that we are in we won't want to be more like her or less like him and seek to find the best mix of all of the personalities that are around us. We also connect and create and build friendships and relationships with people who are similar to us who like similar things that we like to do and also may have new insights to share with us.

As with everything may grow and change friends and your interests also will grow and change but ultimately we all developer major part of ourselves through how we relate to others every the vehicles are my relationships and friendships. Whether it's the friend or bully that taught you to defend yourself the guy or girl who told you that they liked you and pecked you on the cheek or the best friend that was always there for you when you were when you thought you were on your own and gave you the strength to persevere and carry on. Friendships help to support as to nurture and grow and can provide some of the most supportive and long-lasting relationships that will carry you and support you and create moments and memories of Joy that will last you well on into your life.

Authority / Duality Reality

We all are in some ways aware of the lesson of dealing with Authority. Whether it be in school with the teachers, at work with your manager or even with the police in your personal life. We manifest these learning experiences as a way of understanding how we deal with rules and regulations and honouring the authority of ourselves and others and ultimately Divine Authority and Right Order.

When we manifest or experience negativity or resistance in our life it can be easy to put the blame on something outside of yourself. But my understanding from my life experiences and vine teachings is that, whatever we manifest or experience on the outside in a direct manifestation of what needs to be observed and rebalanced within.

We live in the realm of duality, of cause and effect and one of the clauses for being here on this planet is that we learn that we create our own reality, whether collectively or individually, consciously or unconsciously.

In my life I went through the polarities of shifting from being totally subservient to the system and to the roles imposed on me, not wanting to upset the balance or speak out. To begin a rebel and experiencing resistance and the need to fight for my freedom or rights as I learned about being on the opposing side of the system or status quo.

Ultimately these experiences brought me the lessons of order, balance and personal power. I understood that authority figures that presented any negativity or resistance for me, represented my own internal judgment system bringing me back into alignment. Once I acknowledged where the misdemeanour was and sought to centre and rebalance myself, all resistance was gone. This is the nature of Alchemy within the experience of Duality.

Even in our global community, the negativity and corruption, wars and unfair politics and governance, that we see manifesting in the world is a direct result of the seething negativity that we hide within the consciousness of our being and the way in which we have been programmed to deal with each other and our world. We are seeing ourselves on all our glory and through seeing this we are also working together to erase it within ourselves and in our global community.

Duality is a 3rd dimensional experience, the illusion of separation and accession through the consolidation of the opposites, the understanding that there is both light and dark, good and bad, right and wrong in the ALL and ALL is ONE. This revelation and understanding presents the ending of the need for the experiences of duality, and entry into the experience of oneness with all things and that of the 5th Dimension.

Work relationships

Work Relationships are another dynamic and environment in human development and relating story.

Provide an environment of structure and order depending on the type of work environment that you are working in and offers many opportunities to develop your drive driven and purpose in relation to others and can also help you to nurture and understand your adult relationships and gain valuable insight as to how you work with others.

The dynamics of the work environment and work relationships you are such that your main function and focus is to serve the purpose and intention of what you have been hired to achieve your focus is the collective Focus and goals of the business. And the environment will usually be conducive to that.

You usually get a mixed bag of personalities or groups of people with the same personality type depending on the type of job or environment but more than likely as much as they may be similarities they may also be widely contrasting differences that create opportunities for learning and development also may cause friction.

In the workplace you must learn to get on with all different types of people. How to learn the tools of conflict resolution collectively towards one focused goal or outcome.

Depending on the dynamic there are many lessons that can be learnt in these types of relationships about order discipline hierarchy system and authority and being a part of a system or having to work closely with people of whom you have nothing in common outside of the work or job that you do or don't even particularly like.

Work relationships offer us about our ability to learn how to get along with others and informs us about our passions and drives in relation to other people and help us to know our strengths and weaknesses and also opportunities for learning and Growth

In the workplace you are regularly assessed and this is an assessment of both your relationship with self and the ability to work with others. you are encouraged to develop your own out of work and demonstrate your passion drive and tenacity.

You may also learn to see things from a more detached perspective so that you're better able to find a solution to any problem.

The skills that can be learnt in the work environment and through your relationships with work colleagues can be very useful in helping you to develop an effective and intelligent personality that can help you to support both the goals of yourself and others. And work together for a Higher Cause

Romantic Relationships

"No matter what the question, this is the answer: we are here in each other's lives to facilitate in one another a higher state of consciousness. We are here to open each other's eyes to the God within. We don't talk about that; it certainly isn't the spoken goal of most partnerships. But that is what is at play."

Romantic relationships are the spice of life, they make us feel alive in a way that nothing else can.
Genuine romance exists when two people show that they care for each other through small acts of love and affection.
We feel loved and cared for when we know that our significant other is thinking about how to give us the most pleasure.
Romance is the key to keeping the sparks flying. Without it, any relationship will soon lose its shine.

Romantic relationships teach us about love the absence or presence of it how we understand it how we Express it how we received it and how we share it.

They teach us about how we are in relation to ourselves in an opposite form. and can healing challenging as with all other relationships but the wounds in our romantic relationships can cut very deep.

Romantic relationships teach us some of our biggest lessons in life and so therefore can be very traumatic or very liberating they can be healing or harmful but ultimately their goal is to assist us with connecting to the love that is within ourselves and can help us to truly connect to the Divine self within all things

Ultimately Romantic relationships are about balancing the opposites within you your, light your dark, your passion and your power and your ability to share and connect with the other side of yourself to experience oneness and wholeness.

Romantic relationships are your gateway into the realm of sacred or and sacred sexuality and allows you the opportunity to embody and create one of the most powerful and Potent energies known to man, sexual energy.

Root and Sacral chakras are the most affected and connected to our sexual and intimate relationships and also the heart and the route as well. Love and hate are two sides of the same coin and it's through our relationships that we learn these sacred facts.

All relationships are where we first learn about deep levels of intimacy and sharing ourselves deeply with another. Relationships are about how you connect with your yourself and with others romantic relationships encourage you to get intimate with yourself.

It can in uncover your deepest fears taking you to your deepest power may take a whole lot of healing before you get to that point but romantic relationships are key restoring balance and harmony within oneself defying all aspects of self within the heart.

We are also starting to understand our relationships on a much deeper and conscious level finding your twin mate and soul mate has become the latest new craze and intention for many without fully understanding what the nature of these relationships really are and how they support us in our growth and development

As you start on the journey towards healing yourself, you start to vibrate at a frequency of love for yourself within yourself and in-service to yourself.

From this space, you are able to successfully maintain that vibration and find a harmonious balance of giving and receiving and sharing of love with self you will naturally manifest and create the direct reflection and divine counterpart to match your current vibration.

All of our relationships a reflection of who we are now, and can be helpful in helping us to understand where we're going and who we are to become.

A Relationship is vehicle that are taking you somewhere out yourself up to you to decide whether whatever the destination know and trust that something is being held within you because yourself is always seeking to know more of itself in relationship with itself and that anything that doesn't allow for this or does not match the vibration of the highest love will be brought up for healing clearing and release.

You will always a check the relationships that all good the offer your soul's highest good and development looking for love you must be loved and if anything within you is not of love you attract did invite match to help you to heal that.

Romantic relationships can be very complicated but they can also help to uncover some of the deepest deep rooted trauma I'm on leash the most powerful forms of healing energy.

Soul mate Relationships

A soul mate reflects back to us that which is unhealed while testifying to what is already perfect. Soul mates provide different things at different times: sometimes a safe haven from which we can branch out and explore, and sometimes challenges that bring us to our knees. In every case, they help us as we make our way along the path leading to the innermost sanctum where Spirit resides.

Your soulmate relationship those who are a part of your soul group and have chosen on a spiritual level to be a major part in your life story and part of your journey towards healing and taking your soul lessons.

The purpose of soulmate relationships is for each individual's growth and development.

You know your soulmate mate by an immediate feeling of knowing when you meet them you are not truly drawn to them you and you feel happy and comfortable in the space although sometimes you may be challenged but they will be easily resolved.

Your soulmate relationships could be with anyone from your soul family. Your mother, your father, your sister, your brother, your friend, boyfriend, girlfriend or partner may be your potential soulmate. Contrary to what many people think your soulmate does not have to be your partner but in many cases it can be.

The purpose and function of a soulmate relationship is to facilitate a two-way relationship that refines, sculpts and shapes the other into becoming more of its true self.

Soulmate relationships bring out the qualities and strengths within in each soul that prepares you for your twin soul reunion.

Twin Flame Relationship

A twin flame relationship is different from a soul mate, or any other type of relationship. It is the only type of relationship that requires both people to be ready emotionally, mentally, physically and spiritually before a consistent alchemical union can be experienced

Their purpose is to provide the foundation to consolidate all opposites and division and bring experience of oneness and reunification of the once separated or individualised soul.

Before the reunification can take place, each person will experience a set of challenges that seek to dissolve the ego and make way for the soul so that means that whatever you need to experience to do that will manifest within this interaction.

Twin flame relationships can either extremely testing and challenging or completely uplifting empowering an inspiring.

The purpose of twin flames relationships each individual back to the experience of the wholeness.

Only when we have experienced the fullness of separation can we then return to wholeness

Twin soul relationships teach unconditional love and acceptance and how to embody these things before being able to offer them entirely to another. They force their twins to surrender and let go of unrealistic expectations or demands.

The main purpose of Twin flame relationships is that union bring something valuable into the world for humanity. this could be a child, a soul purpose or healing for the collective consciousness.

Their lessons and gifts go beyond that of the individual experience. Two people getting together and learning to heal, harmonise and balance the masculine and feminine energies within also affects the collective consciousness

Twin flame relationships are very intense.

Both people intuitively know that they were brought together for an important reason, and that they have a significant role to play in one another's lives

They can have a strong destructive nature of conflict with intensity between the two people who are experiencing it as they seek to restore and balance

In twin flame relationships, there is a deal of a magnetic pull between the two and this is because it is seeking to be the whole within itself fine to be connected to that but this is also the passion and intensity needed to help you to understand your self fully, both dark and light and bring yourself back to home this and awareness and bring balance restoration and healing to your masculine and feminine energies within yourself and within your relationship.

In the initial stages, twin flames are known to test and challenge one another relentlessly in an egotistical power struggle to achieve and maintain control and balance in their lives. However, part of coming together is the opportunity to break down the ego and the desire for control.

Twin flames are energetic mirrors and when they are in contact, they reflect one another's flaws, faults and insecurities. Although this can feel like a negative aspect of the dynamic, it is an extremely positive one.

To find balance, it is essential to know where unresolved issues and unhealed wounds are hiding.

Twin flames trigger the hidden emotions that weren't acknowledged, accepted or loved in the past. They highlight our shadow sides so that twin flames can find forgiveness and understanding, and learn to love themselves and others fearlessly, unconditionally and limitlessly.

Despite twin flames having a unique and deep connection, they often find themselves physically separated. The reason for this is that if their energy is out of balance, they will struggle to harmoniously merge their energies.

Unfortunately, until twin flames balance within their joint energy, it is highly unlikely they will unite and sustain a peaceful, fulfilling relationship.

We need relationships that challenge our prejudices, and encourages us to grow and see beyond our individual needs and desires. We need people – partners, friends, casual acquaintances, and even strangers – who will walk with us as we make our way to our soul's potential.

Your relationships and interactions with the masculine and feminine within and the partner's you can sometimes be a direct reflection hope how you see or interact with that male or female aspect within yourself and the Purpose and intention of our relationship is to bring harmony through balance of the opposites through love.

We also form relationships with our environment in the world around us. environment plays a very important part and how we see ourselves and also helping us to understand our capabilities if we are sheltered and in an intense environment we might find it difficult to interact with others and be in large groups open spaces. All destruction of mother earth can also be directly linked to the nature of the human condition and demonstrate the lack of self-care and love that we have for ourselves and each other.

Relationships inform us about how we relate to ourselves externally and in relation to all things. They remind us. We are not alone and give us the building blocks that we need to understand more of ourselves and you into the highest vibration of ourselves.

The challenge of finding and keeping a soul mate is the perfect impetus for our metaphysical maturation. Our love relationships bring us face to face with our demons, and we are willing to confront them and learn how to better ourselves because we want so badly to fulfil love's magical promise. It is by using the experiences that arise within the context of partnership – both joyful and painful ones – that we come to embrace the enormous spiritual capacity that lies within us, making us capable of magnificent things, not only in the area of relationships, but in every area of life.

Our spiritual task is to calm our overactive ego, to catch it when it starts climbing into the driver's seat and tell it when to get back where it belongs. In terms of love relationships, we need to become more focused on treating our partners – or potential partners – with respect, honouring the fact that they have their own higher mind to follow and we have no right to push our personal agenda on their lives. We need to stop insisting on getting our own way and allow them to be who they are. We can make suggestions and we can express our opinions, but it gets us nowhere to insist on having things our own way. We can't change anyone else; we can only work on changing ourselves

Power struggles can be a common feature in relationships to help you to understand power, boundaries and will.

Your ego seeks to learn about and expressed itself through your experience with others and ensure its needs are met. Your ego often tries to be the only important feature in your life and relationships can challenge some of the egos needs.

The **Ego** in relationships is driven by 4 common needs

1. The need to be right – this keeps you constantly in space of separation and conflict as the ego tries to maintain its autonomy. The ego, in relation to another, thinks only one can win and so therefore fights for its place

2. The need to be in control – this is the egos way of trying to ensure it feels protected and in control. The need for control is based on fear of letting go and trusting in the interaction

3. The need to be distracted - this is based on the egos fear or being alone and being responsible for its own happiness and growth. some relationships are a distraction firm the work we need to do for

ourselves

4. The need to be inferior or superior - the ego is constantly wanting to make itself feel important and special and keeping us apart from each other by focusing on flaws

The ego doesn't have any understanding of the collective or Oneness and so always seeks to validate itself as the individualized aspect.

This is greatly challenged in our relationships where the ego has to learn and understand how to connect with itself outside of its self and make the transition from separation to wholeness.

These four ego-driven needs present obstacles to our awareness of deep and unconditional love because they keep us focused on what's wrong rather than what's right. They drive us apart rather than bring us together. Each time you see one of these needs arise in your thoughts or actions, recognize it as a warning to relegate the ego to the backseat.

The Ego is an aspect of the mind that serves a purpose to bring balance and oneness. If we stay alert and awake to all the forces at work within us, we can create a well-balanced and soulful partnership

Romantic relationship also helps us to gain an understanding of the love that we have for all selves. Many relationships fail say I found it on a foundation section a lot of self-love and value. We seek relationships to heal avoid that is missing in ourselves and this can destructive for both ourselves and others. this vampiric energy can suck the life force out if all our relationships and you will only attract people of the same vibration if we come from this place.

Like attracts like, and opposites only attract to harmonise with the other and receive something that's it doesn't already have.

but when you focus your intention and match the vibration of what you want to achieve by being just that you will find that the relationships that manifest I'm all harmonious and enhancing to your soul's growth and development

Sometimes when we alone in for love and looking for a relationship that may be the very same time where we need to give that love the attention and that care to ourselves and make a decision to truly love ourselves and the relationship with our souls as much as we love nurture and appreciate the relationships we have with others.

Every type of relationship you are experiencing has a purpose, and therefore, its plain to see, that relationships for my major part of our life and also help us to understand who we are.

They help us to experience more of ourselves and to learn what needs to be in balanced and restored and what needs to be released and when we get that mileage just wiped it can lead us through the gate ways of sacred sexuality and awaken latent hidden power within us to restore heal and create.

Letter to My Sister

Sister, sister, how I love you so
The good times we've shared
How I watched you grow

All the laughs and the giggles
All the stories we've told
How we made plans to always be together
Until we grew old

But hold up
Wait a minute
There's another side to this picture
I also remember the times
When you used to be bitter
Take all of my things
And get me in trouble
Try to steal all my friends
And make me feel embarrassed
And when I was happy
You quickly burst my bubble
Told all my secrets
And laughed at my fashion

There was a part of me mixed with a part of you
And no matter how far we travelled
There is nothing that you can do
To make me forget the love that we are
And how we came together
from our mission from the stars

I remember how I felt

When I knew you were coming
I didn't want another
To take over my mummy
I didn't mind sharing all my things with you
As long as I knew that you would share too
And when you arrived and all came to see
You opened your eyes and looked straight at me
It was that they I knew I would be your best friend
And I would love you and look after you right till the end

Oh sister oh sister
How we've journeyed together
And through all of the struggle
I know I would never
Replace you, because I love you for who you are

The good and the bad times
That brought us together
The gains and the losses
The laughs and the pleasures

As we have grown into the women we have become
A new journey is beginning
We are far from done
I see you now
As a woman and as a mother
And I am proud of who you are
I wouldn't trade you for another
And you've taught me a lot
And to this day you still teach me
How to stand in my own power
Never let others make me doubt me

My sister, My sister

My reflection and friend
A reminder of the real me
Let our love never end
And although we may drift
And argue from time to time
I am so happy that I have you,
Because together we shine

I have in me what you may not have in you
But know we can make a whole,
When we combine the two
You and me together
Loving endlessly
All these years we've wasted
I suppose it took some time to see

Just why we came here together
All those years ago
Now look how far we have come
Which only goes to show
That whatever you go through
And whatever you do
You will always be a special part of me
And me a special part of you

Sister sister, how I love you so
I wish only the best for you
And want you to always know
The love and respect I have inside for you
May it daily grow
I am lucky to have you both with me
Let's always love each other until we grow old!

Letter to My Mother

Mother
This is one of the hardest letters I have to write
In fact it brings tears to my eyes
To know someone so powerful and beautiful
How I loved you from above

I saw the core of all that was
And I came here to make you see
That all the hurt your life had caused
Was hiding something precious underneath

Mum you are so loving and so happy and kind
But I know deep down inside you
A lot of pain you hide
I see myself within you
And all you have become
They say the first is the closest
And I was your first one
The first to make you a woman
And help you to become
A mother in all her glory
And a loving and happy one
To me you were already perfect
So it was very painful for me
When I realised that you were hurting so much
That you couldn't protect me
I never ever blamed you
For what he did to me
I could see that you were helpless
And that it brought back you own memories
I saw your body froze
As I altered your reality

Showed you that I was hurting
And who was hurting me
I saw the pain inside you
I saw the fear in your eyes
I saw that you didn't want to believe my truth
When you told me that my truth was lies
And in that moment I still wanted to protect you
From all that was to come
At the expense of my own sense of freedom
I protected you with my love
There is so much that happened
That's you did or did not see
But I wanted to let you know I forgive you
For not being able to protect me
I saw you were in your own prison
I saw you were trapped in your fear
I wanted to give you the strength
But you wouldn't let me in there

For a while I felt like an orphan
Felt I didn't have your love
I felt so unprotected
And that my only friend was God
At times it was so painful
When all I wanted was love
At times I used to blame myself
And though I was unworthy of love
But now I know different
And I want you to know
That I will always love you
And want our relationship to grow
I want to know you deeper
Like I know you from within
I want to see you happy

And I want to see you win
There is some much you have taught me
You're the reason I'm so loving
And I so want you to see your greatness
And for your happiness can begin

You may not have always,
Thought you'd done your best
But I can tell you now mum
You did what you could so you can now rest
In the knowing that we are all growing
Into the women that we have become
Something you can be proud of
Your beautiful daughters and Son

And mum I just want you to know
That I'm grateful you gave me the seeds
So I can become a mother too
And mother the ones who come from me
In my journey through motherhood
I have learned along the way
That you don't always know everything
And you learn something new every day
It's not about being perfect
The main ingredient is love
But it is also a continuing evolution
That empowers you into what you become

Mum know that I chose you for the power that lies in you
The joy of all the angels
A great way with food
Know that you are magic
Full of power and love
And know that the Creators showers you

With blessings from above

Know that I will always love you
In every single way
I take heed to your guidance
And take on what you say
I see right into your soul
I take in all of you
Because everyone ounce of who you are
Is inside of me too
And although I may do things different
And be part of the change
Know that I am grateful
For you showing me the way
My wish for you is happiness
And to get what you truly deserve
From our pain we gain our power
And that is the lesson we must all learn

But this letter I write to you
To bring forth the healing truth
And to let you know
That I truly love you

Thank you for carrying me
In your sacred time machine
And thank you for giving me life
So I can dream a new reality

I love you Mother
For the past and who you are to become
Know that I am always here for you
And our journey together, has just begun

Letter to My Dad

Daddy oh Daddy
Where did you go
Left a space in my heart
Where no love would grow

Left and rejected
For what I don't know
Confused and abandoned
With nowhere to go

I'm writing this letter
Cause I want you to know
The girl you left behind
Is still lost and alone

In order for her to heal
To grow and break free
I must release the hurt that is in me

My mother, God bless her
She tried and she tried
To hide from the hurt that we both felt inside

She found a new father
To give us support and hugs
But no one could match or replace
A real fathers love

A father protects you
Make you feel safe and secure
He prepares you for the wonder
That life has in store

Tell you that your special
Tells you you're a Queen
Tell all potential boyfriends to steer clear
And that you should study and go for your dreams
But for me you we're not there
To do all of this for me
I wasn't sure
And I so had to question
Why my father didn't love me anymore

When you left my pain began
And you were not there to help me deal with the pain
You left me
And even when I called you
You pretty much did the same
I was never a priority
And you will never know my pain
But I accept you for who you are
And I no longer feel shame
It took me so long to see
That I had chosen for this to happen
So I could learn the life lessons
That I had chosen for my expression
But that doesn't make it any easier
But at least I can see
That your love for me wasn't absent
Which is what I was left to believe

Now that I am older
Know I can understand
That inside you were here hurting
And showing emotions was not usual for a man
Inside you heart and mind was confusion
And you tried the best that you can

I understand that you were hurting
And in need of comfort too
Confronting all your demons
Trying to make your way through
Looking at your family
And not knowing the right thing to do
Feeling disconnected from your woman
Left you lost and confused

Now I see the fullness of you
And deep inside there is a little boy too
Who was missing his own father's loves
And could only rely on the love from above

So I hold you and comfort you
As you should have done me
But grateful in the knowing that
It took me to see
That we are the creators
It's nobody's fault
We chose the experience
We opened the vault
And this is the purpose
And divine plan you see
Because as I release and clear
We both become free

I thank you Daddy and love you
For choosing me
To be the special person
To help you to see
How special you are
And how great life can be

When you push through the fear
And allow yourself to heal

I forgive you for all
That you did or didn't do
And I want you to know that I am here for you
Whenever you need me
As I have always been
I am happy and healthy
A mother and a Queen
And when you return
You'll see the legacy we created
And what you could have enjoyed
If you waited
So much would be different
So different from now
But all is perfect and harmonious now
So I hope this letter find you
Where ever you are
Love from your daughter
Goddess of the stars ☺

Nurturing the Seeds

Seed- 8 Understand Your Relationships

We learn about our self through the very many different relationships and interactions that we have with the various people and groups on our life journey. Equally is the nature of the relationship that we have with our self.

Time to Do the Work

Air – Know Your Mind

- ❖ - What are your thoughts about the relationships in your life.
- ❖ - Think of 5 of the most important people and relationships that you have in your life.
- ❖ - What are the 5 key memories that come to mind when you think about these relationships. Make notes and reflect

Earth – Know your Body

Our material relationships are also of great importance and we learn on understand our nature through our interaction with the things and world around us

- ❖ Take a moment to reflect on how you interact with the world around you? do you feel at home in nature? Do you spend time observing where you live? do you throw litter or are you respectful to your environment?
- ❖ How is your relationship with your body? Do you exercise regularly? do you speak lovingly to yourself?

- *Examine your relationship with money? Do you spend frivolously or are you frugal?*

Water – Know your Emotions

Our past relationships can weigh very heavy on our hearts and affect our moods and emotions

- *When you place your hands on your hearts and think about your relationships, what are the feelings that come to heart and with whom?*
- *Are there any relationships in your life which are painful or traumatic and in need of healing? Make a note as we will deal with this later in the section*
- *What do you like to feel in your relationships? what do a good relationship feel like? What does a bad relationship feel like?*
- *Make notes and review*

Fire - Know your Passion

Passion is a great energy fuel in our relationships. But when unbalanced it can also fuel lustful or explosive situation in our life.

- *Bring to your mind one of your most passionate relationships?*
- *What does passion feel like to you? what do you feel passionate about and why?*
- *Make a not in your Journal*

Spirit – Know Your Spirit

All relationships need work and energy to build up and connection and get the best out of the experience. The same is said for your connection with Spirit and your Higher Self.

- *Examine your spiritual relationship with yourself. When did your spiritual journey begin? What did it feel like? What were your thoughts?*
- *What have you learnt so far? Where are you now in your journey?*
- *Where do you want to go? What do you want to learn more of?*
- *Identify one way you can develop your connection to spirit further*
- *Journal and make notes*

Love – The Spirit of Love

Love is the active force within all relationships and all of creation. Love is so powerful that it can be misunderstood and transformed into the lower vibration of hate. But even hate can lead to healing, transformation and inner-standing, once self-reflection and a return back to the source of the intention is re-established.

- *Which relationships in your life have taught you about love?*
- *Who were these relationships with? Name each one and include:*
  - *What you experienced?*
  - *How you knew it was Love?*
  - *How it felt and what you learned*
  - *What does Love feel like to you?*
  - *Can you connect with the feeling and power of love now?*
  - *Make a note in your journal*

Star Seed Journey

Even our most painful relationships can hold powerful and transforming healing for us. During this journey through the Halls of Amenti and into your hearts secret chamber, you are going to learn how to heal and transform the pain of the past relationships and bring understanding and positive resolution in this moment that will have a great impact as you move forward.

in the section about, you were asked to identify a relationship in your life which still needed healing and resolution. Make a note of this relationship and set your intention to bring understanding and clarity.

Guided Meditation Journey

- *Find yourself a nice comfortable space where you will not be disturbed. Either lying down or sitting in a chair or on the floor*
- *As before, we will begin by taking a few deep cleansing breath and prepare to make our connection with the earth and the stars*
- *Ground yourself and connect to the Earth - drawing the light from the star above your head, down through your body and out through the roots of your feet into the Earth*
- *Set your intention now to take a journey connect with your higher self through the gateway to the halls of Amenti – Through the Heart*
- *Notice a Green ball of light energy at your heart chakra space*
- *As you breath, see yourself going into this bring green light and seeing yourself drawn into a tunnel of green light*
- *You see a mist before you and as the mist clears you see Anubis to your right holding the scale with the heart and the feather.*
- *Bring to your mind and consciousness, the person or relationship that needs to be healed*
- *Through your heart, Ask Anubis to show you how your heart measures against the feather on the scale in relation to this relationship or purpose*

- ❖ Make a note of the reading on the scale and any feeling within your body
- ❖ What need to be healed and re balanced in this relationship? what are you holding onto that needs to be released? Aske you Higher self to shed any light or wisdom
- ❖ What is the learning in this relationship? Listen to your Higher Self' guidance
- ❖ Remember that you can transform the energy of any thought or experience, past, present or future with the power of your intentions, consciousness and understanding
- ❖ What do you need to release now from this relationship? Can you do this now? Then see what needs to be released. Give it a name or a symbol and with the power of your sacred breath and love from your heart, blow and see how the person or situation is bathed in your love and how his love transforms the feeling and nature of the relationship
- ❖ Think of your relationship with the person now. What does it feel like?
- ❖ Notice Anubis again to your right with the scale and the feather.
- ❖ -Notice the new reading on the scale? how does your heart weigh against the feather? make a note and give thanks for the gift of healing and reflection.
- ❖ If you have any other relationships that need healing, you can bring them forth now are repeat the process again when needed.
- ❖ When complete, give thanks to all your guides and make you way back into the green tunnel of light within your heart.
- ❖ Take a moment to bring your consciousness back into your body
- ❖ Make a note of your experience and any learnings or nuggets of wisdom

Journal Page

Use this page to make any notes of your experience.

Golden Seeds of Wisdom

Relationships are the very nature of our experience here on this earthly realm. It is how we experience ourselves in connection and relation to all that we see, or don't see, and all that is.

We learn about Love and Hate and all the Vibration in between!

Our relationships can either take us to our highest points and keep us lifted or take us to our very depths and teach us our biggest lesson.

Whichever you are experiencing, just know that all is really you in relation to you!

When you understand the nature and intention of your relationships, as a vehicle of learning and growth, then you will find that you attract, only the best relationships, that inspire and empower you for growth and change.

To love and to be loved, that is the Blessing of Life.

Seed 9

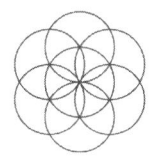

Connect

to

Source

Spiritual power is the eternal guide, in this life and the life after, for man ranks supreme among all creatures. Led forward by spiritual power, man can reach the summit destined for him by the Great Creator.

H.I.M Halie Selassie

SEED 9 – CONNECT WITH SOURCE AND SPIRIT

> *"We must stop confusing religion and spirituality. Religion is a set of rules, regulations and rituals created by humans, which was suppose to help people grow spiritually. Due to human imperfection religion has become corrupt, political, divisive and a tool for power struggle.*
>
> H.I.M Halie Selassie

It would be very difficult to further explain the importance of Spiritual Development and understanding, without first taking a moment to define or at least highlight the current state of being in our reality around Religion and spirituality.

There is no doubt that the belief in a higher power and authority, is something that not many can deny. From the beginning of time there has always been information of on religions, Higher beings, Inner and Extra terrestrials and all nature of things. Some information from the bible and some from other sources and scared texts including the Sumerian Tablets.

Many a war has been fought and blood shed, in the name of Religion and Supreme authority and yet still we, the masses, are walking around seeking a deeper meaning to this life of chaos and destruction in the name of Religion and of 'God'.

We have been pushed and pulled from pillar to post, whilst the rulers of our society, use the sacred texts and wisdom, to pull people into a false imprisonment based on improper application of Spiritual knowledge and wisdom, to the point where many of us are members of faiths, that we do not fully know how to operate within, in order to experience the real power of and connection to the Most High Creator.

There has been a deliberate deception and confusion, created by those who wish to control the masses through Religion. However, within each religion is a sacred truth, however obscured, that can help us to live our live in harmony and accordance with natural and divine law. And in this time of awakening and revelations, it is the responsibility of each individual to seek and find the truth within the scared scriptures and practices of religion, so that they may support us in creating a harmonious reality based on oneness and self awareness and mastery

Spirituality and Religion

"Due to human imperfection religion has become corrupt, political, and divisive and a tool for power struggle"

H.I.M Hailie Selassie

What is Religion?

Religion has been the root or foundation of spiritual doctrine and governance, that informs most of humanities ideas around what God is and what spirituality is.

The definition given in the Dictionary for the word 'Religion' is as follows:

Religion rɪˈlɪdʒ(ə)n/noun

- the belief in and worship of a superhuman controlling power, especially a personal God or gods.

"ideas about the relationship between science and religion"

And as we can see from the break down, Religion, it speaks of 'belief in something of a super human or controlling power." So in short Religion is about belief or worship, in an external and controlling super power.

This definition, to me echoes, some of the experiences that many of us have had and have been confused by, regarding our connection to religion or spirituality and the real function of religion.

From this description or definition, we are shown that Religion requires belief, but not self knowing and that you are required to externalise your power and worship something outside of yourself.

In the past Age of Pisces, we have experienced the age of separation and this has been the main thread of religion and spirituality as well. The past age was brought into consciousness, by the story of the birth and life of Jesus (Yeshua) and even our calendar, references his birth and death as the beginning of a cycle of time i.e. BC is before Christ and AD - is after this death.

This story became the foundation of our collective experience and expression of our identity. In Christianity, we were taught that we are sinners that have been born of sin and that Jesus Christ is the saviour that died for our sins. And we are told through our lives that we are still sinners and our purpose here, on this realm, is to atone for those sins and become 'clean'.

This ideology, takes us away from our power and even the message the Yeshua (Jesus) gave, when he stated that we would go on to do greater works than him and that we were exactly the same as him, not a sinner, but a child of The Most-High, and endowed with the same qualities and powers.

We were stripped of our connection to nature and elementals and magic and told that it was witchcraft and no longer allowed. we were encouraged to look to the church for all of the answers to our life experiences and made docile in the pursuit of our own knowledge of self and our true purpose of creation and intention.

The Feminine energy became separate from the masculine energy, and they no longer worked in harmony as they did in earlier ages. The image of ancient Egypt for instance, is that of Creation from the unit of Man and

Woman, which was depicted by Osiris and Auset, and Akhenaten and Nefertiti. They symbolized the previous golden age of Taurus, love beauty and progression.

In the Christian story we see the demise of the balanced and harmonious union of Mother and Father, equal in their standing and actions, and we are then given the story of the Virtuous Mother of Christ and the Harlot, Prostitute woman, that is Mary Magdalene.

These stories others demonstrated the ideal of separation on all levels.

Separation from Source, Separation from each other, Separation from the magic and wisdom of the heavens and then sentenced to sin and eternal damnation.

Even separation from each other, based on philosophy and/ or minute differences in belief, is something that has been common place in this last age.

Wars have been started in the name of Religion, that have devastated the world and humanity for times to come. Much blood has been shed, lives destroyed, fertile lands damaged and souls left shattered, in the name of Religion and we are no closer to living in the 'peace, harmony and balance' that theses 'so called' wars, were set to bring about.

We are not all free, we are not all living as the Most-High intended, in honour of us as the children of the creator and the custodians of all of the creation on Earth.

The discourse used within some religious texts or at least the effect that is imposed on the minds of the masses that we are here to pay for sin and not as we truly are, blessed Children of the Creator of All, here to learn more about ourselves and to experience the effects of those creations.

The Religions of the past age, all contain very simple truths at their core, which inform us on how to live with each other and in harmony with all of creation. The purpose and intention of religion, was supposed to be to assist us - humanity, in developing a framework of understanding of self in relation to the All and to help us to develop a connection with the creator within us and within everything.

To enrich us with the knowledge that would encourage us to know ourselves deeper. To understand the world that we live in and how it functions and maintains it balance.

What we should eat or not eat and how we should live cohesively amongst each other.

And this is the beauty that is hidden within the confines of religious organisations. Within the heart and at the core, the message is about love and unity and oneness, but along the way these messages and truths have been distorted by 'man' in his attempt to 'deify' himself and render all others to give power unto him.

Now although I share my view with regards to the purpose of religion and what it has done for humanity, I speak mainly from the perspective of the system of Religion and not the information shared within the scriptures and sacred texts.

Ancient wisdom has been filtered down to us all through the sacred scriptures and texts that form the Bible, the Kaballah and many of the world respected books of wisdom. This information, is there to ensure that those who seek, will find the answers and the truth, that facilitates and initiates, the path of Self discovery and Self learning.

When you dig deep into the bible and other sacred texts you will find the experiences of others, that are there to help us to see ourselves also and to navigate our way through life. all of the stories to some effect are based on human experiences and experiences of human engaging with the world of spirit and consciousness.

The parables, scriptures and other sacred texts, offer us opportunities to gain knowledge and wisdom and to think about life and challenge our perception of whatever it is we think or are going through.

They lay the foundation on how to live in accordance and harmony with the universe and also how to conduct one's self. it tells of the realms of the heavens and hells and the experiences of others so that we ca understand our own experience and become masters of our reality by understanding ourselves better.

Many of the original teachings have been hidden from the masses, so as to keep them disconnected from the source of their true power. we are not limited beings, here to be controlled or work till the end of our days.

May of the sacred books of the Bible, were taken out during the time of the Nicaea Creed, (which was instrumental in ensuring that Religion becomes a means of control and illusion) and other crucial times, to further separate humanity from the true knowledge of itself and capabilities, in favour of scriptures that instead encouraged the collective to give their power away to an external authority which it deemed more worthy than itself.

Book such as the book of Tobias, which speaks on magic and demonstrated the Most-High giving wisdom and rituals to people, to help heal and restore health and harmony.

There is a lot of sacred magic and ritual and alchemy within the sacred texts, however this information was kept from the masses so that they would not know their own power and would in fact give over their power to an external God or organisation. And ultimately so that we would not know how to use rituals and other means to assist ourselves and help ourselves to gain wisdom or healing.

We are here to know ourselves, to master ourself, to connect with other aspects of ourselves and to enjoy free will. and in this new age of Aquarius, the water bearer, we are seeing an outpouring of information and knowledge that will allow us to know who we truly are, release from the lies and illusion and step forward in our divinity and create a world of harmony and happiness. This new age brings with it, fresh energy and insight into who we are, the world and reality that we are living in and will challenge all that we thought that we knew. everything you need to know is inside you and we are being encouraged now to wake up and seek. Ignorance is bliss only to those who choose it.

We are now able to understand our selves more than ever before, to experience ourselves in our full potential and know ourselves beyond the limitation of our physical bodies and the imposed ideals.

Part of my purpose here, at this time, is to be a part of that shift and change and to help others to move through it as well. My perception of myself, is not limited to this 3D reality and neither is my awareness of myself and who I Am.

Each one of us have chose to come back at this time, as you know energy never dies, it transforms, and so we have returned to ourselves to undo what was done and to embody the truth of what and who we are.

There will be many pathways that you will travel on this journey of self discovery. There will be friends that will be lost and gained, wisdom that will be lost and gained and so much more in store that cannot yet be explained.

We are moving into a new perspective and seeing ourselves beyond the limitations of what was, to embody the freedom of what it. And for this stage of journey, is is spiritual wisdom and guidance that will assist you, and this will ultimately come from within.

In this time, we are encouraged to know ourselves deeper than we have ever done before and to heal on a deep level so as to release collectively from the experience of wisdom through suffering.

What is Spirituality?

Spiritualty is the Key to understanding yourself and maintain a connection with all things respective of all things and their creative intent and purpose.

When you look up the word Spirituality, there are many different meanings, which demonstrates that it is something that many find it difficult to define.

The Dictionary states the following:

Spirituality spɪrɪtʃʊˈalɪti, spɪrɪtjʊˈalɪti

noun

1. the quality of being concerned with the human spirit or soul as opposed to material or physical things.

Other definitions include:

- the "deepest values and meanings by which people live, incorporating personal growth or transformation

- Christina Puchalski, MD, Director of the George

Washington Institute for Spirituality and Health, contends that "spirituality is the aspect of humanity that refers to the way individuals seek and express meaning and purpose and the way they experience their connectedness to the moment, to self, to others, to nature, and to the significant or sacred."

Hailie Selassie speaks on Spirituality and states that:

> *"Spirituality is not theology or ideology. It is simply a way of life, pure and original as was given by the Most High of Creation. Spirituality is a network linking us to the Most High, the universe."*

In this way, Selassie demonstrates that, simply put, Spirituality is a way of life and in facts informs all life. it is ingrained in our culture and our ideals, the way we live and how we treat each other. It goes beyond separation or domination, but provides the governance and moral compass that, we should live by, as given by The Most-High Creator.

Spirituality, to me, is the practice of consciousness and awareness about your connection to Spirit and all things. Spirituality is the practical application and development of spiritual wisdom and knowledge. It is about seeking a meaningful connection with something bigger than yourself and learning to master your self in relations to all.

Spirituality is the practice of understanding yourself and the Creator and can provide you with the tools to bring more meaning and balance into your life.

It is not so much about the doctrines and the dogma, as much as it is about helping you to understand your connection to all things and the power within us. It informs us of our responsibilities as custodians of this planet and also as single sparks of divinity.

Spirituality informs all aspects of our reality, which is why the church is at the heart and epicenter of the global and local community. However, the separations that have been caused through religion, have caused confusion and separation not only in thought and doctrine, but also in terms of our connection to each other.

Spirituality should not separate anyone from each other Hailie Selassie says that, "No one should question the faith of others, for no human being can judge the ways of God", for the spiritual journey is a personal one and if you can find those along the way that share the same values as you, then you can walk the path together.

Ultimately, each man's faith is his own; his journey is his own and his truth is his own.

We must honor the God within each other and the truth within, to fully over stand the fullness of the Most High and our connection to all, and respect and know that each one of us, as a unique expression of Source, has a part of the story to share.

Spirituality is a personal journey and expression, but one in which we are all free to understand who we are and embody that knowing and that being into our lives.

It is not just about the acquiring of spiritual knowledge and wisdom, it is also about the application of such knowledge and wisdom, that brings about change.

We are in the midst of change and spirituality is the tool that will allow us to shift from the illusion of being a victim and bring without, to the positions of Living embodiments of Source, knowing exactly who we are and able to manifest our truth

> *If you are open-minded and ready to learn, there are many things which you can learn not only from books and instructors but form the very life experience itself.*
>
> H.I.M Haile Selassie

Why is it important to develop Spiritual Practice?

The Law of Relativity demonstrates that in life, we will go through various testes and events, that assist us in learning more about ourselves, clearing past karma or energy and evolving in our consciousness.

During these moments in our life, when we feel as though we are being challenged, we are actually being challenged and encouraged to see the power within and learn the virtue needed to work within a co-creative reality.

Without these challenges in our lives, we would not have the opportunities to see what we are made of and to build our spiritual power and wisdom.

When we are tested, through life's challenges, we are really being encouraged to see and experience the power within and development tools of self mastery, that help you to navigate your way through the growth and self- awareness that is the journey of life. Without the challenges, the opportunities for growth, and sometimes traumatic moments we would not be able to develop Spiritual Power.

Discipline of the mind is a basic ingredient of genuine morality and therefore of spiritual strength. Spiritual power is the eternal guide, in this life and the life after, for man ranks supreme among all creatures. Led forward by spiritual power, man can reach the summit destined for him by the Great Creator.

H.I.M Haiie Selassie

My Journey with Spirit

Spirituality has always been an integral part of my life and my journey.

I have always known myself to be a Spirit having a human experience. I was always aware of a deeper meaning to life and connected with the omnipotent force and Love of the Most High that is expressed in everyone and everything. I knew Source/God personally, intimately and deeply, in fact I felt more connected to source than I did to anything in this world, and that connect never strayed from me.

I knew that I was invisible and Divine, an expression and spark of the same great power that created me, but as I grew and experienced more of what life here had to offer, I started o question myself and who I was, and it was my spiritual development and practice, that supported me in returning back to that stage of knowing, connection and innocence of a Child of God, or Source, with power and potential to do anything and everything that I wanted to be. It offered me the tools to unlock the hidden parts of me consciously and with intent, and helped me to assist both myself and others to get through some of life' most challenging lessons.

As a child, I was naturally intuitive and had a deep love and appreciation for my spiritual gifts and ability to see life from its highest vibration, with innocent curious eyes. I loved to talk, sometime to much; I loved to read and write, You would never see me without a pile of books that liked to read and hoard and my favourite shop was the book shop and stationary shop.

I loved Science and Fantasy, I loved to make and create things and I love loved loved….to Sing. You would never see me without a pile of books that liked to read and hoard and my favourite shop was the book shop and stationary shop.

My spiritual gifts were awakened very early in my life. I was able to read peoples energy and receive private and personal information about them and as guidance and wisdom that could support them to heal whatever needed to be healed or reach any goals that they had set themselves. One of my spiritual gifts is Clairsentience – which means direct knowing or to just know. And I am able access information from past lives present lives and remember far back into time. I remember after a while, people would pick my brains as a child and ask me questions to either test me or obtains and tips or words of wisdom that could be of any benefit. I enjoyed testing myself and being that I loved information, I enjoyed learning about others through the 'readings'

I could see energy in colours, and would see the auras of others as well. I also remember when I first saw an argument between two people, and how the red shards of energy flew between the two. It was quite scary at first, but once I realized what was happening, I thought that if people could really see how their energy looks when they are doing things like arguing or getting angry, they wouldn't do it!

I could see spirits and other energy forms and receive information on healing and natural remedies from Spirit and from my guides, one of which is my great grandmother whom I had never met in this life. Throughout my life, more of my spiritual gifts and talents surfaced and progressed and I also learned to become more open and empowered by my choice to be myself and embody my spiritual self unapologetically.

I went through lot of experiences early on in life, that contributed to me manifesting an shattered and at times disconnected, personality. At times I felt like I didn't know who I was as a human. My ability to see the highest good In even the most traumatic situations, left me feeling deeply spiritually connected, but very disconnected physically to myself, my family, my environment, my experience and my reality.

My natural instinct was to serve and to but others before myself because I felt that I had a responsibility because I was able to see what others couldn't see, to guide and support and see things from the higher perspective, even at times to detriment to my own happiness and development. (This was the martyr complex that I needed to heal on a soul level and one of the lessons that I had chosen to come here at this time and learn).

I learnt early on that most people couldn't deal with the truth, in fact they would do anything to avoid it. When I let my elders know that I was being abused, I was coming from a place of knowing what was wrong and right and was confident that my family would have my back and support me. Children naturally have this nature about them, but as they grow and develop, people around them and circumstances they experience, slowly kill this natural connection to truth and what is. When I saw the elder I was speaking to exclaim that it can't be true and that I was a liar, and when I saw the dread and terror in their face and the complete denial of the truth, I realized that sometimes, the truth is too hard to take and at that moment I learned that Spirit was all that I had, as people were still asleep to truth and only wanted to hear what was safe. They wanted to stay asleep.

I developed a habit of always wanting to protect others from painful things and from the truth, which I now know was more about me wanted to be or feel protected when I spoke me own truth, but at that time I didn't yet understand that and fell into a habit of using my time, energy and love to serve others and not focus so much on myself or my own pain. I soon felt detached and outside of life.

I developed self-esteem issues and over the years manifested the same lessons and experiences for myself that would keep me locked in the prison that I had created for myself in the disillusion of my own lack of self-worth and love. I manifested relationships with people that either needed healing or saving when really the person who needed saving was me. I went from being really happy, to feeling really depressed and I attempted suicide a few times in my life and developed an eating disorder when I was young and as I grew It got harder to hide the contrast between who and what I was outside and to the world and what I was inside.

I because desperate and deeply yearned to reconnect with myself, my true happy self. The me that is both human and spirit and is happy serving others and happy serving herself. I wanted to know who that was and where she was, so I and she could be whole and one again.

I had gone to see a few counsellors when I when I was in my late teens- early twenties and even tried to admit myself into a mental health centre at my lowest point. But they always seemed to want to applaud me for how well I had coped with my experiences because I was able to articulate the experience and expressed the higher lessons involved and offered forgiveness and rationality.

They didn't understand nor did they have to 'vision' to see beyond the exterior and the conditioned mind and help me to join the pieces of myself back together again.

I knew that the only way that I knew how to understand myself was through spirit and asked Source to show me a way to reconnect with my body, my story, and heal myself, through a medium that is natural and supportive to me and who I AM.

It was through my spiritual was through reclaiming and understanding my spiritual nature and gifts, that I was able to fully understand all parts of myself and make peace with my story and find the power from my painful experiences

In order to make my journey back to self, I had to be guided by my spirit, but I didn't where to start.

I needed to find a way of creating stillness in my mind and restoring peace and knowing in my heart. I needed to learn how to understand and harmonise my emotions, to feel more grounded and connected to my body and Earth and to consciously use and master my spiritual gifts in a way that was structured and balanced so that I didn't leave myself open, unbalanced and drained.

My family were not very religious or followers of any sort of spiritual order or practice and although my mother would share stories with me about what Great grandmother used to share with her, and other little remedies and guidance that was passed on, there was nothing solid that I could use to get me started.

Outside of the traditional religions, it can be hard to know which path to take in order to find healing, connection, practice and community that is right for you.

You may be drawn to a particular faith or religious group, on a search to a spiritual teacher or learn more and connect with those who use the spiritual and healing arts. Whatever it is, make sure that you follow your spirit and go with what feels right for You.

Do not follow the crowd, although if something inspires you in another then by all means follow through, but ensure its from your soul's choice and not something you are just going along with as you will end up wasting time and maybe even moulding yourself into someone you don't know of like and maybe even end up feeling more damaged than you were at the start.

Follow your heart and your spirit, your spiritual journey and developing your connection with your spirit as a human in your soul purpose for being here.

Remember ultimately it's your journey, your life, you experience and your spirit.

Understanding Spiritual Power and Spiritual Practice

Spiritual Power comes from knowing yourself and your part on the story of Life. We are Spirit, having a human experience and therefore We, as with everything in Nature has an innate power that connects them to all things and empowers their consciousness.

In our most natural state of being and consciousness, we know that there is no separation between Us and God. We know how to connect with this energy, we know how to recognise it in another and we know when we experience the power of this connection. But for the best part of our experience, this has been a unconscious connection, one that we have innately, but feel we need to develop and master as we move through life.

The truth is that we already know the source and Most High, we know how to pray how to connect and how to embody, we know what is expected of us, what feels good and what doesn't, but through this journey through life we go through an ignorance and unknowing, so that we can then become conscious of the connection that we have and that which we are, and how it is all connected in the fabric of life.

We go through the conditioning of our mind, to not believe in our innate powers, to think that God or Source dwells in churches and religious doctrines. And we are taught from a very young age, to look out side of ourself for 'God' or Divine Power.

Many people come to me asking me, how to pray or how to meditate, or how to develop a connection with the Most High and cultivate their spiritual power.

And the first thing I say to them is, " You are already Connected. you already know how to pray and you are already aware of your spiritual power, its just that it needs to be developed and cultivated.

We each have an innate moral compass. This can however be affected and manipulated as we make our journey through this life, based on our soul lessons and the reality we are exposed to. Society has a apart to play in how we create our standards and understanding of the world and up until now, religion has had a part to play in how we understand ourselves as Spirit and Human, but many are left feeling as if they do not know God and have to go through years of study tin order to connect with that which you already are.

When people ask me about how to pray, I simply say to them, you already know how!

When you are faced with an obstacle, whether out of your making or not, and you get to that point when you feel like you have done all you need to do, you ask The Most High for guidance. you take a breath, you go into your heart and you speak and ask for what you want, with the pureness and innocence of a child who seeks the help and guidance of their father, in the knowing that when all else fails, that he will not let you down.

This is how you pray, from the the honesty and purity of your heart, your prayer is your truth and your truth is your power.

When you are stressed and things are getting to much for you, you take a moment and you sit, the first thing that you do is to take a breath and your body starts to relax, you feel a stillness, your heart beats in your chest and for a moment you are still.

In this moment you are centred and connected to the Most High or the Divine One Within. You are one with all there is.

There is silence, even though you may feel your heart beating and become aware of your breath, in this, moment you are connected to the creator and to all things. This is where stillness lives and silence speaks, this is the peace that can only be attained by sitting still and releasing sacred breath.

Many of us do not understand the simplicity of spiritual practice. The intention is paramount and from this all else follows.

In this New Age, where spirituality is for sale, people can make money out of the confusions of others, as many of us are waking up from control and suppression from our external reality. but we are also waking up to the power within us and the innate ability to overcome all that we experience, externally in the knowing that all is connected and in truth, our reality, is a co-creation between us all, as we blindly give our power to things outside of ourselves, while negating and even being in fear of, the infinite power that lies within.

In this very sacred and special time on the planet, we are returning to our divinity and waking up to who we are and our true purpose, power and connection to all things.

We are understanding that the destruction in our world is down to our ignorance and that we have forgotten the value and sacredness of life. Its is so very important that each one of us, opens our eyes to what is taking place around us and develop the wisdom and spiritual power within to make positive changes in our reality for the better and for the collective, the whole.

In our slumber, we have forgotten who we are and our responsibility to each other and our innate power as co-creators of this realm. But this is the time of Revelation and remembering, that has been written of in the scriptures and we are the ones who must open our eyes to the truth of who we really are, so that we can once again experience more of the power within us and master our power as souls and spirt having a human experience, in order to know ourselves.

There is no complicated way to connect with Source, you are already connected. All you need to do is trust your inner guidance and be what you need. if you need stillness be still. if you need guidance, ask and then wait to receive. if you want to pray, then pray from the truth and simplicity of your heart. Pray in your own voice. Pray openheartedly in the knowing that your prayers will be answered in line with the highest good and trust that who you are, and what you do and how you do it, will be right for you.

You already know the Most High because you are connected to The Most High and the Most High Dwells within you.

Spirituality, is the gift that offers us the opportunity to make the transition through this great awakening, where, for the first time in a while, we the people, are waking up to who we truly are and our power.

Many scriptures and sacred texts have spoken about this time and have also left information to help us to prepare for the shift in consciousness that we are currently moving through. Spirituality is the tool that will help us to navigate through this change and to be consciousness of its intention and purpose.

Through Spirituality and Spiritual Practice, we understand the nature of all and also acquire the skills to become one with the all. Through mediation we can learn to centre and ground and benefit from the inner voice within that knows all things.

Through Sacred Ritual and Spiritual Alchemy, we can learn about the various dimensions of consciousness and how we interact with them. We learn the importance of the elements and the unseen world. About the spirits, elementals, Ancestors and another energy life forms which exist and how to develop a connection to them.

Through practices such as Yoga, Body work and the information available about our Food, Health and Nutrition and the way that we eat, we begin to understand the true nature of our body, how to keep in in optimal health and how to get the best from it so that it can last us through our life.

Reading sacred texts and pondering on their truths and meanings, helps us to know that, even those before us, encountered and experienced things, visions and connections which at the time they couldn't understand, but now brings so much meaning to us in this present time. And from the wisdom left by the Ancients, we can navigate our way back to spiritual integrity and greatness and once again, have access to the power and potentials that was prevalent in other civilisations such as the Ancient Egyptians and the Sumerians.

Our world is in a state of change, and this change will be for the better of our collective reality. A world in which we are all the Masters of our Reality and work in harmony and respect for each other. We have to learn, once more, how to love each other, how to master our emotions and our energy, to master our mind, to learn to see things, from a higher perspective and to care about each other again.

For this world is a world for all of us to share and at present the destruction that has been caused through glorification of the self and the lower virtues or sins, has made it so that this world has become a world of Fear, Separation, Greed and Division.

The Age of Aquarius, is the age of information and the Age of Unity, Oneness and Wholeness. No more can we say that we 'didn't know' for all the information is there for those who seek. And we can no longer stand by whilst others are being faced with injustice, as we all know too well, the disposable nature of life at present.

But in the midst of this uprising and change, we also have the opportunity to remember who we are, our connection to all things and each other, and our God Given right to live abundantly, happy and free. Spirituality is a tool that will help us to experience who we truly are and a vehicle for change not only for the world but for each individual.

> *We must become bigger than we have been: more courageous, greater in spirit, larger in outlook. We must become members of a new race, overcoming petty prejudice, owing our ultimate allegiance not to nations but to our fellow men within the human community.*
>
> H.I.M **Haile Selassie**

Understanding your Spiritual Power

Spiritual Power is the energy that is generated through Spiritual practice and development. Is the faith and knowing that comes form having your prayers answered and knowing how the universe works, which there fore allows you to be calm collected and conscious.

Spiritual power is very much connected to our emotions, faith and our experience of having our prayers answered or feeling the tangibility of the protection, guidance and present of Source, the Most High.

It is the strength gained from having been through the 'fires', and making your way out, guided by a higher power or force. Whenever we go through a situation in life we have a choice to either be benign to it or become proactive.

When we are benign, we fall into the victim-victimiser blame game, and look at life's experiences or challenges from the perspective of " Why is this happening to me?'. When we are conscious that everything in our life happens as a direct result of us, we instead ask ourselves, "What is it that my Soul/ Self, is trying to teach me here?"

It offers a way for you to be empowered by the challenge, rather than to be in fear of it, which will then render you feeling, "Hopeless" and Helpless' and incapable of finding the way through.

But when we pray, or meditate or even facilitate an oracle reading for ourselves, we are tapping into the truth within all, we are tapping into the wisdom that is available to us, and we find a way. Whether it be from the voice within that tells you, "You can go this" or the voice that says " be still" or " there's another way", in theses moments we develop a way to connect with the highest part of ourselves and we find that strength, that guidance, that power, to know that whatever we are facing, we will overcome and not only that, that we will be better for it on the other side.

When we are in despair and we pray, or when we take moments of stillness, or work on our anger and transforming it into love, when we dance, when we sing with joy, we are cultivating our Spiritual Power.

Many people, whether they believe in god or not, are aware of a higher force or power that governs all. And we know that this power is the sustainer of all things. we know that when in need, we can tap into this power. but the practices of spirituality will assist you in accessing and connecting with that power, consciously.

Spiritual Power is an invisible force, abundant in nature, allowing for the betterment of all.

It is tangible, active an easily invoked through, sound, intentions, thoughts, acts of kindness and developed unconsciously through adversity and the study of life and consciously through the application of spiritual practices that help to develop and strengthen our Spiritual Power and connection.

When we master ourselves and our spiritual power, we will go on to create great feats of magic and marvel. It says in the the Bible that with Faith the size of a mustard seed, we can move mountains, and this is so true. We have to develop this faith and trust and knowing. We have to develop our connection to the creator and all things and we have to learn to cultivate our own Spiritual Power and wisdom so that we can fully over stand our purpose on this planet and the true gift of Divinity that is within us and at our disposal.

The importance of Spiritual Development

It is said that when the student is ready, the master will appear, and this very true.

Within you is the Master and the Student, and once you start to ask yourself the right questions and genuinely want to know more of who you are and help yourself, then the external master will appear. The right people, or person, environment and 'teacher' will manifest for you and the path on the journey back to self begins to clear.

I was guided to many different workshops and courses, 'Master teachers', Readers and Healers on my way and then trained in various healing modalities not because I wanted to become a Healer, but because I wanted to heal myself. I wanted to feel whole.

I already knew that I could heal others, that for me was like breathing and natural. but what I really needed now was to heal myself.

I wanted to feel the same thing that people felt from me. It was all about me.

I was drawn to a variety of different healing and spiritual development modalities ranging from the 'traditional and commercial' to cultural and even more advanced. From Past Life Regression and Hypnotherapy, Wellness coaching, Shamanic Healing, Working with Crystal, Ancestral Healing, Ritual Magic, Spiritual Coaching and Mentoring, to Reiki and Holistic Massage. And every single one was vital in heling me to uncover and heal the different aspects my fragmented being.

I remembered who I was, I healed my emotional pain and trauma, I learned to reprogram my mind and get deeper into my body. And although it is a continuous process of healing, growth and development, I am thankful that I was guided to heal in this way because it allowed me to truly be and find myself.

I collected a lot of tools along the way that over time form a very faithful spiritual tool kit of goodies to keep me topped up and tuned in! If I need guidance I can do a meditation or if my mind is to frazzled I can do some Reiki and ground my energy. If I want some guidance or another point of view, I will consult my cards, if I need to talk to someone and no one is around I consult my journal and release and share my deepest feels and restore my inner peace. And if I'm feeling under the weather, I will make a remedy for myself.

My Spirituality is an integral part of my personality and who I Am. I and Spirit having a human experience and so I need to develop a method of spiritual practice and personal development that will help me to understand my life from a human perspective and use my spiritual perspective to master my life lessons and my reality. They both go hand in hand, and it was in the understanding of that that I am able to find balance and harmony between my one fragmented selves. Now I Am whole, and even though this has always been true, Now I Know and can bring myself back from anything that life or I, throw at me.

Connection with Your Ancestral and Spiritual Guides

As I mentioned earlier, my Great grandmother is my Spirit guide and was my first guardian in spirit who I knew was real and had manifested as a life before, she was in fact the 'Creator' and giver of life for my family lineage.

I remember when she first appeared. I was sleeping at my Grans house one weekend in a room full of cousins sleeping on top of each other, all legs and bodies everywhere. I had had a dream that night and had woken up in the middle of the night, so when I opened my eyes the room was dark. But in the corner, on the wall next to me, the light from the outside street light, shone into the room, through a small window that was open.

It shone right on a picture that hung on the wall of a woman with a strong build, and a proud but loving manner. She was wearing a blue dress with her handbag hanging gracefully off her and white gloves on her hands. I looked and the picture and stared into it, feeling all the energy of this great woman and Ancestor for my family beaming out at me and pouring into me and I was filled with same pride and loving energy that she displayed in the picture. I instantly felt my heart open and this warm feeling take over me. I looked back up at the picture and I saw her eyes wink at me in the picture, I froze, mouth open wide! And then I heard a voice say "its ok, don't be afraid. Now close your mouth ad go to bed. I am with you!"

And ever since that day she has always been with me, guiding me, protecting me, giving me advice and guidance and remedies to help those who come to be and being a light and mentor for me in spirit.

Anytime I have a reading, people always pick up on her. And in one reading in particular I was shown why she came to be with me and how she fought for me to be born and be here, so I truly love and appreciate her and know her deeply as if I had lived a life with her, even now as I write, I feel her in my heart and right here with me, smiling and letting me know all is well. I feel blessed to have such a deep connection with her and I'm sure she feels the same.

Over the years as my spiritual practice and passion developed, I learned how to connect spiritually with your Ancestors. How to create an Ancestor Altar in your home to interact with and nurture your Ancestors.

For a lot of my training in African and Caribbean Spirituality and Ritual, I had to learn to develop and deeper connection with my Ancestors, as they were the one who were my eyes and ears in spirit and could protect and advise me as I facilitated work through the crossroads of the two worlds of the visible and the invisible.

I learnt their likes and dislikes, I learned that some Ancestors didn't like to be placed next others, how to call them and the importance of feeding them and ensuring they depart safely after being called. But besides all this. It gifted me with a now rich understanding and connection with those family members who came before. I had to ask questions about them, gather pictures and information and just through the act of gathering the tools to create my ancestor altar, I head long forgotten stories and reawakened the memory of them within the minds and hearts of the family who still remain in the flesh.

To build and maintain a spiritual connection with Ancestors can be a very powerful and beneficial thing not only for you but for your whole family, those in spirit and in the flesh. And more than anything it gives you a rich understanding of who you are as part of a collective family and remind you of the thin line between the living and the dead, and the reality of everlasting life in its various forms.

Our Ancestors hold so much love wisdom and power for us. And when we maintain a connection with them, and hold them closely to our hearts, they can be a guiding light and source of deep support and love on this journey through life.

Connecting with Your Higher Self

The 'Higher Self' is who we truly are beyond our individual incarnation on Earth and can be thought of as the immortal 'I" the everlasting part of us. It holds all of the knowledge, lessons and experiences of all our physical experiences, past present and future and is therefore also the wise part of us all. When we descend I consciousness and manifest on this realm it is the highest self that remains connected to source and we to source through it. All aspects of our self are one, but as sentient beings we vibrate at different frequencies at different times and have to vibrate at considerably lower vibrations that that of the realms that house or higher selves, to have this physical experience here on Earth.

The Higher self can provide intuition, insight and information that can assist you in circumstances in your life where you may need clarification and guidance. It provides the highest level of perception available to you and works closely with source to influence the Universe in all aspects.

Learning how to communicate consciously with you higher self is a very valuable tool on this journey through life and awaken you to the latent power and truth within that is you and an invaluable source of wisdom and support.

Understanding your Spiritual Power

Spiritual Power is the energy that is generated through Spiritual practice and development. Is the faith and knowing that comes form having your prayers answered and knowing how the universe works, which there fore allows you to be calm collected and conscious.

Spiritual power is very much connected to our emotions, faith and our experience of having our prayers answered or feeling the tangibility of the protection, guidance and present of Source, the Most High.

It is the strength gained from having been through the 'fires', and making your way out, guided by a higher power or force. Whenever we go through a situation in life we have a choice to either be benign to it or become proactive.

When we are benign, we fall into the victim-victimiser blame game, and look at life's experiences or challenges from the perspective of "Why is this happening to me?' which is part of the Victim- Victimiser mindset.

When we are conscious that everything in our life happens as a direct result of us, we instead ask ourselves, "What is it that my Soul/ Self, is trying to teach me here?"

It offers a way for you to be empowered by the challenge, rather than to be in fear of it, which will then render you feeling, "Hopeless" and Helpless' and incapable of finding the way through.

But when we pray, or meditate or even facilitate an oracle reading for ourselves, we are tapping into the truth within all, we are tapping into the wisdom that is available to us, and we find a way. Whether it be from the voice within that tells you, "You can go this" or the voice that says " be still" or " there's another way", in theses moments we develop a way to connect with the highest part of ourselves and we find that strength, that guidance, that power, to know that whatever we are facing, we will overcome and not only that, that we will be better for it on the other side.

When we are in despair and we pray, or when we take moments of stillness, or work on our anger and transforming it into love, when we dance, when we sing with joy, we are cultivating our Spiritual Power.

Many people, whether they believe in god or not, are aware of a higher force or power that governs all. And we know that this power is the sustainer of all things. we know that when in need, we can tap into this power. but the practices of spirituality will assist you in accessing and connecting with that power, consciously.

Spiritual Power is an invisible force, abundant in nature, allowing for the betterment of all.

It is tangible, active an easily invoked through, sound, intentions, thoughts, acts of kindness and developed unconsciously through adversity and the study of life and consciously through the application of spiritual practices that help to develop and strengthen our Spiritual Power and connection.

When we master ourselves and our spiritual power, we will go on to create great feats of magic and marvel. It says in the the Bible that with Faith the size of a mustard seed, we can move mountains, and this is so true. We have to develop this faith and trust and knowing. We have to develop our connection to the creator and all things and we have to learn to cultivate our own Spiritual Power and wisdom so that we can fully over stand our purpose on this planet and the true gift of Divinity that is within us and at our disposal.

How to cultivate Spiritual Power

There are many practices or tools that you can use to help you to cultivate your Spiritual power and develop a deeper connection to all things and yourself. it is a life long journey, in which you will have many experiences and find many tools along the way. There will be many teachers that will cross your path, and knowing that you are the master of your own journey will; assist you greatly.

Also know that as much as others may share and teach you what they know, always trust in the truth that is revealed within your self. develop a deep connection between you and the Divine One Within.

Your faith, your Love, your trust, your joy, your happiness, your confusion, your anger....are all tools of expression and generators of power. Are you cultivating them consciously? are you aware of your feeling and emotions?

Your belief and emotional connection to whatever you want to create in paramount in the successful manifestation of your desires. If you cannot feel what it is you intend then it is unlikely to manifest.

You are the power behind your manifestations and so therefore it is of the utmost importance that you understand this truth. For the knowing of this truth helps you to know that when you are praying or affirming or manifesting, you are doing so from the source of power that is within you. and you must cultivate this power and this truth and send it out into the universe and then it will manifest and be so.

You must learn to listen to your inner voice. And not to deny your inner power. Be humble in the knowing of thyself, but strong in the knowing of thy innate God given power.

Seek to Master this power and become One with it.

Your intuition and your inner voice is your guide and divine compass. Cultivate a healthy relationship with yourself and you will have access to all the wisdom that you need.

There will be many paths to your enlightenment and it is all about the journey, rather than the destination, so allow yourself to grow into what you already know.

Below are a few tools that I have used which have supported me along my journey of self discovery and self-mastery. It is in no way exclusive but I hope it will get you started onto developing your own spiritual practice and routine, to help deepen your connection to your self and cultivate your spiritual power.

Meditation

Meditation is a great spiritual development tool, as it allows you to experience the ability to be able to consciously shift in consciousness and invoke a certain energy or thought, for deeper reflection and understanding.

Meditation is the first step in developing a connection with yourself and preparing your body and mind to move out of the unconscious experience and into one of consciousness and self mastery.

It introduces you to the stillness within, so that you can meet yourself. connect with yourself and hear yourself.

According to the Cambridge Dictionary, the word Meditation means:

Meditation noun UK /ˌmed.ɪˈteɪ.ʃən/ US /ˌmed.əˈteɪ.ʃən/

1. the act of giving your attention to only one thing, either as a religious activity or as a way of becoming calm and relaxed:

2. serious thought or study, or the product of this activity

Meditation is the act of 'Listening to Spirit'. Stillness speaks wisdom. And in a reality where we are always bombarded with noise, opinions, thoughts etc, Mediation allows us to learn how to cut through the external haze and connect with our own truth and hear the voice of the Divine and ourself.

Meditation is another thing that people say that they find it hard to do. and to be honest, I can see why. But this can be properly remedied when you take a moment to understand how your body and your mind works, then you will know how to understand the process that it takes to gain mastery over your mind.

Even when we say " master your mind', it conjures up a thought that you literally have to battle with your mind to find peace and stillness and this couldn't be farther from the truth.

In fact, the best way to Meditate is to just be still.

For many people, even the simplicity of this instruction, may instil confusion or inadequacy, but this is because we over complicate things. We in truth already know how to mediate, and when we look at how our mind works and the reality we are living in, we can understand even further what the obstacle may be, and so we then know what to look out for and how to move forward towards mastering this skill.

The mind has 3 layers, the Conscious Mind, the Unconscious mind and The Super conscious mind.

The conscious mind is always taking in information, but can only take in so much information at a time. Any further information that the conscious mind is not able to take in, is then recorded by the subconscious mind, to be played back at later date.

When we close our eyes, take a rest, or sleep, the information that has been held in the sub conscious mind starts to offload, or download the information that you received during the day, but were not able to take in via the conscious mind.

This is why, when you got to sit down to meditate, although your intention is to connect with the inner peace and stillness within, you are instead met with a flurry of information coming in from your subconscious mind, which distracts you from your peace.

But when you know that this is what will take place naturally, because you understand how your mind works and take in information, you realise that if you wait and allow all of this information to flow and pass, it will eventually stop, and you will find yourself in peace, inner peace.

Most of the time, we do not wait until the distraction fades and the mind quietens, because we create further anxiety in our inability to find the peace and stillness within.

However, though conscious application of this knowledge, and regular practice, you will find that it becomes so much easier to find the stillness within and this becomes the space in which you learn to expand and contract and tangibly experience shifting of consciousness.

Meditation is the gateway to experiencing all of who you are and what the universe has to offer. Astra travel and projection, and so much more, can be experienced through meditation.

It is not as hard as you think. Meditation means to focus and become one with your experience. Through meditation you learnt to master of your own reality from within and it is a powerful tool on journey of Self mastery and Development.

Prayer

Prayer is the act of communication with a higher power. If Meditation is about 'listening to God', then Prayer is about 'Speaking with God'.

Prayer is one of the oldest forms of spiritual connection and cultivation of spiritual power. Even if we are not connected to any faith or religion, we all at some time in our life have had the desire to pray and speak to the higher force that governs all things, for guidance, support, wisdom and assistance.

Prayers can come in many forms, they can be based on Words or sacred verses that have been written down in sacred texts and scriptures. These prayers are seen as words of power, as they have been used by many to communicate with the Most High for centuries.

Other types of prayers include, prayers written by others or special incantations that are part of a particular faith and religion.

But the Most powerful prayers are the ones that come in your own voice and with your own emotional connection and your own power.

Prayer is another thing, that many people who come to me, say they do not know how to do. and it is as if, there is some specific way to pray, that the general masses are not privy to.

Prayer is a simple dialogue between you and the Creator, the same as you would speak to your mother or father is the same way in which you communicate with Creator. Trust that you already know how to do this. in fact, you already do. Even as a child, you knew how to pray. You just speak with truth, knowing and reverence in your heart and know that your voice will be heard.

Prayers are a great way to help you cultivate Spiritual Power and wisdom and also support you in knowing that there is always a way or higher learning within each experience.

Affirmations

Affirmations are statements of intent, which are spoken and repeated to bring about the manifestation of the intention of to activate a shift in consciousness and self awareness. In the beginning there was sound, and sound is one of the most powerful forces of creation in the Universe.

When we combine words, with intention and emotion, then we have the perfect recipe for powerful manifestation and creation. Sound crystallises though and intentions, so any time you think something and then you say it, you are crystallising the intention and setting it forth in motion to manifest into reality. What you manifest and whether it manifests at all, is down to your belief in that which you want and also your belief in your ability to have it and see it manifest.

So many people who work with affirmation, find that they fail or can be slow in bringing about the change that is requested. but the secret to this is knowing the power within your emotions and how they affect your manifestation.

If you are asking for something, that you do not believe that you can have, then the reality is, that it is unlikely that it will manifest. This is because your energetic resonance has to match the vibration of that which you wish to manifest.

You have to believe that you can have what you are requesting. you have to know that you are not asking for something outside of yourself, or begging for assistance, you have to know that you are creating and magnetising what you want to you, with your word, sound and power.

The same in experienced, when you want to manifest something but do not believe that you can. In a way you drive your intention even further away from you with your doubt. Either way, the ability to attract and repel that which you require, is yours and successful manifestation comes from the application of the knowledge that you are the creator and can manifest whatever it is you want to you.

As long as you are able to match the vibration and frequency of that which you wish to create or manifest.

Once you realise this truth, that you already have the power to attract or repel, that which you desire, then you can master this process and bring real change to your life.

You may have to' fake it till you make it' and consciously generate the emotions and visualisations of what it would be like to have what you desire, but this will also be a useful tool in helping you to understand how you transform energy with your thoughts and emotions, and therefore can embody this knowing even if you have not yet seen the success of your intentions.

Affirmations are a great way or stating your intentions and cultivating spiritual energy to empower your intentions. And chanting is also a great way of cultivating spiritual power and matching the vibration of your intentions

Developing your intuition

Your intuition is your inner voice and your greatest gift.

You already know everything that you need to know, you are just here to experience and embody that knowing. Your inner voice is that part of you that knows all things.

It is the part of you that remembers exactly why you are are here, what you are here for and all you need to know along the way.

It is the God within and the moral compass. The good voice that encourages you and the voice that lets you know when you are doing something out of alignment with personal integrity and purpose.

The Ego and The inner voice are the 2 voices (truly one voice) that dwells within and assist us in discerning and learning and navigating this reality. The Ego's voice is loud and personal and the Inner Voice of God within you is encouraging, inspiring, powerful and true and also much more quiet than the Ego.

So we must develop a practice that helps us to learn to know the difference between the two voices so that they can be powerful tools of self mastery and development. You see our inner voice is our super weapon and we must build a connection within and develop a relationship with this all-knowing apart of ourselves.

Some great ways to help you develop your intuition include:

- ❖ **Journaling** - Write don your experiences, thoughts and visons and create a space for dialogue with self. Great for developing Self Reflection, Self Awareness and

- ❖ **Taking note of your Dreams** - Dreams are messages from the subconscious mind and can be very insightful. Upon rising, write down any notes from your dreams. thoughts, feelings, smells, and anything significant that you can remember

- ❖ **Ask Questions** - Ask yourself questions and just allow yourself to reveal the answers. get a pen and paper and just write whatever your spirit guides you too. You may be surprised at how smart you already are and the guidance that your spirit has in store for you

- ❖ **Trust Your Gut** - Our gut, is the seat of our intuitive power. We can feel subtle energy changes in our gut and therefore it communicates to us,when something is not right. When you feel as if something is not right, do not eject your feeling, simply observe them. Then in time you will be able to know how on point your intuition is, and develop that ' gut instinct'

- ❖ **Join a Class of Workshops that focuses on developing your intuition** - there are many classes and spiritual development groups that can support you with even more skills and also support your growth and development. we learn so much quicker when we are around others that share the same perspective and also have had some practice in the skills we wish to acquire. Learning new skills will definitely leave you feeling more empowered and more supported, to explore your self and your inner power

There are many other ways of developing Spiritual Practice and cultivating Spiritual Power, which may include:

- ❖ *Spiritual Study*
- ❖ *Self Love and Appreciation*

- *Helping others- Acts of Kindness and Community Building*
- *Spiritual Service- Honouring the Source/ Most High is All*
- *Developing a moral compass for holistic living- Understanding Virtues and Sin/ Harmony and disharmony*
- *Self Mastery and Reflection*
- *Developing and maintaining a consciousness and open* connection with the Spirit or Essence within all things

Developing and creating a personal Ritual of Self Healing and Spiritual Development is key to living a holistically balanced life.

Rituals are practices which are give sacredness and repeated over again. they have been the foundation of all indigenous cultures, as a staple requirement to maintain the connection between spirit and man. We can create our own little rituals, to help us to maintain the balance between Sprit and Life, Self and The Most High.

This will help to ensure that we always honour our connection to all things and not forget our part in the collective human journey and story.

The Importance of Daily Spiritual Practice

Spiritual practice is about building a relationship and maintain a connection with your Spiritual Self and your connection to all that is. You are Spirit first, but you in an environment which not natural to your spirit and requires more of your physical presence to manifest your reality and lessons here. But your spiritual practice gives you a way of reconnecting with the part of you that knows all you need to know to help you on your journey here.

 It's about nurturing the Creator within and without and gaining the tools of mastery and accessing the wisdom that can be gained from your Highest Self and Source. Seeing yourself in all aspects and making a tangible connection between what you see and what you feel and know in your heart.

Your spiritual practice can be a combination of rituals and activities that help you to feel grounded, focused and connected to source and your higher self. Its purpose is to give you a structure and frame work in which to heal, develop and nurture yourself and ensure that you are vibrating at the highest possible frequency and taking responsibility for the healing and understanding of anything less.

The benefits of Spiritual Practice include:

- Providing clarity and focus
- Facilitates times for own personal growth and development
- Engages your sense on a variety of levels
- Helps you to feel calmer and more relaxed
- Can lift your moods and create joy'
- Provides a sense of focus and self-discipline

It may include things like:

- Meditation
- Mindfulness and Walks in Nature
- Yoga
- Energy Healing
- Prayers and Affirmations
- Rituals and Sacred Arts
- Journaling and self-reflection
- Acts of service
- Reading and Studying
- Reading oracle or Tarot Cards
- Spending time connecting with yourself

Listening to Uplifting Music

This list is just a start of some of the things that you can do to develop and create a Ritual for Personal Spiritual Practice. A ritual is something that you do regularly that has meaning and intention. The important thing is that you create a positive and healthy ritual that is easy for you to do and supports your growth development and healing on all levels.

Another thing to note, is that Spirituality is as much about yourself and your personal practice as it is about embodying that within your daily life and seeing the highest potential and same divine spirit in others. Are you embodying and sharing your spiritual nature and energy with others? Do you smile at people, and help those in need?

Can you be 'Source' and see the same 'Source 'in others and respect and love it as you respect and love self. Everything is connected and we all reflect the Source and Love of Source to each other and through each other.

Service is one of the greatest acts of Love and is the Divine Nature of Source. The Act of helping another and sharing the love is a powerful tool on your journey towards loving and healing yourself. Choosing to take responsibility for your life and your actions and being a positive and supportive influence in the lives of those around you, is all part of your growth and development and we all share this in common.

Spiritual development and practice has helped me on this journey to begin the process of integration between my Higher self and my physical body and all the various levels in between.

I am a multi-dimensional Divine Source Being of Spirit, Energy Will and Flesh and so are you!

It is a way to bring all of the aspects of us, on the various levels of existence together in perfect balance and harmony. As well as giving us the tools we need to navigate our way through this journey of life and be a master of our own reality.

Sekhmet Invocation

We call on Mother Sekhmet
Devour all unrighteousness
Restore Ma'at and order
Bring you might and power
Might Mother Sekhmet
She who burns the flames of divinity
She who drinks the blood of the wicked
The Redeemer
The Might of Ra
Divine Protectress
We call on You
Cast your fires now and consume all that is against life
Draw out from the belly if the beast the eye of the storm that bites

DUA SEKMET
NUK PU SEKHMET
RIGHT EYE OF RA
RESTORE AND REBALANCE
YOUR CHILDREN OF THE LIGHT NEED YOU
COME AND BLAZE YOUR FIRE OF TRUTH
PROTECT US AND EMPOWER US DIVINE GODDESS TO STAND IN OUR POWER
SA SEKHEM SAHU
SA SEKHEM SAHU
SA SEKHEM SAHU!!!!

The Soul-U-tion

The only way is complete disconnection
From the system
That causes pollution
The only solution
Is if we come together
Raise each other
Support each other
Feed each other
Love each other
Boycott the shops
Buy from each other
Spend your time
Helping each other
Put together your agenda
So Humanity can remember
The atrocities we causes
When we were in the fall
But now we rise
With crystal eyes
No longer hypnotised
We are wise
No longer can they divide
Us
From source
Or from each other
As long as we love
and help one another
Work together
See each other in each other
Be a mother to another
knowing together we are stronger
This is the agenda

Of the real illuminated
Follow false prophets
And your sight may be jaded
Your lesson this time is to know thyself
For in the unknowing
You created this state
So take back your power
Give love and receive
The blessings of Unity
Amongst humanity
This is the sacred prophecy
Written for all to see
144,000 guides we be
Standing together
For all to be free!

Amenti the Awakener
30/1/17

Nurturing the Seeds

Seed 9 - Connecting with Source

Spiritual development is Key to helping you to awaken to who you truly are and understand yourself as source energy. Spiritual practice allows you the tools to create rituals that support you to maintain your connection with source and with all aspects of your self.

Creating and maintaining a regular program of spiritual development can strengthen your connection to self and help you to become a master of your reality. It can assist you in handling traumatic situation.

Your spiritual practice should include a range of modalities that can serve you on all levels of your consciousness. It should be something that is not hard to do or too time consuming and also something that you enjoy doing

Time to Do the Work

For this seed you are encouraged to create your own Daily Spiritual Practice, using the Elements. This program that you will create can include things you want to learn and things that you can already implement. Ultimately it is for your benefit so ensure that it is enjoyable and that you can keep to the program you set.

You can start off with one thing, like doing a gratitude list every morning or you can do a combination of things for example: Prayer, meditations, Affirmations and then some Yoga. You can even ask any friends that you know, who are on a spiritual development path if they can share any tips with you.

Whatever you do remember it's about you and ultimately about helping you to create a deeper connection with source.

Air - The Mind/ Intellect/ Etheric

Air activities work with the mind, voice and sacred expressions as a form of communication with spirit.

This could include:

Affirmations, Visualisations, Journaling, Automatic Writing, Chanting or Singing Mantras.

Earth

Earth activities help to connect you with Mother Earth, can be to do with the body or physical activity.

This could include:

Yoga or body work, Reiki healing, Massage, Grounding Meditations, Walks in Nature and also some rituals which include creating or making something

Water

Water activities offer opportunities for reflection and healing. This could include:

Bath and Water Rituals, Journaling, Emotional Healing, Energy Healing, Self Reflection, Dance

Fire

Fire energy is active and creative. It is the passionate and transformative energy that we feel after dancing or most physical activities. Fire exercises bring fresh energy into the body and help to release old and stagnate energy. Fire also inspires drive and a ' can do' attitude.

Some fires activities could include:

Dancing, creating and making things, acts of service, drumming or music classes

Spirit

Spirit is all about shifting and expanding consciousness and becoming aware of your connection all things. It is also about being present and connecting with whatever it is you are experiencing and it is also manifested by the qualities of introspection, peace and mindfulness.

Activities can include:

Meditations, Soul journeys, connecting intuitively with animals or Nature, Reading Spiritual Wisdom and Prayer

Love

Love is about doing what you love, sharing your love and being love. it is about the expression of Love, acts of Love, Self Love and making a conscious decision to enjoy and celebrate each moment.

Ways you could achieve this could include:

Spending time with self-doing what you love, spending time with others, acts of service and kindness

Golden Seeds of Wisdom

Spiritual development and Spiritual practice is about facilitating a connection with yourself and the divine one within and without.

You are already connected to spirit and to Source and Always will be, but through the practice of spiritual development, you can build a connection that goes beyond belief and outs your firmly in the realm of knowing

Spiritual Practice has been a blessing for me in times of confusion and struggle and have allowed me the means to step outside of the matrix and observe myself as master of my reality. From this place of reference, I can find the keys to my success and them come back into my physical and manifest exactly what is needed. I recommend it for all who are embarking on a Spiritual Path of growth and even for those who are not!

Journal Page

Use this page to make any notes of your experience.

Star Seed Journey

Soul Journey - Journey to Meet Your Spirit/Ancestral Guardian

Each one of us has guardian spirits, ancestors and helpers that can support us from beyond the veil, whether we are aware of it or not. Developing a connection with your Ancestors or Guides can be a useful and insightful and invaluable resource in your own spiritual growth and development. You may have many guardians throughout your journey, some hat come and go and others that may have a longer lasting effect or presence in your life. Note that all will come to be pf a positive support to your life and would never put you down or make you feel bad about your choices and decisions.

They know very well the nature of this experience and her to guide and assist.

The next journey into the Halls of Amenti will be the journey to meet with your Spirit Guide or Ancestor who is available to support you through the next stages of your journey and development.

Guided Meditation Journey

- ❖ Find yourself a nice comfortable space where you will not be disturbed. Either lying down or sitting in a chair or on the floor
- ❖ As before, we will begin by taking a few deep cleansing breath and prepare to make our connection with the earth and the stars
- ❖ Ground yourself and connect to the Earth - drawing the light from the star above your head, down through your body and out through the roots of your feet into the Earth
- ❖ Set your intention now to take a journey connect with your higher self through the gateway to the halls of Amenti and meet with your Spirit Guardian or Ancestor for your work in the Halls
- ❖ Notice a Green ball of light energy at your heart chakra space

- *As you breath see yourself going into this bring green light and seeing yourself drawn into a tunnel of green light*
- *You see a mist before you and as the mist clears you notice a light before you. This light is green in the heart and surrounded by white light*
- *-As you move closer you begin to see the light take on a form, within your heart, as you guide to come closer to you and make it self-known to you*
- *Close your eyes within your vision and make a connection to your guide intuitively- what does it feel like?*
- *Ask your guide its name? listen and receive. How does the name feel to you what feeling does it give.*
- *Ask you guide how it will support you in your life? what does it day?*
- *You may open your eyes in your vision and ask your guide to show you an image that represent their vibration.*
- *What is the image? what does your guide look like? Are they Male or Female? In the image of a body or just light?*
- *Ask you guide how you can develop a deeper connection with it*
- *Spend a few moment and when you are ready. Thank your guide and then prepare to depart from the Halls*
- *Make you way back into the green tunnel of light within your heart.*
- *Take a moment to bring your consciousness back into your body*
- *Make a note of your experience and any learnings or nuggets of wisdom*

Journal Page

Use this page to make any notes of your experience.

Seed 10

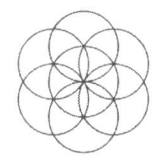

The Alchemy of Ecstasy

"There is a supernal intelligence behind sexual arousal, the true purpose of which is to create for us ecstatic experiences of our own divinity."

~ John Maxwell Taylor, Eros Ascending: The Life-Transforming

SEED 10 – THE ALCHEMY OF ECSTASY

There is a transforming and healing power that is created when two become one for the purpose of bringing healing, harmony and balance.

Amenti The Awakener

The Power of Intimacy, The Power of Alchemy

Let's Talk About Sex

Sex is one of the most powerful tools for personal development and growth when used in the right way and with the right intentions. It can also facilitate the release of dysfunctional energy within the body, which can help to keep one from becoming diseased. It can also assist in opening the higher chakras, and under the right conditions allows a person to begin the process of enlightenment.

When we start to develop a connection with ourselves and our bodies it opens up a whole new world of experience of excitement and mystery.

We learn from our external world and develop a natural curiosity about our sexual organs

We first start to observe ourselves. We become aware of our bodies and all the various different parts.

And observe the bodies of the people around us, our parents or siblings and later friends; and compare and contrast.

We also begin to touch and play with our sexual organs and develop a connection with the feeling of stimulation, pain and pleasure and introduce emotions into the mix.

Some of us may have memories and experiences of when we first started to have feelings towards the opposite sex.

The first time you fancied someone or experience love at first sight first kiss.

Around the age canary School set of puberty your interactions with the opposite sex become much more intriguing and intense

With raging hormone surging through our bodies giving rise to all kinds of exciting and sometimes feelings and emotions we become more aware of and responsive to the subtle sexual energy bubbling under the surface actually want to explore further

Most of the referent points that we have on what sexual relationships are supposed to be about we have seen or observed in our environment.

Perception can be influenced by your environment, the people around you, and the various television programs, films and magazines.

Fairy tales of happy endings and perfect beginnings, fill our minds with expectation or fear all contribute to creating an image of the nature of sex and relationships.

Many of us have not been introduced to the sacred and healing nature of sex and sexuality and the message of it's true power and potential.

Nevertheless, a natural urge within us grows and we walk into embark on a journey to explore ourselves sexually our sexual nature more fully.

Losing your virginity is usually the initiation into adulthood and the sexual journey.

Your virginity is your symbol of purity and chastity, something sacred and cherished by many but not all. We are initially sold a story by the media and society of how beautiful and special it will be and loads other fanciful things.

Religion teaches us of the virtue in keep thyself sacred and celebrates the archetype of the virgin as clean wholesome and pure. And shuns the woman who gives her sex loosely.

But a lot of what is actually experienced is far from that amazing and less condemning.

I attended an all-girls school when I was a teenager and I remembered the different perceptions and experiences of my friends and others around me.

Some were sexually active from a young age, some as young as 13, and they would openly and sometimes boastfully share their stories of sexual exploits. They didn't seem to care much or think that sex was anything special.

Other girls either openly maintained their chaste with conviction and pride, or didn't talk about it at all.

The Dark Side of Sex

For some the initiation into the world of sex and sexual energy is not always a positive one and this can affect the ability to really embody, embrace and enjoy sex.

The dark side of this energy is that it also has the potential to destroy and cause harm when not used with the right intentions.

Sexual abuse is common in the human experience as we learn the lessons of power and control through the Egos need for self-gratification and dominance.

The painful memories of misuse of sexual energy both Ancestral and personal are linked to the imbalance of our masculine and feminine energies within and without.

The collective experience of repression of the Divine Feminine energies and imbalance within the Divine masculine are etched in the emotional bodies of humanity and many souls manifest the experience of sexual abuse in their life, so that once it is healed and transformed the balance, harmony and oneness can be restored in the collective mind.

When you engage in Sexual intercourse from the heart and focused intention from a place of purpose, power, and Love, it is transformed into a sacred act that can facilitate deep transformational healing, liberation and Spiritual Awakening.

For those who have experienced sexual abuse, sex seem a very painful and negative experience in which they dominated or controlled and manifests pain rather than pleasure

The energy transferred and memories created during this type of sexual exchange can corrupt and distort our sexual energy centres and perception of sex altogether.

Sex becomes a painful act of submission and control rather of liberation, freedom and love. But with time and through the conscious intention of healing and understanding, combined with the powerful force of forgiveness, Transformation new love and rebirth can be found through healing power of love and sacred sexual alchemy.

Understand the Healing Nature of Sexual Energy

Making love or having Sex, is much more that something that you do to feel good or to procreate. It is something much more powerful than that and many do not really understand or get to experience the true healing and transformation that can be gained through sexual energy and sexual energy exchange (S.E.X)

Sexual energy is one of the most powerful forces on the planet.

It is s the potent and creative force that brings forth life and when harnessed and understood, brings forth great self-awareness, healing and spiritual growth.

Governed by the Root and Sacral Chakras, sexual energy and intercourse is closely linked to our connected to our lower and carnal self, but in fact, the act of sex and making love can actually facilitate transcendence and support spiritual growth and development and awaken latent healing energies from deep within

All energy is light including sexual energy and light in itself is information

When two people engage in sexual intercourse they are in fact creating an exchange of energy and information between two people, and this Information can either have a positive or negative effect on those involved.

The Sacred Art of Tantra

"The beauty and wisdom of Tantra is that it enhances sexuality as a doorway to the "ecstatic mind of great bliss". Truly, at the peak of orgasm, we pierce through the illusion of fragmentation and separation, and glimpse the unity and interconnectedness of all beings. And through the other—our partner—we fall in love with life. Margot Anand

Tantra is a spiritual tradition found in both Hinduism and Buddhism and which has also influenced other Asian belief systems. The word 'Tantra" means ' woven together' and Tantra is the art of oneness with yourself and your divine reflection. It is about the harmonising and balancing of the masculine and feminine energies

Teun Goudriaan, describe tantra as "systematic quest for salvation or spiritual excellence by realizing and fostering the divine within one's own body, one that is simultaneous union of the masculine-feminine and spirit-matter, and has the ultimate goal of realizing the "primal blissful state of non-duality."

Tantra is the practice of sacred union and the harmonising of the opposites. It's is about the scared alchemical haling practice in which two become one and experience wholeness and Divine Spiritual Connection.

To be one with another Mind- Heart- Soul and Spirit is to be back at one with Source.

The Power of the Orgasm

It was believed in ancient Egypt that the orgasm was the key to eternal life, and that it was intimately connected with the chakra system. The Egyptian system held that the orgasm was intimately connected to the Universal Heart Chakra.

Most people in the world are not fully aware of what happens to their sexual energy after they have an orgasm. Usually, the energy moves up the spine and out the top of the head directly into the eighth or thirteenth chakra (same chakra, different system).

In a few rare cases, the sexual energy is released down the spine into the hidden centre below the feet, the point opposite the one above the head. In either case, the sexual energy — the concentrated life-force energy called Kundalini — is dissipated and lost.

It is similar to discharging a battery into a ground wire. It is no longer in the battery and so it is gone forever. This is what all the world's Tantric systems believe, that orgasm brings one a little closer to death because a person loses his or her life-force energy in the orgasm and is made weaker.

But the Egyptians found long ago that it does not have to be this way.

The Egyptians believed that orgasm is healthy and necessary, including the release of sperm in males, but that the sexual energy currents must be controlled in a deeply esoteric procedure that is unlike any other system. They believed that if this energy is controlled, the human orgasm becomes a source of infinite pyranic energy that is not lost. They believe that the entire Mer-Ka-Ba or light body (the field of energy surrounding and interpenetrating the body) benefits from this sexual release. They even believe that under the right conditions the orgasm will directly lead to eternal life, and that the ankh is the key.

Kundalini

Kundalini is a type of life force energy that sits dormant in the first chakra, at the base of the spine. This energy is released during orgasm through the second chakra, as the body attempts to create a child. It is coiled up like a very tight spring, and when released there is sometimes an explosion of power.

Properly directed, the kundalini will travel up a tube in the energy body that lies close to the spine.

Without proper direction, the release of kundalini can be very uncomfortable and possibly damaging. On its way up, the kundalini both cleans and strengthens the energy body and chakras. You may feel a warm sensation moving up your back.

Kundalini energy is similar to chi and prana and can also be passed on by a spiritual teacher. It also called "serpent power" because this sleeping spiritual force in every human being lies coiled at the base of the spine. It is an expression of sexual energy that can only be awakened and accessed through deep spiritual development and awakening

Sacred Sex

Sacred Sex is when you transform the conscious awareness from that of pleasure to that pf spiritual development and growth.

Sexual energy is all encompassing and when two people engage in the act of sexual intercourse they share mix their energies and body fluids and the two become one and when they climax the emotions generate a powerful release and feeling of Ecstasy create a powerful and intoxicating essence of Ecstasy. Ecstasy is that feeling of overwhelming happiness and joy and in Sacred Sex.

Sacred sex, which is the experience of ecstasy, is the real sexual revolution. Sacred sexuality is about love—not merely the positive feeling between intimates, but an overwhelming reverence for all embodied life on whatever level of existence. Through sacred sexuality, we directly participate in the vastness of being – the mountains, rivers, and animals of the Earth, the planets and the stars, and our next-door neighbours.

Sacred sexuality is about recovering our authentic being, which knows bliss beyond mere pleasurable sensations. It is a special form of communication, even communion, that fills us with awe and stillness.

It is generated in that moment when you are in a space of intense passion and surrender and fully connected as one with your divine reflection and this potent energy can be used to heal and transform our past experiences and set us on our path to ascension and awakening

When you engage your mind heart body and soul in Sacred ceremony with focused intention and love then S.E.X (Sacred sexual Energy Xchange) can become a powerful tool for healing that can heal all past traumas and initiate massive awakening.

When the power of Sacred Sexual Energy is created and shared from a place of love of the highest vibration.

The Art of Making Love

Sex is more than about something that feels good or about procreation. Sex or making love is a sacred exchange of energy on multiple layers and multidimensional.

When you make love you can act physically biologically for your fluids spiritually and energetically and sometimes but not always you connect mentally are your intentions always aligned and for your highest good full stop what is the drive behind your intentions seeking a partner and a mate?

It for lust or self-gratification, is it purely for pleasure, is it for healing and spiritual elevation

lust is the dark side of the sexual energy spectrum. Lust is the energy that feels fuels your Desires and can be vampiric in its nature if not balanced. It is animalistic in nature and based on an intense need for stimulation pleasure and release.

When you engage sexually with someone in a lustful way it is short lived and your connection or interest in the person may not last long beyond the act.

This kind of sexual energy exchange is not sacred or conscious with high intent and so therefore this unfocused energy can fierce by way of argument boredom disconnect racing or desire.

This kind of sexual exchange is powerful but will do to you only lower vibrational entities who will feast on the unfocused energy that is released.

Sacred Sexuality

Sacred union reveals the truth that in our single creations there are two aspects of in the one soul which had separated and become one. Therefore, Sacred union and Tantra is ultimately the practice of oneness and unification with the Source in the physical body.

In Sacred Sex, you combine the Mind, body soul and spirit and set an intention to harmonise the energies of you and your partner to bring forth healing, spiritual growth and empowerment.

You can also use the power of sexual energy to manifest anything you want to create

Sacred sexuality is:

- ❖ The Freedom to express and explore one's sexual nature and power as a part of one's spiritual growth and development
- ❖ It enhances self-worth and encourages intimacy with those who value and see your light
- ❖ sharing yourself freely with your mate in unconditional love and rapture

- ❖ To honour your sacred sexual experiences
- ❖ The ability to be naked and comfortable in one's skin
- ❖ Tapping in to sacredness and sanctity of Divine union
- ❖ Sexual Healing to release old traumas and wounds
- ❖ Conjuring Sacred Power with focus and intention
- ❖ Becoming one with the Divine

The Alchemy of Ecstasy – The Healing Nature of Sex

It is by the consistent living of Sacred Union that twin souls can and shall coalesce with the humble reliance on God to help overcome all obstacles

Aniya Sophia

Love making or sacred sex, is when you partake in the creating and embodiment love and sacred union of the highest vibration with the intention of liberation, healing and growth.

This type of lovemaking is empowering and is the physical act vacation of the hole the Harmony of the polar opposites oneness and alchemy in action.

The orgasm has the power to heal transform or lower vibrational experiences and memories from the body when initiated from a place of love and focused Intent.

And through the alchemy of ecstasy the true healing power of sexual energy can be cultivated end use for liberation awakening and spiritual awakening.

Male and female energies when brought together with purposeful intent have the power to heal and harmonise each other and when they unite in love they are the closest to source that we can get.

To experience this kind of love and healing is a beautiful and soul empowering experience.

Sacred sexual energy can be healing and empowering if you are open and allowing.

> "When we practice sacred sexuality we are working with cosmologically rooted principles, balancing the heavenly yang (male energy) of the Universe with the all-knowing, life-giving yin (feminine energy) of the earth within ourselves."

My Sacred Intention :-) My Divine Mate

He knows my strengths and my weaknesses and he takes pride in helping me to grow.
He is proud of me and thinks I'm precious
and wants to ensure that I know
He never makes me feel less than any other woman,
cos in his eyes I'm a queen.
He celebrates my talents
and believes in my dreams

He knows I can be stubborn
and shows me the benefit of learning to bend.
He is my home, my homie, my lover
my brother and my friend.

I am his keeper and he is mine.
We know that our union is part of a grand design.
We both see and know the value in each other
And look forward to the hidden parts that we will discover
.
Someone to hold my hand and love me deeply,
Stroke my hair when I'm sleeping.
Remind me that my purpose is of value, and with all my talents there no end to what I can do.

When I'm feeling low, depleted or down, he runs me bath, gives me a rub and readjusts my crown.
And in the stillness and receipt of all of him,
My passion stirs as I proclaim what I'll be to him

Someone to love him, remind him of who he is.
When he feels empty, with my sacred breath and words of nourishment,

His cup I fill
To remind him of how grateful for him that we are.
He is our protector, our strength, our guide, our star.

I make him nutritious meals to keep him healthy and strong.
I run him a bath and sing him a love song.
I remind him with every breath, that I Am here,

To love him, and guide him, support him and show him that I care.
Stoke his body, massage his feet,
stimulate his mind,
give him spiritual food to eat.

Take the time and interest to see the truth in him,
to see him in his fullness, stirs my passion within
To let him know that he's never alone,
and after fighting the battles of the day,
he is welcomed home.
With open arms, that nurture and embrace.
And let him know together there is nothing we can't face.

That our union was written in the stars
and by living in our truth we will always go far.
By him being him and me being me,
we make the perfect recipe
for all the wonders that God did create,
within our union our purpose, greatness awaits

The perfect union of all there is,
wrapped in a loving package of me and him
And from this deep passion,
from this all-encompassing space
We merge in each other's greatness
and from the void we procreate

As we connect in sacred union
Our love a portal of transcendence
Creation arousing within me
I feel the energy, I open up, embrace our fate

Floating in the expansiveness of our love for each other
I bask in the stars and the power of my lover
Bringing that magic down into carbon density
By the power of our love, our union of 2 is now of 3

Continuing our legacy of Love, passion and purpose
with the magic of giving birth
We welcome an evolved aspect of us
To enjoy a new life on this Earth
A new manifestation of all that we have become

A new life waiting to unfold
A testimony to the effort we made to nurture each other and be bold
A new creation birthed on a foundation of pure unconditional love
As above so below,
our paths merge into one

This sacred union nothing can beat
And from our sacred love
The world did a receive
A gift, A God a returned ancestor
To remind is of the power when we come together
In love Sacred union, peace and harmony
When I'm loving you
And you loving me

This is the reality we Co create
In our hearts and our minds

So on my lover, I'm willing to wait

Kissing all of the frogs has helped me to see
That my relationships reflect the balance on me
I make a commitment to love and reflect on self and get my heart in optimum health

See the power in the other half of me
I cultivate my soil
so that he can plant the seeds
in good fertile soil of self-knowledge and faith
When my King man appears,
there will be a Queen in his face

A woman steadfast in her purpose, full of wisdom and grace
Open to live and respect you
Whilst being totally empowered in her space
Ready to embrace all of what they will become

The bending
The shaping
The moulding
The love

The masterpiece of love and harmony in action
A fiery ball of intention and passion
This is my vision of the love that is for me

And with open arms I am ready and prepared to receive
Thank you to the frogs I kissed along the way
But this time I'll have patience
Whilst my perfect match, finds his way :-)

In to me see (Intimacy)

See the reflection of all that is
In loves kiss
In ecstatic bliss
The heavens insist
On the truth that lies within

The darkness holds the key
The hidden rainbow and kaleidoscope
Of all our many colours and expressions
Into the void
Between the two pillars
The halls are awakened
Life is rebirthed

In to me see
What do you see
In me
Divinity
Prosperity
Virginity
Purity
Ugly waiting to be
Transformed
Beauty and greatness
Waiting to be adorned

Intimacy
You
And
Me
Exactly how
are creator intended us to be

IN TO Me See
IN TO WE SEE
THROUGH THE EYES OF INTIMACY
WE SEE
ECSTACY
DIVINITY

Sacred Sexual Power

I am Awakened
My alive and glistening eyes have the power
to hypnotize and mesmerize
Deep into the depths of my divinity
And see
Me
The Dakini goddess in her glorious majesty
Hips so power filled
Send ripples across the Universe
Arousing heavens potency
The phallus of righteousness awakens me

I dig deep
Into all that is me
Unbridled in my sacred sexuality
All of the goddess Is Magic
Expressed through theses lips
And between these hips
I am vast and expansive
Ecstasy and passion
Initiation and transmutation
Death and rebirth

My breasts- givers of life

Pleasure centres
Bringing Orgasmic Adventures
And climatic expressions
That give birth to creations
Of the highest intention

I give Life
I give birth like mother earth
I QuakeEarth Quake, Earth
Whilst I lie in wait
and mentally masturbate am risen higher than before
Rising through my passion
Opening the secret holes I explore
Galaxies and dimensions
Gateways and portals of Ascension
I rise to meet the highest Part of me
Awakening my kundalini
In tantric harmony
From the root to the tip of the tree
This is me

The sorceress of manifestation
The source
The manifestor
The Creator
The life giver
Orgasm bringer

My sexual fire burns with a desire
To take you higher
Resurrection is what I inspire
Burning away transgressions
Releasing all depression
The sacred intention manifested through my divine expression

My sacred sexual power I devour all ungodly and transform it with my heaven essence
My sacred presence
And the darkness into pure light

I erupt
Volcanoes of consciousness from within
Arousing me to begin
To dig deeper
Deeper into the Seas of me
And him
And we

Passion
Magic
Intention
Purpose
With every moan and every breath
Life is excited into expansion
contraction
expansion
just like breathing
we are one and the same
and together we can to bring the fire
to bring the truth
the bring the divine through all that we do
I see you
and you see me
Together we manifest oneness and harmony
Sacred sexual alchemy
love is flowing freely
The Spirit of Love And Truth burn within
How could this be of sin

My sacred magic
My sacred sexual power

My feet stomp the beat of the rhythm of creation
Bated breaths in the anticipation of ejaculation
Concentrated intention
Nurturing the seed of creation
Placed in the centre of the womb
to be birthed in to manifestation

My lips
The lips that hold and caress
The lips that receives remove and undress
All of you
All of him
All of me
My lips
My hips
The gateway to Eternity

Sensitive, plump and easily aroused
To the touch of you
Anticipation of you
Bated breath
I breathe
I breathe
I inhale you
The magic of you I inhale
I embody
I transform

My sexual fires I drink of you
I taste of you
Bring healing to you

Nurture you
I am you
And you are me

Orgasmic seas carry the blessing of Divinity
The Ark of the Covenant within me
Through our Union comes a gift for humanity
A child made of Love for our Earth Family
All created from our sacred sexual alchemy

The knowing of divine self
Repression bad for your health
Each movement what's a good intention bringing for sacred expression
I hold
A flower in my hand
And smell it
And drink of it
The nectar in heels and awakens
Alchemy in me
Healing of I, Us, We
Releasing the Essence
Smelling sweet
Heavens sent
Good enough to eat

My liquid flows
Red white and gold it flows
Bringing Life
Clearing Death
Transforming
Erupting
Exploding
Popping

Liquid gold don't you know
Have you tasted from the sacred fountain of youth
Have you explored me as I explore you
Do you know the truth of the sacred chalice and the holy Well
Or are you under the illusion
That it will cast a Spell

All the greats of antiquity have drunken from this divine Cup
To seek wisdom power and initiation
Into the sacred mysteries that dwell

Holy waters flow
Holy waters flow and bring blessings
Sacred holy waters flow

how can you be afraid
How can you be afraid to know
And come to know all of you
Be More of You
The sweet smell of home and nurturing
How can you be afraid

They told you it wasn't Powerful
so you play into their game
Powerless
Sex for sale
low it's vibration
A journey straight to hell
void of all its magic
and all its wisdom too
drawing to you the demon
who in the depths of the abyss they dwell

From my place of sacred power

I Devour
All on truths
And dig deeply within me
Outside I'm naked for all to see
The truth and the power
Through our sacred sexuality
With highest intent and purest love
The potential for all to be made free

Dig deep into your seas deep
into the destiny when two souls meet
Awaken your passion
hold on don't let go
release your fear
make an intention to Know
All of you
The power within your sacred flower
Awakened by your lovers power

Dig deep
The rod of righteous Intent
Dig deep
Into the void it's sent
Dig deep
And feel the waters within and beneath
Dip the tip to the back
Explore the depths of you and him
Know that the journey is about to begin
dig deep and love abundantly
And bask in the magic of I, us, we

Sacred Waters
Sacred showers
Sacred sexual god goddess power

Black magic
Black gold
Impossible to imitate
Too powerful to hold
They Corrupted your perception
Of the power in your sexuality
Lower the vibration
Of Ritual Planting of the seed
To allude us from its power
A true gift cast as sin
To stop us all from truly embodying
The Healing Creative Power
Created between you and him

But I Am here to tell you
That in myself I am free
Now that I know the power of
my sacred sexual energy
I know that it on of the most
powerful forces on earth
and through its sacred practice
I am a mother who will give birth
to more than just my pleasure
more than a baby
through my sacred sexual power
I gave birth to the Goddess in Me

The Sacred Alchemy of You and Me

Love abounds
And surrounds
As I open to all of you
Swimming in more of you
We two

Are likes stars twinkling from afar
Gazing lovingly, wondering who we are
To each other
No other lover has held me so tenderly
So deeply
Filling all of me
Completely
In rhapsody
I
Us
We

My inner erupts as you fill my sacred cup
With you magic
Your wisdom
Your love
Our beginning
No separation
Never ending
Only revelation
Of the highest intentions

I caress you
And feel the sacred expression of me through you
1 and 1 is two
And as I hold you
Firmly in my hand
Whilst you stand
Firm In your intention
And direction
Not to mention
The penetration
Of mind body and soul
We take hold

And bathe in the
Alchemy of Ecstasy
The Alchemy of you and me
Combined in all our glory
Blessed in divinity
And sacred sexuality
Majesty
And regality
I into you and you into me
No mystery
For inside of us we hold the key
To fulfil the prophecy
Of sacred destiny
For humanity
When I become you and you become me
We 3 bring forth Divinity

I take a breath
And breathe in all of you
My spirits food
Tastes Oh So Good
So Good
So Loving
So Living
So creative, creation, creating Love

What a blessing
Yes
Yes
Yes
I and Him
He and I
And We
In unity

Oneness
And feeling free

Love abounds and Heaven is the destination of our journey
Hidden between the sacred walls
We both fall into our rapture
Nothing can capture
This divine blessing
Everlasting
And ever giving
Balance and harmony
Land and sea
Me and you
You and me
And we
Sacred
Alchemy

BLESSED risings :-)

The power and the potency
Deep within
In the darkness
Life does begin
Seeds are planted
Like planets in the Universes sea
Magic within
Waiting to break free
On the divine vehicle of ecstasy
My higher self
My inner God
Desires to meet me
In between
The hidden realms of

12 Seeds To Awaken Your Spirit

Me and You
My womb does swell
With power potency and liquid rich
That contains all of life within it
Aroused by my sacred nature
Every centre opens
As he enters
Spiritually into my sacred space
No flesh of man dear enter this place
A God manifested in carbon density
Knowing all he is
And all he truly came to be
Not physically
But spiritually, mentally
Intimately
We
Dance in the magic of what is meant to be
And the Universe and stars dance inside of me
As the hormones raise my kundalini
I'm set free
Into a sea of potent Ecstasy
My divinity
Carried me beyond
The physicality
Into the realm of all that be
Rising higher
Shifting my frequency
To the highest vibration and potency
Awakening and activating my Kundalini
To the centre of all that is he carries me
On the orgasmic rivers of sound frequency
The stars hold me and the Universe is my bed and sacred sanctuary
I and laid bare
For all to see

And the magic of the divine feminine builds with me
I chant a psalm, and hekau as I call on the God's to fill every cell
and rise me above
Everything that can make this experience less sacred
Less full of love
Lifted by the magic of the earth's potency I open to the magic deep
with me
as the ripples of the Universe
Hold and take heed
I feel the power build in me and I am take hold of
In fill embrace
By the Most High Source
To help manifest his face
In the children of earth his creation
He will used my seed to mother a nation
To give birth to a whole race through me
And the power hidden in my sacred seed
I take a breath as I fill with potent expectation....

Nurturing the Seeds

Seed 10 – Sacred Sexual Power

Sex is something that is quite taboo for a lot of people and not many of us are truly connected to our sexual selves, or even allow ourselves to experiences it. As we are moving out of a male dominated experience of the world, we are moving in the feminine energy of Sacred Sexuality. The introduction of the sacred harmony and oneness of the Divine Essence of the Creator, or God, you and your divine reflection. The questions below will help you to get an understanding of where you are with your Sacred Sexual Power and maybe uncover some food for thought.

Time to Do the Work

Air – Know Your Mind

What do you think about Sacred Sexuality?

- ❖ What are your thoughts?
- ❖ Have you experienced it before? if so what made it Sacred for you and what is your reflection on the experience
- ❖ Can you see yourself engaging in this type of relationship? spend a few moment thinking about what it might feel like

Earth – Know your Body

- ❖ What is your connection like with your body?
- ❖ Do you like your body? if not why not? and what would you change
- ❖ Can you describe you most empowering sexual experience? how did it make you feel and why?

Water – Know your Emotions

- ❖ How do you feel about the idea of Sacred Sex?
- ❖ have you experienced an Orgasm before? if so what was it life you?
- ❖ How does the word 'Sacred Sexual Power' make your feel?

Fire - Know your Passion

- ❖ What arouses you sexually?
- ❖ How do you tap into your sacred Sexual Power?
- ❖ What do you use your sexual energy to create?
- ❖ How do you let your partner know that you want to connect sexually?

Spirit – Know Your Spirit

- ❖ What do you understand about Tantra?
- ❖ Are you comfortable with the idea of Spirituality and Sex being together?
- ❖ What defines 'Sacredness' to you?

Love – The Spirit of Love

- ❖ How versed are you in the Art of Making Love? do you feel comfortable with yourself sexually?
- ❖ If no, what could you do to change this
- ❖ How do you make your partner feel loved and special?
- ❖ What can you do for yourself to make yourself feel sexier and loved?

Golden Seeds of Wisdom

The Alchemy of Ecstasy is the ability to transform the illusion of Separation into the reality of Wholeness.

Sacred Sex has the power to erase the traumas of the past and bring elevation, liberation and Spiritual Wisdom

Through the Power of our Sacred Sex in connection with our sacred self with bring forth the true essence of the only constant within the Universe.......LOVE

Journal Page

Use this page to make any notes of your experience.

Seed 11

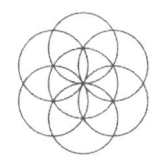

Understand the Power

of Love

" Love is the most healing force in the world. Nothing goes deeper than Love. It heals not only the body, not only the mind, but also the soul" **Osho**

SEED 11 – UNDERSTAND THE POWER OF LOVE

Love

Love is such an expansive topic that to be able to fully do it justice, as a topic, I would really have to write a whole new book. But for the purpose of this text, I intend to discuss Love from the perspective that we can all experience and understand it tangibly.

Love is as natural to me as breathing and is the first thing I knew how to do before I knew how to do anything else. But as I grew and experienced more of this realm, I realized that love and come in so many different and sometimes confusing ways, that even the world alone means so many things to many different people.

There is the love that you have for your parents and your family, the love you have for you friends or favourite things, the love you have for your personal passions and the love you have for humanity amongst other things.

A Mothers Love is one of the most powerful gifts on Earth, whether it be your own mother of the mothers in life who afforded you this beautiful and nurturing energy. It can bring us back into harmony with divine sour e and is the very essence that reminds us that at the core we are love and love.

There is also the dark side of Love, which unrequited love, possessive love, jealous love and 'single white female' love!

Love Connects Us All

Love can come ins so many form and teaches us so much of ourselves.

Bob Marley has a famous song with the line "Could you be loved and be love" and not many people can truly understand the meaning of that phrase.

When we are loved it is this energy that fill our and nourishes us. It nourishes our mind, body spirit, it energies our actions and spreads healing to all those we meet.

But when things go wrong we can get sour and not be that love that we have received. We can be loved by another and not be loving to others. This is our ultimate test. To love and be loved and the honour the sacred gift of love that we share with each other.

People do all types of things in the name of Love, whether they are for them owns gains or for another. Love teaches us so many things about ourselves and about our nature.

But in reality there is only one real type of love and that is…. Love! You know that love I'm talking about.

That real love that makes your whole being light up and feel enriched and it's so contagious that it spreads without you even saying a word.

That love we feel when we connect with likeminded others, that Love that we feel when we are happy within ourselves and in our joy. Love of life, Love of Love!

Take a moment and allow yourself to connect to the feeling and power of love. Allow your higher self to reflect to you a memory that reminds you or puts you in the vibration of Love!

Love is such a powerful gift

Some call it unconditional love, and yes that is a quality of it but love is ultimately the source from which were all created, in fact everything that has ever been created is created from Love.

Love is one of the many emotions of experiences that we have in this experience of life to help us to lean about ourselves and each other. We all go through times when we have had string feelings of love with another only to find that some action or misdemeanour, steals out love away and it soon turns into hate, disappointment, or neutral energies.

Many suffer in silence and trauma, due to the experience of the absence of Love in their lives. This can sometimes off there a traumatic or challenging experience but ultimately when transformed can gift them with the knowledge of how powerful love is and encourage them to give it to themselves and others.

The true fact is that on the real, love is what we are!

To seek it is an illusionary experience on this realm as you cannot seek something that you already are. But at times on this journey the lesson may be to come back to that understanding and to see ourselves as love so that we will no longer seek it in longing -ness but be empowered by the knowing that we are already that and continue to be it and enjoy it and allow it to power amazing experiences and interactions with others in our lives.

My experience of love has been an eventful one. My original knowing is that love is all there is and I came into this world with a love for everyone and everything. My understanding was that Love was something that is eternal, natural and everything that we are do and create is love.

Like however was based on choice. We love our family whether we like them or not but we like our friends because we choose to.

We love all the shoes in the shop but there's a particular shoe you like.

You can choose who to like but you love everyone, this was my thought form.

My love was unconditional and I would show love to everything, but I became jaded by expectation and the knowing that all people do not think like that.

The people who you feel are supposed to Love and protect you, sometimes don't' based on conditions sometimes out of control. If you did something that they liked, or if you did what they said they loved you but if you didn't, they didn't.

I was confused by this kind of love.

As I learned more about love through my life, it became something that made me anxious. Love wasn't truthful and honest, love was temperamental and fragile and I felt as though by being myself and loving in the way that I did, I left myself open to the abuse of others who were jaded by their own experiences of Love.

Understanding The Various types of Love

According to Greek philosophy, there are different types of Love that we encounter and experience within then human journey.

These Love types and their definitions are listed below.

1. Eros - Erotic Love

Eros is the Greek God of Love and Fertility. Eros, as an expression of Love, represents the idea of Sexual Passion, Masculine Potency and the Creative Masculine Force.

This kind of energy is Lustful, and Passionate and can also be dangerous if not balanced. This is demonstrated by the carnal desire within men to procreate and also dominate in sexual interactions. It involves loss of control, through the primal impulse to procreate.

- ❖ *Passionate and intense form of love, that arouses romantic and sexual feelings*
- ❖ *Primal and Primitive*
- ❖ *Burns Quickly, is fickle and is about Self- Gratification*
- ❖ **Love Catalyst: The Body**

2. Philla - Affectionate Love

Pilla is Affectionate Love or Friendship. This was seen the type of Love valued most by the Greeks because t was based on Love of equal measure. This is the nature of most platonic relationships, where there is Love without Physical Attraction. It is the type of Love that is felt between two friends who have ben through much together.

- ❖ *Physical attraction is not a necessary part of this connection*

- ❖ *Platonic and dispassionate virtuous Love*
- ❖ *Love that is shared equally*
- ❖ *Loyalty and Sacrifice amongst friends*
- ❖ **Love Catalyst: The Mind and Heart**

3. Storge - Familiar Love

Storge, is similar to Philla, in the way that it is also a Love that is expressed without need for physical attraction, however it is primarily to do with kinship and familiarity. your relations, family and can also include those of whom, you have developed a relationship, similar to that of family. It is a natural form of affection that often flows between children and their parents and vice versa.

- ❖ Affections between kin and family
- ❖ Based on blood or loyalty
- ❖ Can block you from moving forward and making choices for personal growth and development
- ❖ **Love Catalyst: Causal/ Emotional / Memories**

4. Ludus - Playful Love

Ludus is the playful Love that is felt between those who flirt with each other, or the affection that is felt between to young lovers. It is similar to Eros, in that there is the potential for Erotic Love and Desire. However, Ludus is about the playful nature of Love. Playfulness in love is an essential ingredient that is often lost in long term relationships. Encouraging playfulness in your relationship is a great antidote to the stresses, that life can bring.

- ❖ Affectionate, Attractive and Playful interaction

- Felt during the early stages of Love
- Interesting and exciting
- Flirting, teasing etc
- Brings feelings of joy and Euphoria
- *Love Catalyst: Astral/Emotional*

5. Mania - Obsessive Love

Mania is the type of Love that, in my opinion, really isn't love at all. It is obsessive in nature and can lead to madness and loss of self awareness and respect. its occurs when there is an imbalance in Ludos (playful love) and Eros (Erotic Love). For those who experience Mania, it can be about possession and low self esteem.

The intention of the relationship or interaction, becomes more about the need for self love and acceptance, that it becomes about sharing love. The persona wants to love and be loved, but somewhere in the mind-set, needs to find the balance of self love as well. Love can be such a powerful and uplifting thing, but the reality, is that it can also be destructive. love is a thing that is freely available, but not everyone feels like they have it. This can lead to control and suppression in relationships and obsession with the object of affection.

- *Unhealthy and Obsessive attachment to another*
- *Self indulgent and Self conflicting -indicative of need for self healing*
- *Possessive and Jealous*
- *Need to control and supress another*
- *Love Catalyst: Survival Instinct*

6. Pragma - Enduring Love

Pragma is the Love that transcends all space and time. That loves, just because it always has done. It is the Matured love that grows between those who have travelled may roads together.

It is the love that loves, even when all others have left. It is the love that is developed between those who know each other so well, and have each other's back no matter what the cause. this is the love felt between to old people who have lived their lives together. Or two best friends who have been through thick and thin.

- ❖ *This type of Love is not easy to find*
- ❖ *Result of effort from both parties*
- ❖ *Love developed by those who have learned to make compromises and have demonstrated Patience and Tolerance*
- ❖ **Love Catalyst: Etheric (Unconscious)**

7. Phiautia - Self Love

In truth, Phiautia, is one of the most important aspects of Love that we should be encouraged to develop and learn. It is the love for self, which is the sustainer of all life. We all must have the desire and rive to live, to breathe and to love and this should not be dependant on the love of another.

Aristotle claimed that, " All friendly feelings for others, are an extension of a mans feeling for himself".

We cannot give from an empty cup and you cannot share what you do not have. So therefore it is of utmost important to develop a healthy love for self. The only way to be truly happy, is to have unconditional Love for yourself. this will also allow you to have the same unconditional love for others. but you cannot have for someone else, that which you do not have for yourself.

Only once you learn to love and understand yourself, will you be really ready to love and understand another. In truth, there is no separation between you and your partner, so the love that you have for self so the love you share with another.

- ❖ *Self Love, compassion and understanding*
- ❖ *Honouring yourself*
- ❖ *Balanced and Self Preserving*
- ❖ **Love Catalyst: Soul**

8. Agape - Selfless Love

Agape is deemed to be the highest vibration and act of Love. It is love that is Selfless and Unconditional. This is the love that comes straight form source and a deep knowing and connection to all things. This is the Love that flows straight from source. It is the Love of the Creator, that is felt in moments beyond our expectation.

The Love that brings forth miracles and is filled with compassion and grace. It is what the Buddhists describe as "mettā" or "universal loving kindness" and is the purest form of Love that we have available to us.

Agape is connected to Spiritual and Divine Truth

- ❖ *It Is the love that accepts, forgives and believes for our greater good*
- ❖ *The highest power and force on the planet and beyond*
- ❖ *Understanding How We Express Love*
- ❖ ***Love Catalyst: Spirit/ Unity Consciousness***

The Purpose of Relationships

Relationships are a beautiful experience and an important part of our lives ad learning on this planet. We are learning about ourselves and others right from the beginning of our journey here on this earth. And it is through our relationships that we learn.

Relationships can also be seen as a vehicle, taking you on a journey to experience yourself in relation to others. Some of our most intimate relationships can bring about the most change or trauma in our lives.

If you break down the words you can bring further awareness, to what it actually means and the intention for such an interaction.

> **1. Relation**
> **NOUN** (**countable** and **uncountable**, plural **relations**)
> 1. The manner in which two things may be associated.
> 2. The relation between diet and health is complex.
>
> **2. ship¹**/ʃɪp/
> noun
> 1. a large boat for transporting people or goods by sea.
> "the ship left England with a crew of 36"
> synonyms: vessel, craft, boat
> 2. a spaceship.
>
> 2.2 Suffix[edit]
> -ship

So in short a Relationship is a union, that helps you to understand yourself in relationship to another, that will take you to an experience that will help you to define yourself.

When we understand that relationships are not there merely to serve us, but also for us to learn about ourselves in relation to another, they are able to serve their proper functions. Relationships and the partner that we choose can, either reflect to us the best in our selves or the worst or, most importantly, whatever it is that needs to be changed or understood within our selves.

We can lean so much within or relationships, if we stop seeing them as self serving and start looking at it for a more informative and healing perspective.

We can learn about how we and others, communicate and express ourselves, through the knowledge and understanding of the Love Languages.

The Five Love Languages

The **Five Love Languages** are as follows:

1. Words of Affirmation -Statement: "Actions speak Louder than words"

If you are stimulated by the words of others, like to hear how much you are loved and a stickler for communication in your relationship, then your main relationship language may be 'Words of Affirmation'.

This type of person, like to have long talks about their relationship, receive feedback and words of affection. This is stimulation of the mind that brings about feelings and expressions. If you love to 'hear' how someone feels about you then this could be your love language.

- *Uses words to affirm or express love and affection and emotional stimulation*
- *" I Love you ", Little secret Message, Compliments, Word porn*
- *Positive words empower and demonstrate Love*
- *Negative words cut deep like a knife*

2. Quality Time - Statement: "Spending time with me, shows your love and affection"

If you feel that the way someone can show you their love and affection, is to give you their time and their presence, then your love language may be 'Quality Time".

You enjoy spending time together, either chilling and relaxing or doing things and exploring. You believe that if someone wants to be with you and thinks that you are an important feature in your life, then they would want to spend time with you and enjoy your company.

- ❖ *Giving undivided attention*
- ❖ *Talk is cheap, actions show that you care*
- ❖ *Quality time is an affirmation of Love*

3. Receiving Gifts - Statement: "Showering me with gifts shows me your love me"

Now we all like to be blessed with gifts, but for some, this is the main way in which they like to express and experience the love of another. This is derived from a need to provide and nurture. In nature and in some indigenous cultures, one mate must shower gifts upon the other, to prove their status and worth.

Sometimes, in society it can be seen as a negative and materialistic trait, if you are focused on receiving gifts. But as long as it is not about the cost of the gift, but the intention in which it was given, then all is well. Instead, their persona thrives on the Love, Joy and spontaneity, that goers into the gift and sees this a sign of the Love that their partner has for them

- ❖ *Gifts and trinkets of Love and Appreciation*
- ❖ *Like to create and gift to another*

❖ Like to protect or be protected and to nurture or be nurtured

4. Acts of Service - Statement: "The things you do; shows me your Love"

We all love to do a good deed, but for those who are 'turned on' by selfless acts of kindness that someone does for others. Acts of Service, are things that are done to selflessly help others.

When someone is able to help out, this can be seen as a sign of Love. Showing that to care, by helping others. This may be by fixing a neighbour's sink, or giving someone advice, or helping a homeless person. The person with this Love Language, is a humanitarian at heart and believe that lending a hand shows that you really do care.

- ❖ *Preparing a special meal or bath*
- ❖ *Helping out with chores or errands*
- ❖ *Buying gifts and Acts of Service*
- ❖ *Hugs and Kisses*

5. Physical Touch - Statement: "The way you touch me and make me feel"

And last but not least, are those of us who love to feel the touch of another, to experience their love and affection. Theses types are the 'touchy-feely' and 'huggers' amongst us. and those who love to show their love through physical connection with others.

- *Love Hugs, Kisses, Light touching and Caressing*
- *Holding hands and hugging people to show love and affection*
- *Touchy feely and loves to physically express love*

Take a Moment to Reflect

- ❖ *What do you think you Love Language is?*
- ❖ *Do you find that you use a combination of Languages?*
- ❖ *Do you see any similarities in your Love Language and the Language of your Parents?*
- ❖ *What is the Love Language of your Partner?*

When we understand the true nature and intentions of our relationships, the various types of Love and also how we communicate and express our love, then we are a step further towards having more fulfilling and loving relationships with each other and celebrating our differences.

You can find out more about the Love Languages online and can also try out a quiz to assist you in ascertaining what your love language is.

Love languages quiz

http://www.beliefnet.com/love-family/relationships/quiz/the-5-love-languages-quiz.aspx?ec=1

The understanding of this information will assist us in being able to be conscious of the relationships that we have with others and ultimately how we express our love. through life we will go through many interactions that will also demonstrated this learning to us, but to be conscious is to be aware, so that you can make choices that are on alignment with your highest good, and seek to make changes wherever possible.

All forms of love are necessary and non are to be ignored. Understanding ourselves in relation to others, assist us in embodying the true power of love and help us to express it consciously and purposefully.

> *"Love is the nourishment for the soul. Just as food is to the body, so love is to the soul. Without food the body is weak, without love the soul is weak.*

Love is the Elixir

Love is the elixir
Love is the key
Love is permeating through
Every part of me
Love is the elixir baby
Love is the key
Open up your heart and soul
And you will truly see (feel)…….

LOVE!
The portal of creation
And all that you see
Love transforms everything
Open up and you will see

Looking out the window
Birds singing in harmony
Smelling the smell of fresh warm bread
Cooked by mum and me

Soft kisses in the moonlight
From someone you haven't seen in a while
The feeling of a warm embrace
A memory that makes you smile
A feeling in your tummy
Just like butterflies
The rush of love and excitement
When you look into your lover's eyes

The warmth of the sun on my shoulders
The feeling of grass underneath my feet

The sacred kiss from a lover
Every time we meet

Dancing the dance of my ancestors
Giving birth to my dreams
Meeting up with long lost friends
And catching up over hibiscus tea

Running fingers through my hair
The embrace of my beautiful body
The curves and bends and silky softness
Enjoying all of me

The joy of bringing forth life
Being a part of history
Looking into my children eyes
Love Deeper than the deepest sea

The portal of creation
And all that you see
Love transforms everything
And allows you to be free

Love cannot be tainted
Not if it is really real
False love is an illusion
The cause of the hurt that we feel

Real love is gentle,
Uplifting and kind
A gift of deep connection
A dance with the Divine

Real love is abundant

Tender and true
Expanding and hopeful
It lives within you

Real love comes from the heart
Just look and you'll see
Behind all the hurt and trauma
There lies the key

Take a conscious journey
Deep into your heart
Don't you be afraid,
Cos that's where the healing starts

Yes, there may be trauma
Things you think you cannot face
But you'll break through the barrier
And feel real loves embrace

Just look a little further
And then you will see
That love it burns so brightly
Deep in you and me!

And once you have tasted it
Filled you cup abundantly
Enjoy it, share it and give it away
And then you'll truly see
THAT….

Love is the elixir
Love is the key
Love is permeating through
Every part of me

Love is the elixir baby
Love is the key
Open up your heart and soul
And you too can be free!!!

Nurturing the Seeds

Seed - 11 Love is Your Super Power

Love is the most beautiful gift that we can give to ourselves and others. Love is the currency of the Universe and something of which we all seek but have in abundance deep down within us. We are so full of love and love is or true nature, be have also come to experience the illusion of the absence of love and what love is not!

As we continue to nurture our seeds of development, we almost share with others. When we choose to grow and develop we do it not just for ourselves bur for others

Time to Do the Work

Air – What Do you think about Love

- ❖ Think about What Love is to you?
- ❖ What kind of words do you associate with Love?
- ❖ How do you express your love?
- ❖ Write a letter to someone you love and tell them exactly why

Earth – Know your Body

- ❖ What do you love?
- ❖ How do you show your love to yourself and others?
- ❖ How do you show love for nature and Mother Earth?
- ❖ What self-care ritual can you create to show love to your body?

Water – What does Love Feel Like

- ❖ What does Love Feel like to you?
- ❖ Where in your body do you feel it?
- ❖ What makes you feel loved?

Fire - Know your Passion

- ❖ What makes you feel passionate with regards to Love?
- ❖ How do you show someone that you love them?
- ❖ Think of a time when your Love or attraction was not reciprocated. What did that feel like and what did you do? Would you do the same now?
- ❖ Create or make something for a loved one as a symbol of your love

Spirit – The Spirit of Love

- ❖ How do you show acts of Love and Kindness to people you do not know personally?
- ❖ What to you is the 'Spirit' or Essence of Love
- ❖ Do you have a love for Spirit? can you describe your love for the Creator?
- ❖ Find a piece of spiritual writing on Love and list the key points of reference

Love – The Love That Is

- ❖ How do you show love to yourself?
- ❖ What is it that you Love?
- ❖ Who do you Love and Why?
- ❖ Make an acrostic poem about love

Golden Seeds of Wisdom

Love is the active force of the Universe and from love all harmony and balance can be restored. Never forget that the Love that you seek outside, is hidden within waiting to be acknowledged. Only until you can value the Love within yourself, will you then be able to receive the Love of another

Journal Page

Use this page to make any notes of your experience.

Seed 12

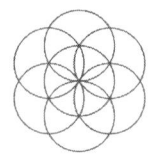

Step up and Step Out

Master Your Reality

The Law of Perpetual Transformation of Energy – All persons have within them everything that they need to change and transform their own life. We have the power to change any condition or situation that we have manifested for ourselves. Higher energies transform and consume lower ones so if we change our perspective on a situation, through understanding of the law, we can change the effect it has on us

— Three Initiates

SEED 12 – BE THE MASTER OF YOUR REALITY

"One can have no smaller or greater mastery than mastery of oneself."

Self-mastery is key

Self-mastery is Key to being able to properly navigate through this reality.

You are Source Energy, the Creator manifested in the physical. You are more than flesh and blood. You are a star returned from the Heavens. Within you is the same substance that makes up the stars, the moons and the galaxies.

You are here to experience yourself in relation to all that is. Anything you want to create in life is down to you?

To become a Master of your own reality, means to take responsibility for one's own learning and self-development. To understand that the true nature of the Universe and the power that runs through you.

Everything in the Universe exists as a quantum probability with Quantum Potential. It has everything inside of it with the potential for greatness. But if this potential is not utilised, if it is left unexplored, then it will remain a figment of what could have been rather than what is.

You are at a point in your journey right now, right this minute, where you are being asked to be the Master. You have taken the journey throughout this book, and grasped an understanding of the make up of the Universe and how everything that has happened to you, and will happen to you, is down to you.

You have been given practical tools and advice and I have shared some of my stories with you, but what are you going to do now?

The Law of Action states:

"Action must be employed in order for us to manifest our desires and intentions on earth. If we do not act, we cannot materialise our intentions. We must engage in actions that support our desired wishes and intentions."

The Law of Perpetual Transformation:

All persons have within them everything that they need to change and transform their own life. We have the power to change any condition or situation that we have manifested for ourselves. Higher energies transform and consume lower ones so if we change our perspective on a situation, through understanding of the law, we can change the effect it has on us.

So the Universe confirms it: You are the Master of Your Reality! Only You can do the work it takes to be that Master! Return to Glory!

How to Create You Own Reality

To Master your reality and bring your intention into manifestation takes an understanding of all the information provided in this book. You are on the journey as it prepares you for the end, which in itself is just another beginning.

A simple formula operates within the Universe which allows you to Master the ability to manifest whatever you desire.

1. Know what you desire

2 Ask for what you desire

3. Harmonise and Align with that which you desire

4. Take actions towards your desires

5. Offer Gratitude for receiving what you desire

1. **Know what you want** – Knowing what you need rather than what you 'want' is an important part of manifesting. You must have clear intentions of what it is that you want the Universe to deliver to you.

2. **Ask for what you desire** – it says in the Bible ***"Ask and it shall be given unto you, seek and ye shall find; knock and it shall be opened unto you"*** Mark 7:7 KJV

    Many ask for things form the Universe but do not believe that they will actually get it or they believe they are unworthy. This is why the preparation work in this book is so important. When you understand the nature of the Universe, you know that everything you need you can create.

    All you have to do is ask and align yourself. Most of us, when praying or asking for something to manifest, usually come from a lower vibration of lack or pleading. When requesting from the Universe, you must know that it will be given. Speak your intention with that knowing.

3. **Harmonise your desire** – Harmonising with what you desire is important. You have to match the vibration of what it is that you wish to manifest. Therefore, visualising and harmonising yourself with the vibration of that which you want will bring your desire into manifestation. Harmonising is not only about visualising, it is also about creating the feelings that go with the vision. How could it feel if you had what you desire? Like attracts like and everything is vibration, so take the time daily to harmonise with the intention of your desires. Live as if you already have it.

4. **Action towards your desire** – As the Law of Action states, "we must act in order to bring what we want into manifestation." So whatever you can do to help bring your desire into form, then you need to do it. You cannot just ask the Universe and wait for what you want to be delivered. Even when you order from the internet you have to act. So

to order from the Universe is quite the same except you pay with your attention, action and energy.

5. **Gratitude for your Desire** – Gratitude is another powerful energy like Love and Joy. Gratitude is the energy that brings about more of what you want to yourself. When you are grateful for what you have and maintain a vibration of joy and appreciation, the Universe responds to that and gives you more to be happy about. The Universe and God Loves to see you happy and winning. So be grateful for everything you have and also for the things that you desire which is already making its way to you. The truth is, it is already manifested but you have to bring it down into the material world, the same way you had to come down and be manifest into the material world.

These 5 steps will help you to really put some of the work from this book into practice and help you to see the power in yourself. Do this practice and see what happens. At the very least you will get what you desire.

That is not a Magic Trick, this is Physics

Step Up, Step Out

Now that you have all the keys that you need to remember who you are and be the master of your reality, guess what? .... It's time to do the work!

It's time to Step up and Step Out!

It's time to be the Co-Creator of your reality,
it's time to put in the work and begin the journey

It's time to put to bed
all of your fears

Because you know,
your power is hidden there

It's time to step out of the closet

It's time to take off your masks

It's time to get connected with your true nature
and connect with your other half

It's time to Step Up to your Greatness
and Step Out of the Dark

It's time to know who you truly are

It's time to live from your heart

Within you is all the magic

All the tools you need

It's time now to Step Up and Step Out

Into a New Reality

It's time to be fantastic

It's time to reconnect

It's time to help each other

It's the release of Karmic Debt

It's time to be the Master
that you came here to Be

It's time that, we together,
live in Oneness and Harmony

Step Up in your wisdom
Step Out and be the Light

Step Up, Step Out
it's time to go

A New World is in Sight

Keep your Head

In the midst of chaos

When all seems a fire

Keep your head

Don't give them right to expire

Our light

Our might

Keep it strong

In plain sight

United we stand

God and God's children

Rise in love

Rise in peaceful power

Rise above

Light a candle for peace and power!

Call on your ancestors

Fight fire with light!

Nurturing the Seeds

Seed 12 – Step Up, Step Out

You are the Master of your own reality and after all is said and done you are the one that needs to **act** in order to **create** it. Within this book I have offered activates and exercises to help you to start the process of doing the work and taking your journey of discovery deeper.

The Law of Action states-

> *Action must be employed in order for us to manifest our desires and intentions on earth. If we do not act, we cannot materialize.*

So it's time now to set the path for your journey ahead and create your Road Map to success and to further support you in your awakening. The question below will assist you in putting together a plan of action so you can start to take Massive Action and bring Change to Your Life!

Everything that you need is inside you, so make a decision to begin and dig deep. Remember you are not alone!

Time to Do the Work

Air – Master Your Mind

- ❖ What changes will you make to the way you think or express yourself?
- ❖ What 3 things will you do to help you keep your Mind Healthy, Balanced, Focused and Clear?
- ❖ Write down 3 affirmations you created whilst on this journey that will help you moving forward

Earth – Master your Body

- ❖ Name 3 things you will do to positively affect your body?
- ❖ What changes will you make to your diet and food?
- ❖ What exercise activity will you do to energise your body?

Water – Know your Emotions

- ❖ How will you balance your emotions?
- ❖ What are your triggers for when you are feeling overwhelmed?
- ❖ How can you honour your emotions and feelings more?

Fire – Know your Passion

- ❖ Write down at least 3 Goals that you want to achieve
- ❖ Write down 3 things you will do to make it happen?
- ❖ Write down the reward you will receive when you are successful?

Spirit – Know Your Spirit

- ❖ How will you maintain your spiritual practise?
- ❖ Name 3 spiritual practices you would like to explore further
- ❖ Name at least 1 thing that you will do daily to connect with Spirit

Love – The Spirit of Love

- ❖ Write 3 things you will do to show love for yourself
- ❖ Write down 3 things you can do to show love to your nearest and dearest
- ❖ Write down 3 ways you can show Love through Service!

A Brand New Day

A brand new day
A brand new Earth
A brand new expression
Is about to be birthed

All we once knew
Now fades away
the experiences learnt
For new ones to make way

It's time for the unfolding
of who you truly are
To reconnect to your soul
and remember you're a star

Break free from the illusion
of imposed mental slavery
Raising the vibration of love
Coming together in unity

Tap into your inner power
Tap into your divine love
Integrate with your higher self
So below as above

Speak from your highest expression
Connect direct to source
Open your heart to know the truth
of who you really are

Weigh your heart against the feather
Make peace with all that has been

12 Seeds To Awaken Your Spirit

Peel off the layers of illusion
Then the beautiful awakening can begin

Love others as you love yourself
and from anything less
There is no such thing as separation
Even that is an illusion just like death

Know that you are immortal
Know that your purpose is meant
Know that your higher self will guide you
To experience your highest intent

Release from all the programs
Release from the untruths
Reclaim your Divine sovereignty
That's all you have to do

Remember the infinite power
That the Most High put in you
To have Dominion and governance
With Love and humility too

Wake up to your reality
Wake up to who you are
With Joy and Love as your currency
You will go very far

Share all that you have
Some food, a smile, some love
Help One another
And we will all rise above

All Illusions of separation

All feelings of lack of love
Cultivate your joy and happiness
Keep your vibration 528 Hz and above

Now really is the time
To be all you can be
To take off your mask and chains
To be a master of your reality

The new world is revealing
and it begins with me and you
Take the step towards your healing
And we'll help each other through

Awaken to your power
awaken to your truth
Awaken to the knowing
Nothing you can't do

Awaken to the love within
And you will truly see
That's the only way forward
Is to walk in harmony

Together hand in hand
As one huge Earth family
Loving sharing caring
In love peace and unity

Step up, Step out

Step Up, Step Out
It's time to be free
Time to remember your Divinity
Step up, Step out
Rise up and you'll see
Stand in your power now
In you is the key

What if I told you
There was so much more
For you to experience
For you to explore
What if I told you
The best is yet to come
You haven't scratched the surface yet
of who you shall become

What if I told you
You're so much more
Than you can imagine
There's so much in store
and what if it told you
That all you have to do
Is believe in yourself
Just believe in you

Life can be rocky
Painful and unfair
Sometimes you may even wonder
What you doing here
Why would you choose
To be in a world

Where you're
'born to suffer'
'born of sin'
Work your whole life
and get old
We have many experiences
that shape our path
Some test the mind
others strengthen the heart

But what if I told you
that you're a creator
So powerful and special
A great inspiration
A creative spark of divinity
So powerful and loved
You can create reality

And what if I told you
that each and every part
of your life story
was decided at the start
That you have chosen everything
by perfect design
Each life trauma and situation
you chose to help you shine
You'd probably glance at me
with a look of confusion
As to how or why you would
create a reality of disillusion
Where nothing seems to go your way
With a life experience
littered with pain
Where it seems only others are able to succeed

Everyone is rising and you think
What about me?

You know only too well
how the odds stack against you
But what if I told you
that they are there to make you
Transform into whom you are to become
And shine your light as bright as the sun

The first thing that you have to do
Is take a good long look at you
Appreciate yourself for coming this far
Hug yourself tightly and kiss all the scars
For they remind you, that you dared to love and dream
To take a risk, to be broken, to hurt and to feel
Take a moment and celebrate how far you have come
And remind yourself that your far from done

Step 2 is Get Clarity and Focus
Release your baggage, your failures and Own Them
Stand up to everything that has stood in your way
Times you should have acted
Things you didn't say
Release all, as beneath the pain is your purpose
All you have to do is breakthrough, trust the process
Take responsibility for the things you should have done
Try to understand your trauma, so forgiveness can be won
Ask yourself what you have learned from your struggles
About Yourself
About the World
About the strength of Spirit
About your connection with others
And take this wisdom and rebirth anew

Allow each challenge, to bring out the greatness in you
Don't be afraid of the skeletons in the closet
Take the out, face them head on
And the put them in a box and shut it
Take with you only what inspires you to grow
That which helps you to remember to honour your divine flow
Make peace with the past, take the best of everything and make a fresh new start
Step 3 is to do the work it takes to heal
After 1 and 2 that's it's a done deal
But you do have to release the pain you make carry
Because if left resolved it could return in a hurry
Me this is the important part
From where you are and make a fresh start
Time to learn and to understand
That everything that you have been through is part of a divine plan
For to be without love
To be rejected or abused
When transformed with the wisdom of healing
Brings out the best qualities in you
Like humility, service, passion and strength
Compassion and integrity
And a will that you cannot break
Learn to understand your pain so that you don't make the same mistakes again
But the Greatest Gift from this that you will ever know
Is when you have the opportunity to share your story and to help another to grow
When you look into their eyes and recognise the scars that do not show
Your heart mixed with joy and sadness
For deep inside you know
This person once was you

12 Seeds To Awaken Your Spirit

But now you have the seeds of wisdom
That can help them to grow
And in this moment the gift into your power and purpose and just finding his
Or hers for all that matter
For at the core we are all the same
Whether masculine or feminine we have all at some time felt pain
Through healing our pain through passion we open up ourselves to so much more
And this takes us on to step 4
Step 4 is when you pay it forward
Step up and step out into your purpose
Using the skills you've learned to heal yourself
You can now share that with others
To know the truth inside
What they should do
Empower others, change your life
Say goodbye and thank you
To all the pain and strife
Remember all your lessons and the moment shared
Your past is now the foundation
On which you build and repair
Image and perception of who you truly are
Born of divinity birthed from the stars
Part of a perfect design
Success is inevitable so you'll do just fine
Just continue to trust that you'll make it through
And that all that you need lies deep within you
The past the present and the future you see
Is all perfect and balanced in oneness and harmony
Testing your metal
And helping you to see
That you are powerful and special
Creator of your reality

So step up and step out into who you're meant to be
And your pain into your passion
so you can set others free
Leave the past behind
And step into your future proudly
Remember you have made it
Let your spirit truly be free
Step up into your power
Step out and share the love
Let your past empower you
Shower the painful times with love
uncover all the learning
Allow yourself to see
The everything that you were looking for
Is now everything that you have come to be
It was hidden deep inside you
just waiting to Break Free
So share yourself with others
And let's heal in oneness and unity

Journal Page

Use this page to make any notes of your experience.

_____

_____

_____

12 Seeds To Awaken Your Spirit

From Star to Seed....and Back Again

The journey of Ascension and through the mastery of this game of life is an eternal on. The Universe is always expanding and contracting, dying and rebirthing and maintaining a perpetual state of harmony and balance and experience for all of creation.

The 12 Seeds outlined in this book are just the beginning of your journey towards understanding your true nature, remembering who you are and becoming the Master of Your Reality!

Nothing in this world is but chance, everything is part of a unique and meticulous design, each part different yet connected to the all.

The journey from star to seed, and back again is the main purpose of our journey here to earth. To begin as infinite divine source consciousness, a spark of light and source energy. And to descend and plunge into the fertile, nourishing and loving soil of mother earth, who nurtures us with all the elements and nutrients we need to live out our lives and experience our self and the manifestation of our every want and need.

In this time, after a long lesson in duality and the illusion of separation, we are about to return home to our divine purpose and intention but within this physical realm and body for as long as we choose to.

When we understand the alchemy in nature and the alchemy of life, it becomes a journey which becomes an empowering and loving experience rather than one of density and restriction. The more readily we are to face any challenges and see them as opportunities for learning and growth, the quicker we take off our masks and reveal our true selves so we can work on being the best self that we can be.

I realised very early on in the inception of this book, that it would be something that I would become, that it would be testimony to my own personal experience and that wouldn't just have the chance to share wise words, I had the chance to share, my experience and show myself how far I have come.

The publishing and completion of this book, is my testimony to how far I have come and how I have taken up the commitment to Step Up and Step out and live and be my authentic true loving and divine Self!

I once found it very uncomfortable to be here on this earth plan, and although I could understand the higher purpose and intention of each experience that I created, I was still not yet sure how to master the healing process and gather the gold from the lead piles.

I had to know that the path to self-mastery and awareness and living out my true potential, was not in the acquiring of knowledge and wisdom outside of myself, or even helping others to find themselves, but that ultimately, it was about uncovering the knowledge and wisdom deep within myself, that was waiting to be understood and then allowing that energy, to transform and empower me to know myself on a deeper level, and become a true alchemist and turn my lead into gold!

Each one of us has returned at this time, having started out as a star shining brightly and then a golden seed planted into the fertile soil and waters of mothers earth so that we may grow in our awareness of ourselves and be nourished by the right mix of elements and energy so that we can create the best opportunity to nurture our seeds and transform them into a luminous tree of light and of life, from which we can enjoy our experience here and create and experience even more of ourselves, until we finally make our way back home to the stars.

This is the true journey of nature and of life at this time.

Each one of us a golden seed of pure potential and it is our purpose to manifest re true potential and shine brightly from within and without.

I truly hope that you have found this book inspiring and insightful and that it has in some way allowed you to awaken to the true magic and divine power of your soul, your nature, your power, your purpose, your passion and YOU as a Divine Sovereign being of light!

It has been an absolute pleasure sharing my 12 seeds to awaken your spirit!

I trust that it has and will continue to be as magical an unfolding for you and it has truly been for me.

I thank you for taking the time to read my words, share in my journey and receive a few nuggets of gold.

Much Love and Abundant Blessings To The Most High and Divine Source within all things.

Namaste

Other Books by Amenti the Awakener

Current

Sekhmet Rising by Ra Sekhi Arts Temples – Contributing Author

Forthcoming

Wisdom of An Oracle

Journey Through the Gateways

12 Keys to Self-Mastery

The Alchemy of Ecstasy

To keep up to date with Amenti the Awakener visit…

http://is.gd/AmentiSpeaks

About the Author

Holistic Health Expert, Light Worker and Spiritual Teacher

Amenti the Awakener is Inspirational Speaker, Soul Coach, and Spiritual Teacher who uses her own life experiences and skills to help awaken others to their true potential. She is the founder of Amenti Healing Space and Halls of Amenti Academy of Higher Learning, which is a school dedicated to reviving the Healing Arts and Spiritual Development.

Coming from a lineage of Healers, Priests and Shamans, Amenti draws on here cultural and ancestral heritage to bring forth knowledge, healing and communion with Spirit.

An initiated High Priestess in the Order of Melchezidech and Ancient Kemetic Order of Auset and the Sacred Blue Lotus Temple of enlightenment, she brings a wide wealth of knowledge and experience on all ancient rituals, spiritual wisdom and healing.

Having travelled to many sacred sights and worked with Spiritual Mentors and Teachers including Caroline Shola Arewa, Stewart Pearce, Ras Campbell and more, Amenti is committed to sharing her knowledge and wisdom with all who need it.

She is committed to supporting others to Awaken to their true God-essences and live the life of their purpose!

She began her career in youth work and working part time in the gynaecology Dept. at St Thomas Hospital, London. Since then began training in a succession of healing therapies with the aim first and foremost to heal herself. A survivor of Child sex abuse, domestic violence and depression, she knows and understands the struggles life can bring but has always been guided to know that all was for a purpose…And this purpose is to learn, heal and share. Amenti used her traumas to help her understand her greatness and does the same for others.

She has now been working professionally in the world of healing and wellbeing for 11 years and has hosted many workshops, lectures and demonstrations on many health and wellbeing topics.

Amenti is a fully qualified Reiki Master Teacher, Past Life Regression Therapist, Hypnotherapist, Holistic therapist and Wellness Coach with a wide range of tools including Crystal Healing, Inner Child Healing and Medium ship. She also offers courses and workshops in Healing and Spiritual Arts.

Celebrity clients include Brian Belo, Emilie Sande and many others.

Specialising in working with 'Awake & Gifted Children' Clearing Ancestral blockages, Womb Wellness, and Spiritual Development, Amenti shares a wealth of experience and support, delivered with a down to earth feel, non- judgemental approach and an open and loving heart.

Amenti is committed to supporting others through the Ascension process or elevation of self, by being a living example. She truly believes that we each have a purpose so great, we may not see it yet, and her purpose is to guide you to your Highest Potential.

Your Review

Thank you for reading *12 Seeds to Awaken Your Spirit* by Amenti the Awakener.

We would appreciate it greatly if you could leave some honest feedback.

Please click here to leave a review on Amazon UK
http://is.gd/12SeedsUK

Please click here to leave a review on Amazon US
http://is.gd/12SeedsUS

For this book's Bonus Content please visit http://is.gd/12SeedsBonus

To keep up to date with Amenti the Awakener please visit
http://is.gd/AmentiSpeaks

12 Seeds To Awaken Your Spirit

Printed in Great Britain
by Amazon